The Pipes, The Pipes Are Calling

By Jim Smyth

First Published in Ireland, in 2010,
in co-operation with Choice Publishing Ltd.
Drogheda, County Louth, Republic of Ireland

ISBN: 978-1-907107-60-3

A CIP catalogue for this book is available from the National Library.

Contents

Preface

This book tells my own journey through life in the Liberties but it is much more than just the telling of a life, it is a tale woven around the adventures I had with those dear ones I met along the way. Since I was born, raised and spent most of my adult life in the Liberties in Dublin Ireland this was where my tales began.

I loved the Liberties, from my first remembrances of the streets and alleyways. As a young lad I was early on amused that an alleyway could be called Dirty Lane, and right behind it was a street called Mullinamack, and Cherry Steps were nearby. There were two world famous breweries located in the Liberties, the Powers Distillery as well as the Guinness Brewery. Also there were countless churches in our parish. It seemed nearly every block or so there was a church and each one seemed to have lovely little patches of grass or flowers around it and many had enough land to have beautiful, large parks. So we had a rich church life with priests all around us.

And last but most important I loved my days with the people in the neighbourhood, who were rather like my family. Of course most especially I loved my very own family. There was my dear mother and father and eight children, three dear girls growing up in the Liberties and five boys. Three of the five young lads were later to become the *Three Smyth Bros.,* who began singing together in the mid forties and sang professionally together for the next twenty years.

In the mid 1960s we eight children were all getting married and began to drift off from the Liberties into our own family homes. My dad and mom were the last to move from the Liberties. They moved to a lovely flat in Malahide. Soon after, in the seventies, my dad died and mom continued to live a few more years in their Malahide flat.

I remember I was sitting with my mother on her porch in Malahide, one Sunday, talking. She reached over, took my hand in hers and said, "Jim dear, as a family we were very loving of course, but each one of us had our own adventures during our own growing up in the Liberties. In a way our family was a lot like every family in the Liberties, I know that, but we kept being pulled close together by our wonderful, funny – or sometimes not so very funny - adventures. Jim, one day will you write about all this?"

I said, "I will of course dear mother."

And so I am.

I remember the Liberties was an 'up-and-down' area, we were always walking steep up and low down the streets, up and down.

For many of our young Liberty years there was old lady who every day pushed her big wicker basket up and down the streets, piled with all the apples and fruit for her outdoor stall that day. She was pushing the basket up and down the hills long before I was born, and walking the streets of the Liberties.

The story goes that one morning as she was passing Halligans Bakery which was situated at the top of Church Street, she looked in the bakery and as she did so she saw a young boy under a lorry. She shouted at him to get out,

"Get out son or you will get killed!"

There were soldiers all around in the street, British soldiers.

The soldiers caught him and took him out.

The young lad was none other than our ...

Irish Patriot Boy, Kevin Barry.

He was hiding under the lorry. The soldiers took him away and they hanged him in Mountjoy Jail.

He fought for Ireland, he died on the streets of Ireland down there in the Liberties, he died for Ireland.

My mother said, "So Jim it was a mistake. But she paid dearly in her poor old mind. God love her," Mum said.

"I second that mother."

I did meet her, I met her every morning when I went to the Brunswick St. School. I passed by Halligans Bakery and met her on the way up the hills to her stall location. After my mum told me the story I would be enthralled looking into Halligans Bakery as I passed by. I would often stop and look at it and you know I used to say a prayer for Kevin Barry. God bless his soul.

""Sure, only for you, Jim," my mother said, "remember when you wanted to go and join the priesthood, I should you have let you go."

"No matter, I still have my religion and I still have you."

"You won't have me much longer, Jim," Mum said.

"But I love you with all my heart dear mum".

Three weeks later my mother passed away.

My dear mother's love has always been near as it has been in the lives of all our family. She taught us love. She gave love, guidance, help to we children from the very beginning as well as to all our neighbours around us in the Liberties. This is how we saw our lives as we grew up. Dear mum and dad, thanks for the memories, a walk down a loving memory lane in the Liberties. May all who read of it feel its loving presence near.

Top of the World, MA! ...

Top of the World, DA! ...

"And I can still hear the Pipes Calling ..."

Jim Smyth
Co Dublin
2010, September

Chapter 1

The Young Days

"Travelling through life I have had many wonderful experiences."

And so it began:

I was born on the 14th of June in the *Rotunda Hospital* in the year 1932. There was a Eucharistic Congress that was held in Phoenix Park on the date so it was to say a memorable occasion to have a birth.

Furthermore memorable: I was born with a caul. I was covered with it. Saying goes it's very lucky to carry it around with you. Sailors go extra wild for it when they go to sea for they say, if you carry a caul you never drown at sea. It's a centuries old sea tale. The doctor attending my mother asked her for it, which she gave to him after much persuasion.

I was a blond baby. My mother's name was Chrissie and was a very attractive woman. She had lovely auburn hair and took extra special care about her appearance. My father was a handsome man, tall and dark of hair, whose name was Terry. He and I were very close to each other. He would take me everywhere with him. I loved him very much. This bond between us was to continue until the Lord took him from us many years later.

In my early years we lived in a top back room at 59 Queen Street in Dublin city centre, over Thundercut Alley. I was an alley cat! The Alley ran from Queen Street to Smithfield which was a busy market place. The farmers brought their cattle, pigs, sheep and horses to be sold from early morning till late every afternoon.

I first went to school in *Kings Street National School.* Right behind our school was Christian Brothers which I was to attend in later years. At that time we lived in a top story tenement room overlooking Thundercut. It was well-known because Gypsy O'Brien, a famous fortune teller lived there. They came from all over Ireland and England to have their fortunes told. I well remember all the cars pulling into the Alley.

In those days, at the top of Queen Street, was the famous Cherry Steps. They were six or eight huge steps leading up to a couple large houses. On the Steps all the young men would gather to converse with each other or share work.

My father took me with him when he went to the Steps. He was popular with all the men and he got most of his work from Fusco, a big, handsome Italian guy who called me Ming Ming – I don't know why. Fusco was very sweet on my mother. He would always get me to take her some ice-cream in a carton, which I assure you I enjoyed more than she did.

My best pal on the Steps was a young man called Bunny Doyle, a good Light Heavyweight professional boxer, a very big, well made man. He did all his boxing in Belfast or England. I loved it when Bunny returned from a fight. He would bring back Mars Bars and Spangles and we would chew to our heart's content.

I loved to watch Bunny sparring on the Steps, setting his opponent up, then dropping him with a left hook. I stood mesmerised, watching him. Then he would say, "Come on, little Jimmy," and hold out the palm of his hand. I would hit it as hard as I could and then he would wince and say, "God, that hurt." Then he would smile and ruffle my hair.

Bunny would always catch my dad's hand and put some money in it. I would hear Bunny say, "Pay me back when you can, Terry," and my dad would say, "Bunny, I can manage." "No sweat," Bunny would say, "you always do, Terry".

He would always remember the Holy Days of Obligation with a "don't forget Mass in the morning lads".

We would all be at Mass, my dad was very good to see

that we went. We would all go to receive Holy Communion. I would be brought up by my dad. I stood beside him at the altar and would get a tap on the head from the priest. Then Bunny would bring me back to my seat with my dad behind me. I was proud as punch walking home between them.

Many loving memories.

It was nice in the evenings on the Steps, the last rays of sun, and Fusco would come out with a few ice-wafers.

One nice evening dad and I had come home from across the street where we had been visiting our grandad, my father's dad. At the corner of Queen Street Mrs. Donovan was putting away the fruit from her stall. Someone was roaring. It turned out to be Mr. Brogan, who was not a very nice man. His wife had to leave him on more than one occasion over the way he beat her when he got drunk. The poor lady always had marks on her face. He would lock her out at night when it suited him. He had three lovely girls. He would come home drunk from the pub with one or two of his pals and he would let his pals abuse his daughters.

This evening Mr. Brogan had one of his daughters by the arm. He hit her once on the head and pushed her. Mrs. O'Donovan let out a roar to leave the girl alone and threw an apple which caught him on the side of the head. He shouted back at her and threw off his coat. My father saw what was happening and made for Mr. Brogan. Just at that moment, through the dust and grime and crying in the street, up strode a giant of a man that no one wanted to meet mad, "Big Bunny", and what followed wasn't funny.

Bunny brought his left hand up from his knee, caught Mr. Grogan on the point of the chin and dropped him right on Mrs. Donovan's fruit stall. He never got up. The men carried him up to his flat. Police came up to our street to make enquiries. I will never forget that punch Bunny threw. It was the sweetest left hook I have ever seen. I don't think Mr. Brogan was ever the same. He left the street some weeks after, when his daughter became pregnant but Mrs. Brogan continued to live in the street and her daughter had the baby with help from all the neighbours.

St. Pauls Soccer Club was formed and my dad and I started to play, along with the *Grange Gorman Pysco Hospital* staff and doctors who were also players. Most of the players were "outside men", from other parts of Dublin.

It was Monday afternoon and Smithfield was packed with people and cattle. I was with my father on the Steps. Suddenly there was a commotion. I saw a man leading a bull into the square that had been roped off. The man was standing away from the bull, holding a rope through the ring in the bull's nose. I felt someone's hand on my shoulder. I looked around and saw it was mother with my little brother Paddy. I was glad to see her. I heard someone shouting that the bull was acting up. Dad said to mother, "I see Bunny is gone over." Mother caught my hand, we ran around the corner and saw Bunny with the rope in his hand and the bull well in control. It looked so easy to him. He gave the rope a slight flick and that was enough to subdue the bull. I said to mom, "He's great isn't he!" The farmers all around said, except for Bunny there would have been hell to pay. The man is fearless, all agreed. Bunny gave me a wave and then said hello to my mom. "Do you want to buy a bull, Chrissie", he said to her.

I think of Bunny all those years ago and can still see him, a huge, kind, loving bloke.

Those were my young days and those are my memories. I love them.

My friends have long since gone and so has Queen Street and Smithfield as I knew them, but Bunny will always fill my life. In all the years I knew him he never failed to amaze me. A great guy. His approach to life was unique, always there on the spot to help his friends and neighbours, to use his God-given strength to help those in need.

Chapter 2

Time to Move....And Move

When I was ten years old my family and I moved, in Dublin, from Queen Street into a house over a shop on Benburb Street. This was great news because Benburb Street was not too far away from our old home on Queen Street and we could still go up to the Cherry Steps and see all our mates.

You know, it wasn't too unusual to come down in the morning and find one of the patients from *Grange Gorman Psychiatric Hospital,* which was just the next block away from where we lived on Benburb, asleep on our stairs. Some times they would be aggressive and other times very meek and quiet. My mother used to feel sorry for the man, who ever he was, and she would end up giving him a cup of tea. The porters from the asylum always knew where to look for anyone that went missing. My father would say to my mother, "Be careful, Chrissie, always call me, I'll go down," but mother never called him. She could handle herself as she was to prove to me later on in years.

Gypsy O'Brien's son used to come out to play with me. I don't know why he did, but I used to play with anyone and everyone. We played a bit of hurling, and I wished him good luck in his games.

Fusco heard about us moving to Benburb Street. It wasn't such a big deal but I suppose we were popular, my family, and got along with everyone. Fusco said, "I'll miss you little Jim, but we'll still see each other as you'll still be living near by."

"Okay, Mr. Fusco. We won't say goodbye but the time's coming near to say it."

Our new home on Benburb Street had two big rooms and a shop for me, my mom, dad, Paddy and Fran. My parents were delighted with the shop. We had been there nearly a week when we were told something was wrong. To put a long story short the landlord told my mom and dad that the house had been signed over to another client. Seems our good luck was short lived. We were all disappointed. My dad said we must accept it as there was nothing else we could do and no one to help.

My mother's father, my grandfather, fought in the First World War and was killed in battle. So the rest of the O'Grady family, my Gran O'Grady, her daughters Kathleen and Annie with sons Jim and Paddy emigrated to Bath in Somerset, England. Jim got involved with Hoover Enterprises. He was the first man to bring the Hoover business into Ireland and became a huge influence in the industry.

So our family were turned out on our ear and with no family about. We had to move and find new accommodations. A lady by the name of Mrs. Quinn organised the move for us. The corporation sent a lorry to collect our belongings. Not a lot of things but off we went. The big driver of the car said, "You know we have to take you to Marshalsea Barrack".

Before we left I ran to the end of the street, looked up toward the Cherry Steps and thought I would never be able to come back to see Bunny and Fusco and I started to cry. My mom said, "Jim, don't do that, please. I'm ready to cry, don't start me".

"What kind of place is it, mom?"

She said, "It's nice, Jim, you'll like it. There's nice boys living there." So I was happier. This was a new challenge for me and I liked that idea. I fell asleep in the truck and the next thing I knew Mom woke me up and we were there.

I climbed down out of the truck and walked into our new home. Inside the door there was an all-stone hallway and a flat just inside the door which was ours. All the moving lads had the furniture in quickly. When the driver and his men had finished he said, "Will you sign this form, Ma'am," so my mother signed the paper and said, "There's the price of a drink for you." "No Ma'am, I won't take that," and my mom said, "you will," so he did ... and we had arrived in Marshalsea..

We made up the beds, got into them very tired and went to sleep.

I woke up during the night to go to the toilet. I couldn't find it and ended up peeing into a flower vase on the window sill. I looked out the window. It was so late when we came in that mom hadn't put up the curtains that she had already made, but she never said anything to us. She was a good lady, our mom and I know it grieved her and my dad to see how things had turned out for us.

The moon was Full and it was looking at me straight through the window and I know it was smiling at me and saying, "Good luck to you". I gave it a wave and replied, "Thank you, we'll need it. But if God sticks with me I'll make it and will be here many years later telling you all about it."

My God was with me after all. I had good times mixed in with a few bad ones. I looked out that night and said to myself, 'I'm going to be a Priest'. I said and thought this many times in the future ... but it never happened. It was so quiet there that night. I lay where I stood and fell asleep.

We were now in Marshalsea Barracks. It was known at one time as a debtors' prison. Our flat was one large room and a smaller room, with a lot of cockroaches. There was plenty of room and in a couple of days my mom had it ship-shape. She was a great organiser.

We slept well that night. Next morning we woke early and it was a lovely, sunny day. My mom had been up early and went up to the *MayPole* store for our groceries. We had a nice breakfast. Afterwards Paddy said to me, "Don't go out till dad gets back." Wrong to say that to me because the first thing I did was go out and get acquainted with our new dwelling place.

The entrance hall where we lived was fairly large. As you stepped into the hall from our room you turned right and were in a huge barracks square It was a monstrous yet typical training area. On the left was a big house which was the care-takers house, Mr. Cheevers.

I walked into the square and right in front of me was a large two storey house with many windows in it but no glass in any of them. Pigeons were flying in and out and cooing a lot. It was mind boggling. I stood mesmerised. What a place for our neighbourhood.

There was an archway on the right leading into another smaller square where families lived upstairs. I walked through the archway. I didn't know what to expect. Everything was spotless clean and whitewashed. There were women and children, dogs and cats all around.

One woman called out to me, "Hey young fellow, what's your name, what do you want?"

I said, "My name is Jimmy Smyth."

One lady said, "I met your mammy this morning. Oh she's a lovely girl."

One big black-haired girl said to me, "I'm Liz Gibbons. Give us a kiss, will you? Oh he's lovely blonde hair." She came over to me and ran her fingers through my hair. Then she kissed me. I tried to get away but couldn't. She put her arms around me and started to squeeze me.

A lovely lady then said, "Will you leave the lad alone, Liz. You're embarrassing him". She smelled nice, this Liz, and looked nice. I was ten years old and big for my age and I had never met anyone like her.

The nice lady, Mrs. Roache was her name, said, "leave him alone, go on off with you". So Liz let me go and Mrs. Roache said , "I hope you do well for yourself, Jimmy. If you want anything tell your mother not hesitate and ask me."

I said I would, "Thank you, ma'am."

I went into the square and looked up at the big pigeon

house. It was a nice morning. Then I was about to go in to see mom and tell her what Mrs. Roache had said when two boys came out of the pigeon house and stood looking at me. I looked back at them. I couldn't make them out.

One boy was trim, slight and very pale with jet black hair. He had on a white shirt with black trousers, no shoes. I said, "You've no shoes." He said, "So what, it's warm anyway."

The other boy had red hair, was strong looking. He had on a grey jacket, black trousers and one of his front teeth was missing. He let out a fierce whistle which startled me. His face broke into a grin and he started to laugh. He looked funny. But I liked him.

Just then the nice lady came up behind me.

"Jimmy, this is my son. We call him Redser.".

Redser said, "Hello, ma'am."

She said, "This is Jimmy Smyth." She playfully cuffed Redser on the head. "Now you look after him and don't forget, no going up to the canal. And oh, by the way, this is my best fella Mickey Doolin,"

Mickey began into a fit of laughing and couldn't stop. He seemed to always go into fits of giggles for the least thing. He said, "Hello Jim." and I said "Hello".

Mrs. Roache said, "Now don't forget what I said, no canal, Redser," and she turned and went back through the Arch to her house.

Redser looked at me, "Well now," he said, "who have we here, little Blondie.

I said, "Why do they call you Redser?"

He said, "A comedian, we're in luck." He never changed in all the years I knew him with his teasing. "Come on, I'll get you inaugurated into the order of things around here," he said.

I said, "I had had a great teacher where I lived before, his name by the way was Bunny Doyle. He was a great Pro Boxer."

"I do a bit of boxing myself," Redser said.

"You're well built," I said

He thanked me. I was delighted with my two new friends. I said, "I'll see you later. By the way, what is the canal, Redser?"

But he wouldn't tell me, said, "Later". Then he asked, "Will your mother let you stay out late? And you might fix up a bit of a get together with this Bunny Doyle."

I laughed and went into my flat. Mom asked how I had got along with the lads. I said, "Great. I met Mrs. Roache. She said you were a lovely girl and she liked you. What happened to all the cockroaches?"

Mom was pregnant again. She was always in a good humour when she was pregnant and now especially.

Meanwhile, I was getting on quite well with my mates.

Redser said to me one night, "I like you, Jimmy. Come on, let's have a bit of a punch up."

I said, "I'm not too good," although Bunny had often said I was very good.

So Redser and me went head to head. I punched him for every punch he gave me. I was enjoying it. I was sweating. But Redser wasn't doing too bad. I was giving as much as I got. Redser said, "I think you're good."

I said, "You're great." I caught him with two straight lefts and then wacked him with a lovely right cross

He stopped and spit a mouthful of blood at a pigeon

walking along the ground in front of him. It hit the pigeon right on the head who let out an unmerciful roar. Mickey, Redser and me started laughing and couldn't stop. Mickey put his arms around me and said, "I love you, Jimmy. We won't ever break up, we'll always stick together."

I loved him too. He was so quiet and so gentle. And Redser always took up for me.

The Thompson Twins were tough boys. Christy, one of the twins was vicious. He was messing me around one night in the square over Liz Gibbons.

A couple nights later we were all in the hall, Christy and me and Redser and Liz, and she turned to me and said, "You and me will stay with each other, Jim."

I was a bit nervous over this as I knew she was going with Christy. I wasn't interested in this kind of situation. One way or the other I did not want to get involved with the Thompson Twins.

Liz said, "That's alright Jimmy."

I looked at Christy. He was livid. I knew he was not pleased.

Redser said, "I'm going. I'll walk you over," he said to Liz.

I stood up, it was late. "Yes," I said, "I better go too." I looked at Redser.

He said to Liz, "I'll leave you up the stairs."

Redser turned and said to me, "I don't pal with Thompson. He's chasing Liz and that's why he was there. Watch yourself. I'll get over the wall after I leave Liz up to her flat."

Liz said to me, "Give me a kiss, Blondie."

I said, "I'm going, Redser."

Redser to me, "Would you give her a kiss and let's get going!"

So I kissed her. She was a lovely girl, long black hair and smelled nice.
"Leave her up the stairs," said Redser, "I'll see you in the morning."

"OK," I said.

Liz and I stayed and talked about fifteen minutes and I got to know her that night. It was my first time talking alone with a girl and it was a lovely sensation. We became great friends.

I said, "Good night."

She said, "I love you."

I said, "Me too."

Right now I wish I was home. I got to the bottom of her stairs and she shouted down, "Next time you can have me. I love you, Blondie."

I ran across the square into my hallway. At that moment something smacked me in the face. I lashed out and hit someone. Then someone caught me by the hair. I could feel the blood running down into my mouth. I was so scared. I didn't know who it was. I pulled myself outside into the light. It was an older man. He said, "You don't know me but I'll tell you who I am. My name is Thompson and you're fucking around with my son's girl."

I said, "No way, I just left her home."

He said, "A likely story." He hit me in the face and it hurt. I swung at him but he had me by the hair. I was going to shout for my father when somebody pulled me off him. I saw it was Redser. He jumped and hit Mr. Thompson smack in the face. He fell back, spitting blood and teeth onto the ground. It wasn't a pretty sight.

"Redser you fucking destroyed him. Thanks. He was chocking the life out of me. I nearly had it."

Thompson was roaring and roaring and cursing at us saying, "I'll charge you, I'll get the police."

We walked away.

Some people came out to offer help to Mr. Thompson. They were people who were afraid of him as he was quite a bully all around the neighbourhood.

My mother came out. "Jim, I heard voices, what's wrong with you?"

"I fell but I'm OK now".

Thompson was gone.

Redser was telling the rest of the neighbours to go home. I said to him, "What's going to happen to you?"

"Not a sausage, nothing. I know what Mr. Thompson tried to do to a friend of mine, namely my little friend, Liz. He tried to have her one night. He was so drunk."

Redser was right. Mr. Thompson never opened his mouth and his two sons, we didn't see a lot of them.

Redser, Mickey and me continued to stay around with the odd visit from Liz. She was lovely.

My Uncle Jim, my mother's brother, was a constant visitor to our flat. He had become a big man for Hoover Enterprises in Ireland. He was always dropping in to see us. When my mom and dad moved years later to the Old Folk Flats on Malahide Road he came to see them to tell them he wouldn't be keeping in contact with us because of his position in life and his job. In other words, there was no room for us in his life. We found out later that he began resorting to drink, two bottles of whiskey a day and dying way before his time. I hope he sleeps peacefully with his Maker but he did break my mother's heart because he was the "Golden Boy", the one who made good starting from a room at the top of our house on Queen Street.

Redser Roache, Mickey Doolin and myself monopolized the Liberties and were frequent visitors to the canal at Guinness Brewery in James Street. We were always prepared with our fishing nets, and jam-jars to put our catch in.

Chapter 3

Marshalsea Barracks

There were so many adventures – and misadventures – for a young lad living in the Liberties. I had my share. This one stays with me.

I remember Redser asking me one day while we were waiting for Liz and Mickey to join us, “Can you hear me?”

“Of course I can hear you, I’m not deaf,” I said.

“Right,” he said, “You know Mrs. Collins from the Lane? Their name is not Collins.”

This amused me but Mickey Doolin came along and sat down beside us.

“What kept you,” I said, “you’re late.”

“I had to get coal off Mrs. Collins for my mother”.

“Now do you know,” I said, “that Mrs. Collins is not her name?”

“Go on, Jim, she is Mrs. Collins to me and it’s Collins over her shop. Her son, his name is Tony Collins, so now.”

“She had to change her name,” said Redser..

“Let’s hear it,” I said, “what was her name?”

“Her real name,” said Redser, “ is Slap-arse”.

Mickey and I started laughing and we couldn’t stop. Mickey kept shouting the name out loud as we were laughing at Redser who, I might say, wasn’t very impressed.

“Now hold it,” Redser said, “just a minute. My granny told

me so, are you implying she's a liar?"

I said, "Wait a minute, no fighting please." He looked at me with his big eyes.

"I'm not," he said.

I wasn't taking any chances. Redser could change his mind at the spin of a penny. As he came near me I gave him a kick in the leg. I started laughing and then Mickey joined me while Redser was hopping around on one leg, roaring his head off.

Mickey and I walked into the Square. I looked back and Redser was following us. He was starting to do his Jimmy Cagney impression. He put his arms out in front of him, then he would shrug his shoulders, stick his chin out and say,

"Ma, Ma, I love you. They got me, Ma, look I'm full of holes."

In one of Cagney's films he was left at the door. When his mother opened the door, Cagney fell into the kitchen near dead. This was the act. I used to tie Redser's coat around him. But I would tie the arms of his coat very loose so, when he came near the ground, he was able to throw off the coat and his arms would stop him from falling on his face.

Redser would then run up the steps of the Caretakers House where there was a ledge at the top by the door. He would stand on the ledge and roar at the top of his voice, "top of the world, 'MA' ".

He was some performer. Then he would jump down off the ledge on to the handrail, then on down to the ground. I don't know how he escaped getting a broken leg. He then looked at Mickey and me and said, "Come on, how about some applause?"

We gave him a hand clap and he gave us a bow. I enjoyed him doing this routine, he was great and very athletic.

Mickey said just then, “Well fellas, will you look who’s here”. It was Tony Collins, delivering some logs. Redser said, “Shut your mouth or I’ll slap your arse,” and we all started laughing.

Tony got as red as a beetroot. He pushed his cart against the steps. “Piss off, Roach,” he said, “I’ll tell my mother.” This got some more laughs from us all.

Mickey said, “Jim, I’m going up.” Redser said, “Me too”. I was about to go as well when Liz came down the stairs.

“Did Tony leave these logs here, Jim?” she said.

“Liz, come on, I’ll help you get them up.” Between us we managed to haul them up. We made it to Liz’s flat. Her mother was waiting near naked, as usual. I don’t think the woman had any clothes at all. I eventually got the logs into the flat, dodged Liz’s mother who wanted me to feel her tits and made haste down the stairs.

Liz called after me, “Bye, Jim, thank you.”

I didn’t see her many times after that. She was a nice, friendly girl and I liked to be around her, she always smelled so spicy, so nice, but soon after we were to leave the Barracks.

Remembering the time Redser did his impression of Jimmy Cagney, he always asked Mickey to tie his coat around his shoulders so that when he fell down he could pull his hands loose. But one time Mickey tied his hands very tight so he couldn’t move. When Redser fell forward he couldn’t get his hands out to break the fall. He fell on his face and broke his nose. I wasn’t there but it was mother who told it to me. Redser’s mom said he was not too amused.

One morning soon after, my mother and I and Mrs. Doolin and Mickey were in the *Johns Lane Church* at 10 o’clock Mass. We were about four rows from the Altar and Fr. Heffernan was the Celebrant. He was about to administer his sermon when Redser and his mother came into the church. He had a plaster across his face and a bandage on his head. He looked so funny, I couldn't take my eyes off him. Then Mickey saw him and his laugh started and he couldn't stop. He lay across the seat and continued to laugh. Fr. Heffernan wasn't too pleased. He took a look across at Mickey and that shut him up. I helped Redser up to receive Holy Communion. It took the priest about five minutes to get through the bandage to get the Host into his mouth. Eventually he was successful.

Mass came to an end and my mother brought us all back to our flat where we tucked into breakfast. A nice finish to our morning.

Years later I was in *Johns Lane Church* and all the memories came flooding back, Mickey Doolin who never could stop laughing, Redser Roache and his broken nose and "say it again, 'Top o' the World, Ma, Top o' the World'".

Chapter 4

Christmas in the Liberties

Christmas in the Liberties was something special to see. Thomas Street and Meath Street were covered with lights and the stalls were full with fruit and Christmas decorations. The magic of it!

"It's only a day, you know," Redser said, "and then it's St. Stephens Day and then it's all over."

I said, "We'll all get together on Christmas Day."

Mickey Doolin turned to me. "Have you any money, Jim?"

"I have. My Uncle Jim gave me a three penny bit so, how much do you want?"

"A penny will do," said Mickey. So I gave him the three penny to get change.

"By the way," I said, "what do you want it for?"

"I want to buy a raffle ticket in Mrs. Collins' store."

I said, "How much are they?"

"A half penny," he said.

"Get one for Redser and one for me. What is the prize?" I said.

"First prize is a *Roy Rogers Gun*, second prize is a *Shirley Temple Doll.*"

Redser said, "I bet you win second prize. By the way, how about us all going in to Grafton Street to see Switzer's window. I heard they have great Christmas decorations, a great Christmas Santa and a big sleigh."

At this point Mickey was in knots of laughter. He was nearly chocking.

Redser said, “What are you laughing at, Doolin?”

“You and Shirley Temple,” Mickey said.

I laughed too but not for long. Redser wasn’t too happy so he grabbed Mickey, pulled his trousers off and slapped him once or twice on the arse. It was funny, Redser swinging Mickey’s trousers around over his head. Just as he was about to give them back to him Mrs. Collins came into the hall from the shop, on way to deliver oil to someone in the Barracks when she came on to Mickey’s bare arse. “Jesus, Mary and Joseph, cover yourself, you’ll get a cold. Mickey Doolin,” she said, “cover yourself, I’ll tell your mother. I might have known, with Redser Roache and Blondie Smyth.”

We all started laughing. Mickey was the loudest. There’s a great deal of fun out of Mickey. I liked him a lot

My mom heard the commotion and came out. “Jim, keep your voice down,” she said, “your dad is trying to get some sleep, and the baby’s very cross, I can’t get him to sleep.”

“I will, mom.”

“Come on in then,” she said. “Say goodnight to the boys.”

“Jesus,” Redser said, “he’s a fucking nanny, what next?”

“We’ll go to Grafton Street tomorrow,” I said.

My mom said, “you’ll go where tomorrow? Grafton Street?”

“Ah, no ma’am,” I said, “don’t forget the Sweet Afton for your father.”

Mickey was laughing, Redser was in knots, Mickey was trying to put his trousers on and wasn’t doing a very good job. He toppled over and landed with his legs in the air.

Mrs. Collins passed by and said, “Mrs. Smyth, they’re not

going in the head, they're coming back."

We eventually got sorted out, Redser and Mickey said goodnight to mom. I said, "I'll see you in the morning, Mickey, good night Shirley."

Redser said, "Don't forget the baby's nappy." We were good mates, that's all that mattered.

Next day after school we went into Switzers, a day of great enjoyment. It was just like I had anticipated it would be.

Believe it or not, the next week I won the *Roy Rogers Gun*! It was magic, the winning! Plenty of caps came with it and the three of us were in business.

I really enjoyed that Christmas, with my father, mom, Paddy, Fran, Des and me, and of course with Redser and Mickey. We spent most of our time in the pigeon house. We had one of the rooms cleaned out and it was quite nice.

The day after Stephens Day Redser said to us that the Thompson boys wanted to come back. They said they were sorry, he said. "You're the boss, Redser, but I don't like them," I said. "I think they're snaky gits."

There were lots of boys and girls in the Barracks but our life was built around us three. We were always together. I was never happier. My mother used to make sandwiches for our meetings in the pigeon house. One night Mickey put his arms around me and said, "I love you, Jimmy, you're my best pal."

Chapter 5

The Move

My dad said to me one day, “Jim, get Redser and Mickey.” I got the lads.

He brought us over to the Cherry Steps. It was in the afternoon. All the boys were on the Steps, Bunny, Juicy Leonard, Christy Dignam, Tony Boland the cyclist. Bunny put his arms around me, gave me a big hug, and to my dad he said, “How’s it, Terry?”

“Okay. I might be joining up, I don’t know yet, I don’t know yet.”

‘What did that mean’, I thought. I looked at my dad. Where was he going?

“Bunny,” I said, “these are my two pals, Redser Roache and Mickey Doolin.”

He shook their hands and said, “You know, any friend of Jim’s is certainly a friend of mine.”

Mickey said, “I heard you’re a great boxer.”

“Well, I don’t know about the great boxer but I do alright,”

Then Redser said, “I do a bit of boxing myself. We must get together sometime.”

Bunny said to me, “Throw me one, Jim.” I flicked a punch and he caught it in his hand.

“Just like old times, Bunny,” I said.

“You’re getting big lad.”

“I’m in the *Christian Brothers School (CBS)* on Brunswick

Street."

"Good for you." He winked at me and said to Redser, "Throw one, Ginger, you've a great pair of shoulders on you."

Redser squared up and Mickey put his hands over his eyes, laughing as usual.

Redser caught Bunny with a left and then a right. Bunny said, "They were two good punches, Ginger."

Redser said to him, winking at Mickey and me, "I hope they didn't hurt you."

"I'll live, Ginger."

Dad was talking to Fusco who had a plateful of ice-cream and wafers for us. We tucked in.

Redser said to Bunny, "I'd like to take a trip down to Belfast with you."

Bunny was really enjoying himself with Redser. He said, "Okay, that's a date." Bunny didn't take him down to Belfast but he went to see Redser when he boxed at the CYC League – and said he was good.

We took our leave and I said goodbye to Bunny. He said to me, "You be a good man, Jim. Don't forget God, he's always with you."

I said, "I won't." I liked Bunny. He was someone very special. I never saw him lose his temper with anyone except the Bull that day in Smithfield. I won't forget you, Bunny. I never did. He got sick in later years. He didn't know many people.

One day my dad went up to see his mother, who was my gran, so I went along with him. She was a lovely old lady. I loved her. I was just going out the door when Redser came in to the room. "I'm Jim's friend," and he shook her hand. When we were leaving Redser said, "I'm a boxer, ma'am, I'll be fighting in Belfast soon." I heard Mickey laughing down the hall. I said to Redser, “you’re priceless”. Redser said to me, “I think Bunny was impressed with me, wasn’t he, Jim?” I said, “He was, Redser”.

We got home to the Barracks. I said, “Dad, we’re going over to the clubhouse.”

Liz was outside, she looked nice and said, “Hello, where were you?”

“If you had been here you could have come with us.”

Redser said, “I’m turning pro”.

She said, “What’s that?”

“I will be getting paid for fighting,” Redser said.

Liz said, “The Thompsons were just here. They were looking for you,” then she said to me, “Do you want to kiss me?”

I kissed her.

She said, “I don’t like the Thompsons. They are not nice.”

I agreed with her. “So stay away from them,” I said to her.

“I will,” she answered.

Redser came out of the house. “Were you inside with them?” he said to Liz.

“No, Redser.”

“I hope not. You’re Jimmy’s girl.”

I said, “Is she? That’s great.”

Redser said, “Jim, I’m thinking of turning Pro.”

“That’s great,” I said and was waiting to hear Mickey laugh. I looked over in the corner and Mickey was fast asleep. I sat down beside him and told him I was sad about my dad.

"I liked your father, Jim," said Redser.

"I'm glad because he liked you too."

I went in to my mom and asked, "Is dad going away?"

She said, "He's going to join the British Army."

I said, "We'll miss him."

"I know we all will but your father has to get work."

I said, "I'm leaving Liz up to her house," and I went outside and had a good cry that went on for about half an hour. After that I felt some better.

It was a sunny Saturday morning. Redser and I were going up fishing. We called up to Mickey to ask if he would come along. He said, "Yes, I'm with you."

We came down the Steps and as we came out onto the Barracks the Thompsons were there. They saw the fishing nets and asked, "Are you going up to the canal?"

"Yes," said Redser.

"Can we come?" asked John Thompson.

Redser and Mickey said okay so we got organised and were off. We got to the corner and my mom was there.

"Jimmy, I want you to go down to the MayPole stores. Mr. Doherty has meat for me."

I said, "Okay". She gave me money and I put it into my pocket. I gave my fishing net and jar to Mickey. John Thompson wanted me to give it to him but I said, "No, Mickey will carry it for me. I'll follow you up."

I legged it down to the MayPole. It was all parcelled up for my mother. The man behind the counter asked, "Is your mother not with you?". I replied no, and took the parcel off him as quick as I could. I raced to the flat where mom was waiting for me. I gave the meat to her.

She said, "Be careful up at that canal, I don't like you being up there."

"It's shallow at the side, I won't be long," I said. I was away up the lane. Mrs. Collins was outside her shop. "Hello, Mrs. Collins Big Arse," I said.

"I heard that Jimmy Smyth, I'm surprised at you."

I laughed and made it across James Street and cut up Crane Street at the side of Guinness's Brewery. I kept running, around the corner. Someone was shouting. 'Something's wrong', I thought.

The Thompsons were running towards me. They were shouting, "He's in the water." I asked who was in the water. Redser was trying to swim into the water although none of us could swim. I kept running. It was Mickey who was in the water. I don't know to this day what I was saying.

I saw one of the men on the Guinness barge jump into the water and start swimming towards us. I fell into the water. I felt someone catch me by the hair and pull me out. I saw Mickey's head go under. His eyes were shut and his face was pale. He was gone.

'Oh my best pal, you're gone ...'

I came to. I was spitting out water and was getting sick.

"That's good, son," a girl was saying to me, "you'll be alright."

Redser said, "You'll be okay, Jimmy."

Mickey drowned.

They wouldn't let us look. They took us home. We were

very upset. He is still fresh in my mind. All these years. All my life.

My mom kept me beside her all the time. She really looked after me.

I went up to Mickey's flat to see my pal. Mrs. Doolin was sitting by the bed. There was a white sheet on it with a head rest. Mickey was laid out on it. He had a white shirt on and black trousers with suspender belts on the trousers. He had shoes on. I said to Mrs. Doolin, "He never liked to wear shoes." Mrs. Doolin was crying. She said, "Alright, Jimmy, we'll take them off." I said, half laughing "He wouldn't wear them." I looked at Mickey. He looked great. I said, "Good bye, Mickey old pal." Mom put her arms around me and we went.

I'll never forget you on the day when they put you in that box and took you away. How I'll miss your smile and the laughter we made. You will always be there in my memories. I will never forget you as time goes on, your laughter will ring out again and again in my heart and in my song. For you were the one who laughed life along and those days would be nothing without you. I'll always remember the secrets we shared and the way that you showed me how much you cared. When I asked for your help there was nothing you spared.

Life wasn't too happy about the Barracks. Redser and I were always together. John Thompson got himself into trouble and was sent to Borstal, a prison for young offenders in Cork. It didn't matter very much. He wasn't missed.

I went over myself to see Bunny.

My dad went into the British Army.

Then one day my mom said to me that we might be moving into a flat. I said, "Great." She said, "You will miss Redser." It was nearly a year since Mickey died. We always talked about him. He was part of our lives. We never went up near the canal. We always had a fear of it, since Mickey's death.

Mom continued to talk about moving quite a lot. I never saw Bunny or the Cherry Steps very often after my dad went in the army. I more or less kept to the Barracks. I would give mom a hand around the flat. Redser and me would talk a lot about Mickey. But mom would say, never dwell in the past. Mickey is gone up to heaven. You will be together one day with him. The Hardy family, Paddy and Christy, becàme top class amateur boxers. Christy in later years joined the professional ranks and did very well for himself in England. A few more girls came into the Barracks. It was becoming quite congested but I still liked it.

One day my mom said, “Jim, we got a flat in St. Audoens House in Cook Street.” She looked at me and said, “We have two bedrooms and a big front room, our own toilet and bathroom.”

I said, “That’s great, mom, I really mean it, I really do.”

I loved my mom. All my life I loved her because she understood me. She was always there for me. Even in later years. When I got myself in trouble she always stood by me. She never let me down, so I was pleased for her and the new flat. All she ever wanted was the best for her children. In her lifetime she bore ten children into the world. Two would die in childbirth, eight would continue to live on in this world. All eight of us would marry and bring our children into the world. Now they have children. I was proud of my mom when I was a little guy and I never stopped being proud of her.

I told Redser about the move. He didn’t say a lot, “We will see each other ... don’t forget me.”

How could I forget him. He was part of my life, the same as Mickey was. Then Redser started to cry. He just went on and on. I started then. My mom came on the scene with my Uncle Jim. He said, “Come on and have a good cry,” and we did. Uncle Jim put his arm around me and said, “Come on, Jimmy, I’ll give you a lift to your new home.”

So Marie, Anne, Paddy, mom and myself were off to St. Audoens which was still in the Liberties and that was great.

There was no goodbye. Redser followed me out to the car. I was wiping my eyes and roaring out to Redser, “Good bye mate.”

Redser said, “I’ll be down to see you, Jim.”

“I’ll be waiting for you.”

I thought then of Mickey, my old pal, how much I loved him.

It was a van we were in. We swung down past Oliver Bond Flats. There it was in front of us, with it’s big clock in the top of the flats. We drove inside. The caretaker Mr. Downey came over to my mom and handed her the key. He said, “Welcome to St. Audoens House, Mrs. Smyth.”

Chapter 6

Redser vs Adams

I didn't know what to make of the flat but I could tell it was going to be one hell of an experience. I knew that already, don't know why. Also I knew I was going to miss the Barracks, Mickey Doolin and Redser Roache. And Liz. Already I missed her. Never got to see her before I left but no matter, I would drop up to see her the weekend. Somewhere to go and nice to look foreward to it.

Our flat was Number 313. It was small but very nice. There was a lovely bathroom, and the flat had just been wallpapered and painted and was spotless everywhere. Having electricity was a great novelty. We only had gas in our last flat. My mother got things sorted in no time and I could tell she was very pleased with this new place.

Our first night, we had something to eat, washed up and got ready for bed. I went to the front door to look over the balcony (I found out later that's what it was called). It wasn't a cold night. I looked down at the big square below me. It looked impressive. There was a huge clothing factory on the far side of the square

A man was standing on the balcony a bit apart from me.

Just as I was about to go inside he said good night to me. I said, "Good night to you. Hi, my name's Smyth."

"John White is mine," he said. "Nice to meet you."

I smiled and went inside. "I met my first neighbours," I said to my mom.

She was writing to my dad and said, "What, Jimmy?"

I said, "The eagle has landed", said good night and went in to bed. It was a great feeling, we were all starting another phase of our lives.

I quickly adapted to the flats and made new friends. I still went up to see Redser and spent long days in the pigeon house. We always mentioned Mickey Doolin but not too long did we dwell on it. Liz came down at the odd time but that was as much as it was. Redser was doing a lot of boxing in Joe Foley's club called *St. Frances Boxing Club*. He was good. He was strong now, very strong and a great mover.

I was still in *CBS* on Brunswick Street (often referred to as *Brunswick Street School*). One of my Masters was Master Paddy Crosby, who would receive much fame years later as the Presenter of the very famous TV program, "School Around The Corner". He was also the writer of it and quite a clever man although heavy-handed. He and my mother were great friends.

I liked school. I got on well with the lads except for one big guy called Johnny Adams. I didn't like this boy. As a matter of fact, no one liked him. He was ignorant and loutish, and tall and fat. When he would pass the younger boys, he would wack them on the head and hard, take their school bags off them, empty them out on the ground and take whatever he fancied.

I channeled my annoyance by having a go at boxing for *Arbour Hill.*

As it turned out, boxing became quite useful to me. I had many a go off Adams, and mostly came off the worst, but he never tangled with me although he continued to lash out at any young kids around. I could see the fear in their faces whenever he came near. We were most of the day in Master Kelly's class and Adams was his pet. I wasn't going to tell the Head Master because that wasn't on, so you sang dumb. Life at school could have been great without this guy, but no one listened to me. I was mad about the situation but no one listened.

I told my mom and she said she would tell Master Crosby.

I said, "No way, mom! You don't do that, that's not on."

She understood and said she would do nothing, although, she said, "If he touches you I am not accepting it. I am going up to see my friend. Mrs. Collins in Marshalsea, will you come with me? You can go up to see Redser."

I said, "Great."

"Mrs. Collins is making curtains for our windows. Now come on, Jimbo, lose the face, it doesn't suit you. Everything will be alright, you'll see."

"I hope so, mom."

On Saturday I got ready and first we went up to Thomas Street into Frawley's shop. My mom knew one of the women in the shop who got her the material for the curtains.

"Oh wait," mom said to me, "I want to get something in Mushatts Chemist." Mr. Mushatt and his son were in the shop. Mr. Mushatt knew my mother and I often went up to him for stuff for my mom.

"Hello, Mrs. Smyth," he said to her, "how is Mr. Smyth?"

"He's great, thank you Mr. Mushatt."

"Nice to see you, Mrs. Smyth. The son says, 'are we going somewhere tonight?' "

My mother said, "Does that include the kids as well? No thanks," she said with a laugh, "I've enough to take care of."

"He's a new boy," I whispered to mom, "he's got plenty of money."

"So what," my mom said, "I've plenty of money haven't I, I got you," and she kissed me.

Sarah May who was selling fruit at her stand, said, "Ah, Jimmy, will you give me one of them?" so I went over to her and obliged. She was nice although I sorta' over did it with the kiss.

"She is a good looking woman," mom said to me, "she is going with that Higgins man."

"Mom," I said, "she is married to him!" So off we went.

We made our way to the Barracks. "By the way," mom said, "who is that nice looking bloke I saw you going across the bridge with the other morning?"

I said, "That's Bob Gallagher, out of the terrace. He's a nice enough boy but I miss Redser."

Mom said, "Ask him to come down to see us some day. He can stop overnight."

"I'll ask him," I said.

We got up to the Barracks. Mrs. Collins lived just a bit down from the Barracks. "I'll see you when you're finished, mom, I said.

"Okay, don't go home on your own."

"I won't."

I went into the hall. Our old hall door was still standing. I heard that nobody lived in the rooms now. I knocked on the door for old times sake. Someone opened the door. I got a shock. "I didn't think anyone lived here."

Standing at the open door was a little man with a kulchie accent. "Off with you, you fucking little bastard."

I was taken aback. "Wait a minute ... ," I said, then I made out someone I knew.

"Redser! you frightened me."

He laughed, his teeth sparkled. I said, "You got false teeth!"

"God, you're very observant."

“Good to see you,” I said.

“What’s doing in the flat? I saw you outside with your mom.”

I said, “She wants you to come down for a few days.”

He said, “I’m going away next week to my Uncle Johnny in Liverpool. How are you getting on?”

“Okay,” I said

“Not very convincing,” he replied.

“You know ...”

“No, I don’t, tell me,” he said.

I said to myself, ‘I have to tell him’. I said to Redser, “It’s that prick Adams. He’s killing us all, all those little guys. I feel sorry for them. He’s getting away with it. I don’t want to tell anyone,” I said, “but it’s doing my head in”.

“I know how you feel,” Redser said.

“What did you do?”

“I bought a pinch-bar for protection,” Redser said.

I laughed and stayed with him for awhile, a good hour or so. Then he said he had to go. “Okay, see you soon,” I said.

I waited for mom outside Mrs. Collins’. She made the curtains for mom so about half an hour later the door opened and mom and Mrs. Collins came out together.

“Ah, here’s my lovely son,” mom said jokingly. “How is Redser?”

“He’s great,” I said, “but he’s not coming down to see us. He’s going to Liverpool to his uncle.”

“Oh,” said mom.

Mrs. Collins said, “Here’s a few pence for you, Jim,” and she gave me a ‘thru-penny’ bit. I said, “Thank you, ma’am.” She was a lovely woman and a great friend to my mom. She was by all accounts sweet on Uncle Jim.

We made our way home, got into the flat and started to make dinner. We had a radio which mom got out by the week. It was a Crosley radio and we used to love to listen to *“The Fairy Tales of Ireland”*, always at 5:50 in the evening. We wouldn’t miss it for love or money.

Mrs. Wilson came to our door to ask my mom something. She said the curtains were lovely and helped to put them up. Another nice woman who became a great friend with my mom. It was a good weekend, getting to know people in the flats. We were getting on.

Monday morning I made my way to school. I wasn’t looking forward to it. Master Kelly was not a nice man but it was Adams who was the real prick in the class. I didn’t want to tangle with him. I got into the class room and looked around but Adams wasn’t in yet. Maybe the bastard wasn’t coming in. I might be lucky. A lad called Conachy whispered to me, “Adams said, he was going to get you, Jim, Thought I would put you on guard.”

“Thanks, it will.”

“Go out and buy a pinch-bar,” he said.

I heard him coming in. It was Adams. He hit against me as he passed by. He went up to Master Kelly’s desk and put a parcel on it. It looked like a bottle. I thought, ‘teacher’s pet’. I was not a happy chappie. Master Kelly came in then, saw the parcel on his desk and gave a nod to Adams. Master Kelly picked it up and went outside, then came back well nuttered, very happy.

Meanwhile, I got the shock of my life. I looked over to one side and saw Redser sitting at the desk against the wall with a huge grin on his face. I nearly freaked out. I thought, ‘Jesus, what’s he at’. No one seemed to notice anything was wrong.

Master Kelly said, “Adams, clean the blackboard.”

Adams went up to the board.

Redser looked at me, I nodded my head. Redser brushed his hair back out of his eyes, rubbed his hands together, got up from his seat and walked out of the classroom. I had not an idea what he was going to do. At about eleven o’clock Master Kelly said, “Outside, class, for a break”.

I went down the hall to see if I could find Redser but he was no where to be seen. I thought he had gone home. I had some biscuits. I started to eat them. I was upset to say the least. ‘What was Redser going to do?’ Whatever it was he certainly wasn’t getting me involved. I knew he was capable of anything.

I didn’t have to wait long.

The toilet room was large. It would hold a fair amount of boys. I made for the toilets. The noise seemed to be coming from there.

“He pissed on Adam’s shoes,” someone said.

“Who?”

“The guy with the red hair.”

‘ This is it,’ I thought. ‘Redser is in business.’

I broke through a crowd of boys, into the inner circle. Two boys were sparing. Redser and Adams. They were throwing punches. Very fast. Redser was giving a good account of himself. He was ducking and weaving between punches that Adams was throwing at him. Redser threw a nice left. It caught Adams in the stomach. Adams lurched forward. Redser stepped forward and caught Adams full on the mouth. Adams stopped, spit out some blood on the ground. He lost his head and threw a wild swing at Redser, who stepped into Adams and caught him again with another right hand into the mouth. Then he continued to punch Adams with a succession of left hooks and right crosses which destroyed Adams. Redser never let up. He just kept going, on and on. At this stage Adams was in bits. The bully just hadn't got what it takes. Redser was awesome. He was breathing heavy. His chest was heaving. Adams just didn't know what was happening. His hands fell by his side, his head dropped forward and at that moment Redser caught his head in his left hand, paused for a second steadied himself, then cracked Adams with his right, stepped back and Adams dropped on to the ground. He never moved. He couldn't. He was out to the world, or to put it simply, out for the count. There was complete silence.

Redser went over to the sink, turned on the water, threw some on his face, wiped his face on the hand towel, picked up his coat, nodded to me and walked out the door and was gone.

One of Adams' cronies helped him to his feet. He hadn't a clue where he was. He was out of it. Just then a Christian Brother came in to the toilet and took over, taking Adams to *Richmond Hospital* across the road. They dressed his wounds, a broken nose, four ribs broken.

"Some nacker done him," one of the lads said.

Redser was something else that day, he was great. I knew then Redser was something special. His performance was world class. Adams was head and shoulders taller over him and he was good. But Redser cut him down to size.

I finished school at 3:30 and ran home. I met John Chapman at the gate to the flats. "I'm leaving my bag with you, John, will you bring it up to my flat?"

"I will, Jim," he said.

I legged it up to the Barracks and caught Redser before he went away. He was going that night to England. I got the feeling Redser and me were beginning to fall apart. I said, "You were great."

"I told you I was. I wanted to do something to show you how much we mean to each other."

"You certainly did. He won't bully any of the lads or the young ones in school again."

"I'm glad," said Redser

And Adams never molested the boys in school again. He stayed in school about six months more after that, then went down to another part of the country.

I will never forget the day as long as I live. It was something very special that Redser did for me. I'll always remember him punching the head off Adams. I only saw Redser a few times after that. My brothers and I took up singing together and I lost track of him, but I always had a thought now and then of those days and nights when Mickey, Redser and I reigned supreme. What were we going to do with our lives?

Redser went to England, became a professional boxer and was 'a good 'un' as they would say in boxing circles. One Sunday morning his body was fished out of the River Thames with his throat slit. They took him away from me but my loving memories are forever.

Chapter 7

Strawberry Picking Tomorrow

During the summer holiday time Mrs. Thompson would organise the strawberry pickers. I never did go in my young days, only as I grew older.

This particular summer I asked Mrs. Thompson if she could fit me in to pick strawberries. The pickers would gather outside the flats early in the morning, and Mrs. Thompson would organise a way for us to get out to the fields. Sometimes we would use a C.I.E. bus, or take a lorry she ordered from the nurseries. Let's face it, any transport available, it didn't matter how you got there as long as you did.

"Certainly, Jimmy, I would be glad to fit you in," she told me. Mrs. Thompson and my mother were great friends and so she always had time for me. I would always bid her the time of day and she would return the compliment when we met. I liked her.

"I'll be seeing you in the morning," she said.

"You will, Mrs. Thompson."

"By the way, my name is Molly."

"Okay Molly, I'll be there."

I told my mother and she was glad for me. I was always looking to earn some money.

"You don't waste much time, Jim," my mother said.

"Why not, mom. I'll be able to give you a few bob."

She said, "Get some new clothes for yourself, Jim."

"We'll, see, I will make some sandwiches mom. I'll make some for Molly and for yourself while I'm making."

"I think she has a smack for you, Jim."

""She is one nice lady," I said.

"Right, Jim. You've convinced me." We laughed awhile. I liked those times together. My mother always had time to talk to me.

So, I was to go strawberry picking tomorrow. The bread and biscuits were all parcelled together, all ready. I got into bed and said my usual prayer to God. I looked over at the other bed. Paddy was asleep. He slept with Des and I slept with Frances. Paddy snored very loudly. If he was too loud I would wake him up. He would give a little groan and a little sigh, so then I would hit him with a container. Then he would wake up and start shouting so mother would come in to us. Then Fran woke up and that finished that. Paddy started of course to throw bouquets at himself, saying he had to be up early in the morning. At this stage he was getting to be a pain in the arse. My mother was trying to keep the peace and not doing a very good job at it. I could see she was starting to laugh a little. I got into bed saying, "I'm going to the country tomorrow." But Paddy had the lights on and he was putting Optrex into his eyes. This never failed to amuse me. He would then use his Gordon Moore toothpaste. Then he would spend about twenty minutes on his hair, pressing the front of the hair into a 'quiffe'. After that he would wash himself in the bathroom. This would be done with carbolic soap. That used to turn me off when I smelt it. I eventually got off to sleep thinking about Molly and strawberries.

Next morning, it was Monday morning, I rose early before Paddy. I got my breakfast, took my lunch and mother had made a flask of tea for me. It was half past six and the sun was shining. A couple of the girls were already waiting outside of the flats so we had a little chat together. I knew three of them but there were another two I didn't know. Two blokes and John Chapman joined us. I liked this. I was very pal-sy with John and his sister May as well. She was a nice looking girl.

I said, “Hello May, how are you?”

“I’m tired, Jimmy, how are you?”

I said, “Come over here to me, May, let’s talk.”

When she came over close to me I caught hold of her and kissed her. She let out a scream. I said, “Be quiet, you’ll wake up the whole flats.”

“I didn’t expect to see you here,” she whispered.

“I need the money,” I said. I ran my hands over her thin calico dress and she let out another scream.

“Can we have a little bit of quiet, please?” said Molly, she wasn’t too happy with us.

“I ‘m sorry,” I said, “we were just clowning around.”

Molly didn’t answer me.

I walked over towards John, sitting on the steps. May was sitting on the steps behind him.

“Are you coming with us, May?” Molly asked.

“If you don’t mind, Mrs. Thompson.”

“I don’t mind, May, but I should have known yesterday.”

“Sorry, I should have told you,” May said.

“Molly said, “It’s okay, I’ll write you in the book.”

Just then a familiar figure strode into the flats. Redser Roche. How did this happen. I would see Redser casually and liked to see him. But, what was he doing here this morning, I thought to myself.

"Who is this?" Molly asked.

"Liz told me about him. I know who he is, he's a good worker. This I could vouch for," I said.

"How are you, Jimmy," he said to me, "nice to see you."

"How are you, Redser?" I said.

"Top of the world," he said, "how's your mom and dad, Jim?"

"Keeping great," I said, "Dad's home from the army."

"That's great," said Redser. "I have money for food."

I said, "Don't worry, I have a good few sandwiches and a flask of tea. We will get it organised." It had been a few months since I'd seen Redser but now after so long it was good to see him again.

Molly started to talk to Redser so all was okay.

The bus was outside the gate and we were off. I was ready to rumble but with Redser being with us, that was something else. I knew that with him on board anything could go wrong. The bus took off and we were mobile.

We got to the strawberry fields soon enough, somewhere out near Swords. There was nothing there but the fields of strawberry plants and a couple of huts strung together. One hut was to be used as a toilet but the problem was it was for both ladies and gents. Molly was annoyed with this as her arrangement with the owner was to have two toilets, one for each.

"I told Joe the owner that it just wasn't on to have the girls using men's toilets, Jimmy."

I agreed with her and sympathised with her, but no matter what was said, there was still only on toilet.

Molly came back to me, gave me a smile and said, "We'll

manage."

"We will, Molly," I said, putting my arm around. She gave me a little smile and said, "Where the hell were you over the last two years."

"Not to worry, Molly. I'm here now." She always needed someone to be with her. She had a hard job, looking after the girls. They were under her care so they were her responsibility.

Redser was in his element. He had a big smile on his face and was singing his Guy Mitchell song, 'Trudy Fair'. "I'm doing well at the boxing, Jimmy, are you?"

I said, "I'm at Arbour Hill."

"I like the black haired young one," Redser said, "what's her name. I think she might want me."

I said, "Redser, you never change, pal." I could see this was going to be one hell of a journey. I wouldn't like to predict the outcome. With Redser on board anything could happen.

The bus stopped at our destination and we all spilled out. It was a lovely, sunny day. Molly let out a big shout for her boys and girls to stay together. Basins were laid out ready to collect the strawberries. We started picking at eight o'clock and we would work right through until one o'clock. I worked pretty hard, never letting up and I can tell you it was hard going. But I was a strong young man in my youth. There was money to be earned and I was in the mood of earning it.

One of the girls came to Molly and told her the toilets were out of action. Molly said, "Leave it to me, Lilly." She came back to us after awhile saying that she had made a make shift toilet behind some bushes. It was rough and ready but it had to do.

There were a lot of girls who would like privacy, so Molly organised it to good advantage which worked well in the beginning till one of the girls caught a man spying on her.

Molly was told about it. It turned out the spying man in question was with another group of pickers.

It happened that Redser was around to hear this and he decided to get involved as only Redser would. I too heard the talk and knew that with Redser involved it would have a funny ending.

Molly went off and made a new toilet, a big square box affair, with a hole in the ground which had already been there.

One of the girls headed inside the bushes in the late afternoon. At this point Redser had already seen a man who also headed inside the bushes and had completely taken off his trousers. So Redser relieved him of his trousers. He took them and started to run away with them, swinging the trousers above his head, to the delight of everyone, especially Molly. The man started to shout and took off through the bushes, without trousers. I don't know how the man got home minus his trousers but we never saw him again.

Once again Redser came out on top. We all had a good old laugh about it. Redser hung the guy's trousers out of the bus on the way home and they were blowing in the wind all the way as we made our way home.

It had been an eventful first day. I was very tired when we reached the Brazen Head. It was the end of our twelve hour day and I must say the end of a perfect day. We were tired but very happy little chappies.

"Do you want your wages now, Jim?"

I said, "Please Molly," so she paid me.

She said, "You worked very hard, Jim."

I said, "For you, Molly, any time," and I meant it.

She smiled. "I'll see you in the morning, Jim."

Redser said, "I'll take a few bob of you, Molly."

"Right, Redser," Molly said, "and thank you for today. You were my friend, a great friend if I may say so."

"You can," Redser said, "and thank you for this money. I'll see you both in the morning. Goodnight."

Molly said to me, "Leave me over to the door, Jim," which I dutifully did. She thanked me with a can of orange from Tullamore. I enjoyed it, sitting on the step outside her door. It was a warm night, the orange was cool.

I said, "Goodnight, Molly. I had a great day."

"Me too, Jim. Get some sleep," Molly said.

I did a couple weeks of work with Molly. They were great weeks, great memories. Redser was fun through it all. He was like a young Lugs Brannigan, looking after the young girls. These days were happy ones, lots of laughter and we without a care in the world. I remember the promises we made to each other in our youth and once again the sun shone for us. The happy times were ours for now.

Chapter 8

The Forty Steps

Our life started a second cycle when we moved into the flats. We quickly made many friends. Weeks became months and they were happy ones.

One new and good pal was Bob Gallagher who lived in the terrace beside *Adam & Eves Catholic Church*. I would meet him every morning to walk to school together. Adams had long gone and school was a great place now, thanks to Redser.

My brother Fran also went to *Brunswick Street School (CBS)* and some mornings I would walk with him to school. Fran was a very quiet person. There were brown marks on his hand. Master Crosby, who had a thing about smoking, said Fran was smoking and he punched him a hard one on the face. Fran started crying.

I never hesitated. I let Master Crosby have it. I was sorry afterwards. I let myself down.

"That's it," he said, "get Head Master Brother Ryan."

"Suit yourself," I said.

Brother Ryan came down to me. I told him what had happened. He said, "Go home, Smyth," so I went and Fran had to return to the classroom.

My mother was home when I got into the flats. I wasn't too happy in the telling. My mother put on her coat and we made our way back to *Brunswick School* where she sorted it out with Brother Ryan and I was reinstated. Nothing like it ever happened to me again. I spent many happy years in Brunswick and got on quite well with Master Crosby.

My pal Bobby Gallagher went on to become Father Bobby

Gallagher of the Franciscan Foreign Missions and was sent out to preach the Catholic faith in the African Foreign Missions. God bless him.

I was always on the mooch for an extra bob or two and was looking for work after school. I first got a job with Neddy Hayes helping him with his paper delivery.

Then Sarah May knocked on our door one evening and asked me if I would do a bit of work for her. "Certainly," I said. She was a lovely woman and I was delighted to work for her. The job was to push her cart up to Thomas Street and get all the stock from the fruit market into it. Then I pushed the cart back down Thomas Street to her fruit stand. I would get up at six o'clock in the morning to start this job.

After I was finished with that job I would go on to help Guisie White with his pigeons. Guisie was one of the lads out of the flats who would pop the pigeons. He used a sling-shot and was great at it. I would meet him in the mornings. When Guisie had gotten enough pigeons in the mornings he would collect them to pack and send to a cross-channel buyer. My mom said I would get up with the lark to make a few shillings. I was really in business so it was nice to relax in the evenings.

At night times me and my pals would go outside to watch the traffic on the Forty Steps. These Steps were located on Cook Street beside the old *St. Audoens Church*, a very old Protestant and Catholic Church, back to back. The Steps ran right up from Cook Street to High Street, to the Corn Market to be exact, on High Street.

We could watch the people when they hit the top of the Steps. We'd sit outside the back gate to our flats and watch all the proceedings.

We knew all the prostitutes who used the Steps. There was old Rosie, a big, blonde bustie lady. She would wave to me and call, "How is my good looking Dublin kid?"

I would go down to her and say, "How are you, Rosie, here's a cigarette for you."

She was always spotlessly clean. She would give me a big hug which I must say I didn't half relish, and a big kiss. John Chapman, Marty and Peter would say, "Smyth, you want to be watching yourself."

"We're only having a bit of craic."

It was great to see the girls. It was keeping body and soul together. I said to Rosie, "I see you have a new girl."

"Yes, she said her name is Elizabeth, come on over and meet her."

I said, "Hello, it's nice to meet you." She was a good looking girl with long, jet black hair.

"Have a cigarette?" she asked. "I only smoke these majors."

I said, "I will, Elizabeth."

I took a cigarette and she touched me in the lower part of my stomach. I laughed.

"You're full of tiddles."

"I'm not," I said, "I'm just on a first time with you. You're nice, I'll see you around." I would be soon leaving school. Hope I don't end up like these girls. But they were nice girls. Hope they don't get dosed.

One of the girls was a blonde haired girl. Her boy friend would meet her at the back of the Church. One day I saw him giving her money behind the Church. John Chapman told me her name was Eileen and she had a kid for him. He had a top level job in the government and was already married with children. I remembered Chapman showed me his picture in the paper. I saw him in the papers again just a couple years ago.

The Forty Steps on Cook Street was the oldest part of Dublin. We were sitting around by the back gate of the flats, sitting calmly and minding our business, giving the girls a wave now and then. It was a nice clear night. I was tired. Mr. Downey, our flat's Caretaker, passed us by with his two daughters. They were lovely. I said, "They're nice, Mr. Downey."

He said, "Goodnight, Jim."

"Good night, sir".

He went on in front of the girls. We were looking at the girls from behind as they went down the Steps. Just as Kay, the eldest, passed me by I let my hand slide down her arse. She gave a little start, then looked at me and started laughing. She was a well built girl, lovely. She looked back as she got up to Mrs. Ryans' shop on the corner. I gave her a wave and she waved back.

I saw them first. Two young men in long brown habits of the Franciscan Order with the double cord around their waists. They passed us by at the gate and said, "Good morning, boys."

They went on up and around to Lower Bridgefoot Street. Then they continued on up the hill to the Corn Market, up to the very top of the Steps, walking up the Steps from bottom to top. We could see them doing something to their habits. Then they ran down the Steps. We were mesmerised at what was happening. There were about four girls on the Steps, where they spilled out on to the ground at the bottom, shouting and roaring. The two Brothers were shouting and lashing the girls with their cords.

I said, "To hell with this." It wasn't funny, it had lost its fun when the cord hitting began

I was in among the crowd and succeeded in taking the cord off one Brother. The other had his taken by Rosie who had given him back what he had given her. I cooled down. I sorted it out but the girls just wanted to go home.

I spoke to Liz. I asked, "Could you not get another job?"

She said, "Not really. I get a lot of money out of this."

I said, "With this hassle going on, who needs a hole in the head."

I walked up to her car with her, a little blue *Porsche-to-Hire*. "Mind yourself."

I went back to the gate. I was fuming. This wasn't on. I didn't know what way it was going to end, but I soon found out.

The girls came up to us. I didn't know what to say. "Forget it for awhile, you know."

Rosie asked, "Where is Elizabeth?"

I said, "She went home."

One of the other girls said, "I think we will too, What do you say, Jim?"

"I think so too. Good night, girls."

As they left I said to myself, 'Jimbo, you fucking idiot, why did you get yourself involved in something like that'. Now I did not know what would happen.

I was soon to find out, and PRONTO!. It came in the form of a giant man on a bicycle.

He said, "I want to speak to you lads, John Chapman," then he turned to me, "I don't know you, what's your name?"

"Jimmy Smyth."

"Are you going to ask me what is my name?"

"Not really," I said.

He said, "Well, my name is Guard Jim Brannigan."

I said to myself, 'Well, bully for you.' But I was impressed. He was a big man. He got off the bike, as was his habit of action now and ever after when I would see him in action.

He would take out his gloves, put them on. Some other times it would be his Cosh, a long swing-type weapon, but not now. This time, he put on his gloves.

He said, "There was a belt up between some priests and the ladies on the Steps. That's not right," he said, "but I think it's over now."

"Did you sort it out, Mr. Smyth?" he said to me.

"Not really," I said. "Firstly, those two were striking the girls with the cord that they had around their waists." I said nothing else. It seemed to satisfy him.

"Jimmy," he said to me, "you do some boxing don't you, for *O.L.G.C. Boxing Club*?"

"I do."

"Good," he said. "I heard you're not bad."

"I am, thank you."

"Do you play hand ball?" he asked.

"I do."

"Come up to Kevin Street Police Station," he said. "I'll give you a few lessons."

I looked at my mates when he left. I had just met the great Jim "Lugs" Brannigan, and we became the best of friends for a good many years to come. He was one hell of a man, always in the thick of trouble, whenever and wherever it struck. They erected a statue to him years later in the Liberties for all the good work he had done for the people there.

We became great friends and often met at boxing tournaments and stadium youth council fights. He was always there. I will never forget our hand ball games. He was also a great friend of my mother.

The *Forty Steps* continued to house the girls of the night for a good long while. Once or twice in my travels I saw the two Brothers. Bobby Gallagher told me that the priests of *Adam and Eves Church* were not overjoyed with the two Brothers. They were eventually shipped to England.

There were other fond memories for us all of the *Forty Steps*.

One day I was coming down the *Steps* with John Chapman, Gladys Wilson, Johnny and myself. As we came to the bottom of the *Steps* I heard a noise. It sounded like a little crying voice.

"Hold on," I said, "Wait a minute."

There was a little opening, about two foot wide and two foot deep. It's still there to this present day and that's how I got inside to the back. Inside the small opening there was a little bundle. I pulled it out, opened it up and inside was a new little crying baby boy. We were all knocked out with shock. Gladys started to cry.

I carried the baby to the flats. The first ones I met were my mother and Mrs. Wilson, "We found a baby," I said. Mrs. Wilson took it into her arms, and my mother and she went into Mrs. Wilson's house. Someone called the police, and the squad soon came into the flats. The place was in an uproar.

What was to be done?

The inspectors and Lugs Brannigan came. Mom said to me, "Good boy, Jim, for finding the little one. I'm proud of you."

I was pleased and even more so when Mrs. Wilson said to my mom that she was going to adopt him and his name was to be Finbar Wilson.

Chapter 9

The Boys Brigade

In my young days I joined the St. Joseph's Boys Brigade, a Catholic organisation for young boys, located on Church Street near where we lived in the Flats.

Me and my pals were about eleven to thirteen years old at the time. Our Boys Brigade had about two to three hundred boys although there were never that many there at one time. We met in a big hall with an adjoining building to it. It was a popular place for we lads to meet and pass our free time. It eased our parents' minds and made things happy for us all.

If I was late to home my mom would say, "Where were you, Jim?"

And I would say, "I was in the Boys Brigade, we were training," and somehow things seemed better for her. It was a good excuse. I liked it. It seemed to attract girls as well which was another bonus for us.

The Committee for our Boys Brigade was run by our manager Freddie Bridgeman and Mr. Hudson. They were always organising something or another. On Sunday night they would have a variety show, which was very popular. We always had a packed house with people queuing up from early afternoon for the eight o'clock evening show. The Boys Brigade had their own singers and dancers.

At about this time my brothers Des, Fran and I began to sing at home together and we called ourselves the *Three Smyth Bros.*. It was at our Boys Brigade variety shows that the *Three Smyth Bros.* sang for the first time in public. This was sometime around 1946 at the Boys Brigade Hall.

At first we began to grow with our singing experiences.

The variety shows went well into the winter season. They

were especially popular with the Sunday night audiences, and as well with the shows we were running on Friday nights. One day as we arrived at the Brigade Hall the Lieutenant in charge of our training and marching, Sammy Morgan, got us all together to meet a man named John Flynn who had just come over from Scotland. He played the accordion and was very easy to listen to. He was a handsome man, had a lovely wife, and was friendly and nice to talk to.

"I'm going to start a choir," he said, "and I will be the boss. I'm going to come among you now, so start singing," so we sang our hearts out.

He had all his boys picked but I wasn't one. Des and Fran were picked but not me,

"I'm going to call the new choir the *St. Joseph's Boys Singers,* and there will be someone to take down your names."

I was real disappointed I wasn't in the choir. Just at that moment someone caught me under the arm and practically carried me up on the stage. It was Sammy.

"Come on," he said as he dragged me up, "you're as good as anyone here."

I was delighted with myself.

Mr. Flynn was a great music teacher as it turned out. He had a terrific voice and was a very learned man. The *St. Joseph's Boys Singers* went from strength to strength and soon became very famous all over Ireland and Dublin. We were working about four nights a week performing.

At first Jimmy Bourke was the lead singer with the choir but what a head he had! He loved himself! He started to demand impossible things, he just didn't get it, how life worked. His father had a go at Mr. Flynn, Jimmy lost out.

"He gets to have it his way," Jimmy's father said to Mr. Flynn.

"No thanks," said Mr. Flynn, "I don't want him."

So father and son left. We were not sorry to see him go although he was a good singer. But, hey, you have to have a boss and Mr. Flynn was top man with the *Boys Singers*. Benny Kavanagh stood up and said, "Three cheers for Mr. Flynn," and we all voiced our approval. At that moment the *Boys Singers* went big time.

I got a solo with the choir. *Old Sailor* it was called. I remember the song that went like this:

> *Before you sail away old sailor,*
> *Far across the open sea,*
> *Remember when you sail dear sailor,*
> *You'll be coming home to me.*

Mr. Flynn was very strict on diction. You'd think it was John McCormack he was teaching! But no matter. I never had anything to say to him in argument. He was a great teacher who taught me much of value in my later singing career. I got along well with him.

The *Boy's Singers* went on Radio Eireann, which was a big show. A lad called George Arnold sang the solo in *Ava Maria*, which won for George the award for Best Performance of the Year. He was great and richly deserved the award. Mr. Flynn of course was delighted with us. "You were excellent," he said and so we were.

George Arnold passed away some years ago but his son David Arnold is still a huge force in music today. He composed all the music for many films, including the music for the James Bond movie series.

During week nights, on Tuesdays and Thursdays, we would go to the Boys Brigade. Our *Three Smyth Bros.* singing act was doing great as well. So we were working around but still kept in contact with the Brigade.

Around Dublin in the Queen's Theatre on Brunswick Street there was a singing group called the *Happy Gang*, consisting of Cecil Nash, Mick Eustace, Bill Brady and

Gloria Green. They were famous all over Dublin and had a large following. But they were to be put out of the Queen's Theatre for six weeks. They had nowhere to go until it became arranged that they take their production to our Boys Brigade stage for the six weeks. Since the *Three Smyth Bros.* were very popular, Cecil Nash asked us to appear on stage with them. We went down well, especially with the younger set. So it was arranged: we stated our fee, it was agreed and the show ran six nights for six weeks and it was packed every night. The *Three Smyth Bros.* became a hit, we could do no wrong. The last night was a sensation. We had little conversation with the *Happy Gang* but I was very active in the show, I went into the sketches easily and did well with them. It would be fair to say I didn't put a foot wrong.

Cecil Nash came over to us after the last performance with a note which gave us the name of a man who would give us some work.

Des said to him, "No money, Cecil? What about our wages?"

Cecil gave excuses that they had this to pay and that to pay, but no money. This wasn't on, it wasn't professional.

For future reference, we said, it would never happen again, and to tell you the truth it never did happen again. But it taught us a lesson.

The story was told to Father Green, our parish priest, who came up to see us in #313 St. Audoens House with a cheque for the full amount we were owed. He was not pleased with the *Happy Gang*. They would not appear in his Hall again he said. So Father Green and his Committee said no more to the *Happy Gang*, they had 'dirtied their bib', meaning they had reneged on their contract. And he said to us, "Gentlemen, it's just not show business." But it did us a power of good for we got contracts from the episode and we never worked with the *Happy Gang* again.

Shortly after that we started to work with the Eamonn Andrews Agency. They were located in Henry Street. It was run by big Fred O'Donovan, and his manager was a nice guy called Eddie McQuirk. The work began to roll in to us. We began to do the top, big variety shows.

We still kept in touch with the Boys Brigade. Then Mr. Flynn upped and finished with *St. Joseph's Boys Singers*. He gave no excuse, he just left. I needn't tell you, everyone was very disappointed. Some of the boys' mothers got together to talk to him, but he just would not talk further to anyone. It was a shame, such a waste of talent. I still have great times to remember of those days in the Brigade. They were sweet, gentle times.

Let me tell you:

On a Sunday morning we would all get together at the Boys Brigade Hall. Between sixty to eighty boys marched together every Sunday morning to church. We wore our best trousers, long and black, and white shirt and tie, and then all the marchers had a white sash with "Boys Brigade" in black letters around one shoulder. We also wore a black peaked cap with a green band around it. Promptly at nine thirty, everybody was inside the big Hall, all lined up, waiting for Lieutenant Sammy Morgan. We were a lovely sight to behold.

Sammy gave the order to stand at ease, and we would file up to High Street Church. Large crowds would line along the sides of the road just to watch us. It was a Sunday morning occasion. Sammy blew his trumpet and I'll tell you, he had a great sound! He would march and we would follow him, up Church Street, across to Lower Bridge Street and past our flats, then up the Bridgefoot Street hill to Corn Market and into High Street Church.

Mrs. Kelly would be at the organ, playing us in. She was a lovely old lady. The priests were Father Green, Father Flash Kavanagh and Father Barry. Then there were always church priests Gerry Cramer, the Fetherson Brothers and Harry Derham who served as Men in Charge of we boys.

When the Lenten Retreat came around, it would be the Carmelites, Father Pollard. He was a big, blond, handsome priest and the women would be six seats full outside his

Confessional, waiting to tell their Confession. What a carry on! He would be hearing Confessions for hours, but he never seemed to mind.

Next door to Church Street was St. Michael's Crypt, a famous place now visited by thousands of visitors from all over the world. Down below in the vaults is a special habitant, the skeleton of a one thousand year old man, a very well preserved body. He was a lucky man, so it went, for when you shook his hand you were supposed to get many blessings. We Brigade Boys had a way to get into the crypt. If we had a new lad join our Brigade we would bring him down to shake the skeleton's hand. We got a great laugh out of this but mostly the new one would freak out.

There was a big pitch and toss school up on Ash Street at the Boys Brigade Hall. We would go up on a Sunday morning after Mass. John Chapman was a great gambler, he never lost. 'Trust to God' he would always say. John would have his two half pennies with him, well shined up and his piece of stick he called a "feck". And he was good. And he would always come out winning and have the price of our fish and chips. We would go up to Burdocks and big old Billy Burdock would say, "Smyth, tell me where did you rob it?" and I'd say, "Mr. Burdock, you have no faith in me."

We would get our chips and take off. I'd say goodbye to Mr. Burdock and John always said, "You should invest in a nose job."

"I heard that," Billy would say, "Chapman you're barred, you're finished," knowing he didn't mean it.

Then John would say to me, "He nose, you nose," and he would start laughing, thinking this was great. He'd go on and on until I'd have to say, "John, shut the fuck up, will you, you're doing my head in."

He would reply to me, "My mother said, and I listen to her, she said you're better than Jimmy O'Dea. How about that?"

I said, "Is that Jimmy O'Dea who lives on Ushers Island?"

And on and on.

We had good times in the Brigade. It was a very popular place to be. You were safe in it. This meant a lot to our parents. The men involved in it were nice men. They looked out for us. John was a good mate to me. We got into some scrapes but we always managed to get out of them.

We still continued to win money at the pitch and toss school until the Box Man came, the man who controlled the game. He had a belt and made a big circle with it. The one tossing the half pennies would step into the circle and toss two harps. You lose head harp, you toss again and then maybe two heads, you would win and take the pot. We won on a good few occasions, too many wins. Then one morning we went up and the Box Man stopped John. "You're too young," he said. "Okay", we said, "no sweat." We soon forgot it, we were into *St. Joseph's Boys Singers* and we were off and away.

When I visit the place where the toss school was, at the Boys Brigade Hall, there is now a big fruit market, quite posh. St. Michael's Church is still there, a beautiful place, the skeleton still in his box, shaking hands with visitors. Good times, always remembered. See you John. Now gone.

Chapter 10

A Romp in the Park

High Street is in a very historical part of Dublin which dates back to the time of the Romans. But it was famous to us as young boys growing up in our teen years because it had one famous shop called Dora Byrnes Sweet Shop. Oh my, the honey bees, aniseed balls and nutty bars, to mention a few, were to long for.

We all loved Dora Byrnes. If you were short a few bob she was great for a touch, money wise. Dora was an attractive lady and well liked by all we lads.

There was a nice park, the High Street Park, attached to the High Street Church, which was next to the Sweet Shop. The church had a huge front door, it was massive. It took a strong man to close it. I should know.

One day John Chapman who was a friend of mine and myself were both in the church grounds playing for awhile after school. We had great times after school, the world was our oyster. We hadn't a worry in the world.

Suddenly the gateway started to close. We made a run for it, I was nearer to the gate and managed to get outside but John didn't. I tried to open it but not a chance.

I ran down the Forty Steps and into the flats but no one would listen to me. I saw Mr. Downey who was the Caretaker of the flats and I told him the story of John being inside.

"Don't worry, Jim, I'll take care of it."

So I didn't. I just said, "Thanks" and moved on. Mr. Downey was a big man, about seven foot tall, a nice, responsible man who just happened to have two lovely daughters. A nice man in my thinking. We were good friends.

At about eight thirty that evening, a dark, November evening and getting near to Christmas, Mrs. Chapman, John's mother, knocked on our door.

Actually there was a knocker on our letter box, as there was in all the doors in the flats. And there was always the key to the door. Ours was on a piece of string, hanging on to the door. It was behind the letter box for your convenience and nobody else would touch it. It was for the family, and nobody else but the neighbours used it. The times were so trusting then.

"Mrs. Smyth," she said, "is Jimmy in?" My mother and she were great friends.

"Mrs. Chapman, come in please."

"Chrissie, John is missing."

"Jesus, Mary and Joseph," my mother said, "don't tell me that. Jimmy, where is John?"

"I don't know mother, honest. The last time I saw him he was in High Street, the Protestant Church."

"Jim, it's nine o'clock," mother said, "and the church is closed."

"I know, it closed when I left him, mother. The door closed and locked him in."

My mother just looked at me and said, "Why did you leave him in the church?"

"Mother I could not open the door."

My mother got her coat and said, "Let's go, Jim."

So mother caught me by the hand and, with Mrs. Chapman, the two of us were off. We went up the Forty Steps. Business was good. A woman walked by and said, "Hello".

"Close your eyes, Jim," my mother said to me.

My mother replied, "Nice to see you."

The woman looked at me. Her name was Rosie. She slapped her leg, laughed out loud and said, "Why it's Jim," she said, "How's my boy?"

"Hello, Rosie," I said, "this is my mother."

"Nice to meet you Mrs. Smyth, my, you are lovely."

"Thank you," my mother said to Rosie.

"Jim is an old friend of mine, Mrs. Smyth."

My mother said, "That doesn't surprise me, he's a popular boy and won't we have one serious discussion when we get home, won't we Jim?"

"Yes," I said, "yes mammy dear. Bye Rosie."

"We play in the park, mother."

My mother said, "Jim, you are thirteen years old. "

"Am I that, dear old Chrissie?"

"Yes," my mom said, "but listen, Jim, if you don't come up with the right answers I don't think you'll see fourteen, sunshine." She nodded behind me at Rosie, smiling. "I'm sure you catch my drift, Jim."

"It's cold tonight mom," I said.

" ... and so will your arse be cold by the time I'm finished with it."

"Here's the door. John," she shouted, "Where are you, lad?" but there was no reply. She shouted some more but there was still no reply. It was dark and some men were coming into view.

“Stay by me, Jim. I think he might be gone home.”

I said, “I hope so, Mrs. Chapman.”

She said, “Come on Chrissie, we'll go home.”

Mother caught me by the hand and said, “Let's go home, love.”

I said, “Alright, mother dear.”

My mother stopped, looked at me and smiled. She said, “Jim, if you patronise me one more time with your ‘mother dear’, okay?, I'll give you a slap in the mouth so hard that you will be farting ivory for the rest of the year.” She looked at me and then she started to laugh.

I also started to laugh. She stopped. “But you still have to answer my questions.”

I said, “Okay but who is that on the school roof?”

“It's John,” he shouted, “I'm freezing.”

I got him out through the backdoor of the school.

“I'm really cold Mrs. Smyth.”

“Are you?” his mother said to him as she caught him by the hair and slapped him hard on the cheek, “and here's one on the other cheek just to keep that one company. Now, John dear, tell me that you don't know that lady Rosie.”

“I don't, mam, I swear,” said John

We passed by Rosie.

“Night, John,” she said.

“It's a cold night.”

“I'm bloody sure it is, love,” said Rosie. “Business is very slow tonight. Night ladies,” Rosie said to my mother and

Mrs. Chapman.

"Good night to you," my mother said to Rosie. "It's been nice meeting you."

"You've a great lad there," Rosie said. "I call him 'the good lookin Dublin kid.'"

"I love him too," my mother said, smiling.

"'The good looking kid', how are you? Wait till your father hears this, and your brothers and sisters." She told them and they had a go at me and it stuck with me for a good while after.

The park continued to throw up adventure after adventure, like the big tree with the red berries. One day about ten of us decided to eat the berries, much to our regret as we all got violently sick. It was like an episode from *Casualty* in the flats, we were all lying on the floors in the flats, roaring and they could find nothing wrong with us. That is, until Dr. Hannigan got the message. "Were you in the park eating berries from the tree?"

"Yes, doctor."

"Now I understand."

It got a good laugh and it still does.

The park had its characters, I can tell you. Bang Bang, Hairy Lemon, the Dude.

Now I can tell you the Dude was an original character. He wore an overcoat, shoes with spots on them, and he always had a waist coat on with a rose in his buttonhole. He carried gloves in his hand and if a young lad came in contact with him he would get a smack of the gloves in the face.

One day we decided to sort him out. When he fell asleep lying on a bench we took off his trousers and coat and gave them to Bang Bang. The Dude woke up with no trousers and no coat.

"Did you see my coat, Jim?" he asked.

"I did, in full view, I can tell you."

"Where? Tell me, John Chapman".

I said, "Last time I saw them it was on a #21 bus going toward Inchicore. Someone was wearing them I think. I think they were with Tommy Dudley". Now Tommy Dudley happened to be none other than Bang Bang, a true character if ever there was one.

Fifty years on and High Street Park is still a nice place. The old knock abouts are long gone. There are still some of my mates around, some have passed on as John Chapman and Rosie, but the memories are still blowing in the wind. I still waltz through there whenever I can.

Chapter 11

Joe, My Friend

Joe O'Connor was a pal and funny mate of my young days.

He said to me one night, "I need a shilling, Jimmy."

"It's a lot of money, Joe."

"I know," said Joe, yawning. "God, I'm tired," he said.

"You look it," I said. "A shilling, what's it for?"

"I'm locked out," he said, "I've nowhere to sleep."

"God," I said, "Joe, come on up to my flat."

"Jimmy, I don't want your mother to know."

"What's wrong with being locked out, it could happen to anyone."

"At nine o'clock at night, Jimmy?"

I got the message, the penny dropped.

"It won't be such a big deal, sleeping with me," I said.

"I know," Joe said. "I'll go to the shelter in Back Lane".

"You will not," I said. 'This is an idea I have,' I thought. We were standing outside Mrs. Wilson's flat. Johnny Wilson had a push cart, resting against the wall

"Get inside the cart," I said. He did. I pushed the car up against the wall, then I knocked on it. "I'll see you in the morning. Night, Joe."

"Don't forget to get me out in the morning," he replied.

I duly arrived about nine o'clock and let him out. "Did you sleep well, Joe?" I asked.

"It wasn't cramped, Jimmy."

"Good. Is it going to be an every night occurrence, Joe?"

"No way, honest Jimmy."

I believed him.

"Don't forget to see your mom, Joe," I said. But it wasn't to be, not for poor old Joe.

I came in that night a wee bit late. Joe was waiting.

"I'll have to use the box again, Jimmy."

"It's early, we will organise it later on. Invitation still stands," I said to Joe.

"Thanks, Jimmy. I'm much obliged to you," Joe said

This business continued for a long time afterwards.

Then Joe got real sick in his head and I was sorry to see it happen. He would just stand outside his door, staring into space. After a long while he got some better which was a great consolation for all his family.

I remember those days, I would not dare forget them. Imagine, a box cart as a front room! I would see his sister Ginny when I visited the flats, but I haven't see Joe for a good many years. He's still alive by all accounts.

Joe was a nice looking lad, as were all the O'Connor brothers, Kitser, Michael, Paddy and poor old Frances. Frances, known as Frank, met his death so tragically with Tommy Dunne on the Four Courts Bridge. Tommy, another lad from the flats, and Frank were mowed down by a car on the Bridge and both of them were killed instantly.

Sad old days. I had a lot of them in my life. They keep

coming back, like a song.

Chapter 12

A Sunday in May

It was a Sunday afternoon, around 2 pm. I had just come back to the flats, had lunch with my mom and Des, Frank and little Terry, who was only five years old.

Terry was a great little guy, always laughing. This I liked in him. He reminded me so much of my dear pal Mickey Doolin who just a little time ago was drowned in the canal. I still mourn for him, still shed an odd tear. I loved him so much, I needn't tell you. He was to come with me on my travels that afternoon to the Mass up in Thomas Street.

I met up with my pal John Chapman. Mass was to be held in the same place on Thomas Street where Robert Emmet was executed in 1803. The Mass was especially held there every Sunday afternoon in commemoration.

John said to me, "Jimmy, tell me what was so attractive about Thomas Street?"

I said, "Right, John my dear pal. You see, Robert Emmet was executed right on this particular part of Thomas Street where our blessed Mass will be held."

This pleased him. "Right Jimmy," he said.

I said, "Okay, John boy, let's rock on," so we did, me with my young brother Terry clasped tightly by the hand. By God, I would look after him, my brother.

I saw my old pal, John Sweeney, across the street. He waved over to me which I replied by shouting back to him, "Hello, John."

"Who is that? " Terry asked.

I said, "He is a very good boxer."

"Will you be boxing him any time Jim?" Terry asked.

I said to Terry, "Most probably," which seemed to please my little brother no end.

Terry said, "Wait up for John, he's tying his laces."

I said, "That is most unlikely, little brother, because you see he, John, never wears shoes."

Terry said, "Why not Jim, tell me?"

"Because his mom can't afford to buy him any shoes. His feet have now become used to the hard ground so he never notices he doesn't have shoes on. So his mom doesn't have to buy him any shoes any more. Does that satisfy you, little brother?"

"Yes," said little Terry.

We all made it up St. Augustine Street hill when I saw a familiar figure in front of us. It was Charlie Henchkow, the local bully. As we passed by he tried to catch Terry. I was not having any of this, no way. As he caught Terry I hit Henchikow a hard belt with my shoulder. He fell awkwardly on the ground. He seemed slow to rise.

"Whoa boy," he said, "what's this," he said, "somebody hit old Charlie. You struck me, don't like that, friend."

I said, "That young kid is my brother. Nobody puts their hands on my brother."

Charlie was on his own now. This was Charlie in a different state of affairs. He didn't like this place he was in, not one bit. He moved away from me at a fast pace, looking around for his pals. He couldn't find them or anyone.

Now he was a run of the mill hammer man.

He ran at me, making a kick at me in his new shoes.

"Charlie," I said. I backed away a bit. He missed me.

I retaliated with a kick back which caught him in the knee and he fell on the ground.

Just at that minute someone let out an unmerciful roar. I turned my head ever so slightly to look. It just happened to be my old pal Redser. I stood mesmerised, staring at him. I hadn't seen him for weeks, since I was back in the Barracks. I started to cry. I was looking for Mickey Doolin, I was suddenly out of it. I was a shambles.

Henchkow couldn't box eggs, never mind me, so now I had Redser. Then he had trouble and he knew it.

I stopped Redser as Henchkow ran off.

Redser said, "Why, Jim?"

I said, "It's Holy Day on this Sunday. I say the Devotion to our Blessed Lady. It will start in about an hour." I looked at him, "Your pal is in charge, Father Heffernan. And I miss Mickey being here with us."

"I miss him too, Jim. How are your mom and dad?"

I said, "Dad is in the army. I miss him. You know, Redser, I miss you too old pal. There are a few nice women down in my flats. You're a great looking bloke. You're big!"

"Oh you cheeky chappie, don't say things like that."

I said, "You know what I mean, like, you know, big ears, big nose, big head."

I started to laugh.

He started to laugh too.

So did Terry.

The three of us were laughing and, do you know something, it felt so good. I stood up and roared real loud but with respect,

"Top o' the World ... and I meant it ... *Top o' the World, MA!!"*

We made our way into Thomas Street. No minding Henchkow for the moment. But I knew he would not forget me. He would make it his business to see me again. He was a two faced tow rag no doubt about that, but I would be watching out. It would be a necessity, I would be sure of that.

We stopped outside Dora Byrne's shop and sat down for awhile. She came out and said, "Hello, Jim, who is the little lad?"

I said, "Mrs. Byrne, this is Terry, my brother."

She said, "He's a good wee lad, isn't he?"

"Yes ma'am, he is that, God bless him."

Terry looked at me and said, "Knock it off, Jimmy."

She said, "He's a lot like Des isn't he, Jim?"

I said, "Around the eyes maybe ma'am."

"You certainly nailed it, Jim. His eyes, they are lovely, aren't they. He has such a pretty little face hasn't he?"

Terry went red in the face.

Redser said to John, "Will you for God sake get your mother to buy you some shoes. You have suchy a pretty little arse."

This had me laughing, not at John, but no matter.

We left Dora Byrnes, she asking us not to forget to tell Des to call in to see her. Terry said, "I think she likes Des a lot, Jim. Will you tell Des, Jim?"

I said, "No I won't, little brother. Definitely not. I know he loves himself very much. He doesn't need me to convey any such message I get for him."

Redser was laughing to himself. I heard him mutter to himself quietly, "I think they have gotten mental, honest," laughing to himself, "I think they are mental since they moved from the Barracks. They have lost the plot."

I said to Redser, "It's nice to see you again. Are you still going to England?"

"I certainly am, Jimmy old mate."

This was great. Just like old times. I said, "Nice outfit, Redser." He had on short trousers, white tee shirt, white shoes. "Are you going running, Redser?"

"Something like that, Jimmy."

"Nice one old buddy."

"You know me, Jim, all heart."

Just then a lot of people came around the corner into sight. They were all runners, togged out

I looked at Redser. He was taking his outer clothes off, leaving him stripped down to his running attire. Now this was typical Redser. He had a small bottle of water which he threw over his head to give the impression he had run all the way from O'Connell Street. He took off with the runners. The finishing line was about one hundred yards past where the Mass was about to be held. It was a well organised Race Day, organised by Guiness Brewery. The runners were invited to go into the Guinness restaurant after, which Redser gladly accepted. He also got a ticket from a lady there which entitled him to partake of some ice cream in Woolworths. He went into Woolworths for his ice cream. He loves the ice cream. We were waiting outside Woolworths, to be honest with our tongues hanging out. But good old Redser came out with ice cream for us all. "It was terrific," I said to Redser while lashing into my coronet of ice cream.

The Mass was about to start. It was magnificent, the

statue majestic. Everyone said they really enjoyed the Mass and Redser made the collection during Mass. I just couldn't believe it, he was great in everything he did. I needn't tell you I was proud of him, all duffed up, good old Redser.

We all ended up with something that day. Our respect to our Blessed Virgin Mother. I said it was a great day, lads, great Redser. Don't forget me. Don't forget me. I will always think of you outside Woolworths Shop. We made a circle, put our arms around each other's shoulders outside Woolsworths Shop and shouted up to the sky, "*Top o' the World!*"

Then a voice said to us, "Let me in." It was Big Jim Brannigan.

He said to us; "Were you all at Mass, lads?"

We all said, "YES!"

I had in hand my coat and John and Terry's as well. Redser still had his white surplice on under his red shirt.

"You look good, Mr. Roach," looking at Redser's white surplice "I presume you would be saying the Mass?"

"Very funny Mr. Brannigan, I'm in knots of laughing." He turned to go away but Lugs caught him by the ear. "Steady on," he said to Redser," I meant nothing."

"Okay lads," he said, giving me a six pence, "Get yourselves some sweets.

I said, "Thanky you, sir."

Mr. Brannigan took off.

Redser walked along with us.

I said something with Redser who replied, "No thank you, sir, nothing. Would you like to kiss my arse, Jim, would you just, seeing you are lickin a few arses?"

I said, “Now Redser, I haven’t seen you for months, and when we do you start looking for a fight”

Redser looked at me with his big eyes.

I said, “You are still a great looking guy.”

He looked at me, dropped his head and chuckled. He said, “You know me by now. I’m mostly on my own.”

I said, “Redser, we will mate together again if you like. We both miss little Mickey. I never stop thinking of him. I still blame myself for not saving him from drowning.”

“Oh no, don’t say that, Jim, that’s not so. “ He put his arms around me and kissed me.

I said, “Redser, Mickey was here today. I heard him laughing, honest, he was with the Blessed Mother.”

Redser looked at me. “Jim, you heard him laughing?” All of a sudden he said, “Jim, you’re a psychic. Would you ever piss off and get a Mass said for yourself.”

Terry said, “Deck him, Jimmy, will you?”

I said, “Now Terry, hush and keep it quiet.” Redser didn’t hear him. Just as well.

We made our way down to Thomas Street. John was coming towards us, sauntering along. “Good old John,” I said.

“It’s getting cleared,” he said.

Redser said to John, “You don’t say an awful lot, do you?”

John replied, “Not a lot, Redser, but one day I will be called on to answer and I will. That’s for sure, that’s for dang sure.”

“Fuck me,” said Redser, “now we have a poet. What next, I give up, I give up.”

"Not yet, Redser," I said, "not yet."

At that moment the buses were back on the roads. The #21 Inchicore bus stopped in Thomas Street. A crowd got off with one in particular, which was Bang Bang, in all his glory. Bang, Bang went on and on.

Redser got involved. He grabbed Bang Bang. The James Street Brass Band was in sight, coming towards us. The music was loud and getting louder. They were playing *When Irish Eyes Are Smiling.*

This suited Redser for he was off with Bang Bang doing an old time waltz right in the middle of Thomas Street. The street traffic stood still. Redser had the floor and everybody was absolutely loving every minute.

The band had to stop and it wasn't because of *Casey and the Strawberry Blond*, it was because of Redser Roach. He was the culprit. Believe me, what an atmosphere! The stall holders, anyone who was moving was dancing. The Blessed Mother was there, it was her day. Terry and John and me got involved. This was something I could not forget and never will. No work, no money but lots of good failte. There was magic in the air because love was everywhere. "Our Lady Cometh" and in this afternoon.

I eventually got Redser un-entangled from Bang Bang, who I might say was slightly bemused by all of this. An innocent poor old soul was Bang Bang. Tommy Dudley was his name, or Bang Bang when he wanted you to make his day. He kept on saying to me, "I love you, I love you, honest man," he said.

I eventually disengaged myself from him, much to the delight of the crowd. I knew at this time Bang Bang would in later years be somehow a kind of celebrity. It was to be and it is very much so. But never let it be said that these characters were all there was to the Liberties. No way.

The years have passed on, the Liberties have gotten a little worn in places but it still can command respect, it is still a great part of Dublin, with its famous Irish Boxing

Champions Paddy Dowdall, Dave Connel, Gerry Colman, Cristy and Paddy Hardy, Tommy and Ando Redd and Paddy Kelty.

Then there was Michael Caruth, Olympic Gold Medal Champion, and Jim McLaughlen, Middleweight. I was looking at television at the show *Strictly* Come *Dancing.* I thought of Redser and Bang Bang and, you know my friend, those two were good as amateur dancers go. They compared up well with the best of the amateurs.

I said, “Where did you learn to dance like that Redser?”

He said, “Lizzie taught me.”

“No way, Ginger, me lad,” I said.

Redser said, “If you ever call me by that name again I swear to God I will slap you so hard in the mouth you will be spitting ivory for the next six months. Gottcha, old buddy?”

“Sorry,” I said.

“No matter dear old Jim, whatever you want.”

So it ended a great day.

Religion was always a part of my life. I always felt real good with myself when I was practising it. I remember I had asked my mum if I could go away to be a priest. I received some sort of answer in the form of “No Jim”.

I said, “Right, Mum.” I would have asked my dad but he was away in the army.

“You’re too young, young man,” she said to me. “Please be to God we will talk about it when you get a little older”.

I said, “Okay mother I can wait,” and so I did. I never went to join the priesthood but you know, it always remained in my head. It was tossed around constantly in my travels, but I always gave my time and efforts to any charity when they approached me in my early years. I was with

Tommy Poland and Father Oliver in St. Anthony's Hall, every weekend for years with his wife Kay Delany. We organised variety shows. The money raised by all the shows went towards the building of a dome for the Church of Adam and Eves Monastery in Merchant Quay. It was built by donations to the Church and Father Oliver.

That was a special Sunday day in my life. I love the memories of it, of Bang Bang and Redser strutting their stuff and doing a good job of it by the applause of all the people looking on. There were a lot of people hanging around after a while when we made our way back to the flats. It was a warm, lovely summer's night so John didn't look so odd in his bare feet. But when Terry and myself said good bye to John, Mom was looking over the balcony.

"Was that John with you, Jim?"

"Yes Mum."

"Go down and ask him to come up to our flat. I have some dinner left over, I would love him to partake of it. Call him, Jim."

Which I did and my mum set a place at the table for him. When we finished eating Mum said, "Put these pair of shoes on you, John."

I'd never seen them before. I looked at Mum. I said to her, "Mum, are they my old canvas shoes I used to wear?"

She said, "Yes, Jim, they fit John. I put some whitening on them. You haven't worn them."

I said, "No mum, nice one dear mother."

She said, "I thought so too dear Jim."

"By the way," she continued, "Is that young Roach sitting outside, Jim? Call him up to us, there is some more food for him. I wonder how he has been keeping. Poor little fellow."

I called out to Redser who shouted to me, "Thank you

Mrs. Smyth. I'm on my way."

This got a smile out of mother. I opened the door as he came in to our flat. He had a small, lovely bunch of flowers. He gave them to my mum who was gobsmacked!

"Thank you Redser. How are your mum and dad."

"Mam is great Mrs. Smyth. I will be going away soon with dad."

I whispered in his ear, "The flowers, where did you get them?"

"I got them in a basket cart outside Sarah May's flat," he answered.

I said, "It's alright, I will explain to her."

Redser said, "I had a piece of paper and wrote a note to her saying you took them away and you will pay her tomorrow."

Terry heard him and started to laugh, he seemed to think it was a little funny, and I started to see the funny side of it.

My mother said, "Am I missing something?"

"No mum but someone else is," I said. "No bother, I will fix it."

Redser did not need a second call to have his food. He made short work of it, much to my mother's delight.

"How is your mother, Redser?" mum asked.

"She is well, Mrs. Smyth. We are in a new flat. It is up in the James Street Flats. My mam always talks about you."

My mum was pleased with this. "You give to your mother my very best regards," mum said. "She was very good to me and my family, she helped me through those hungry years and my family as well."

Redser said, "I'm going soon, Mrs. Smyth. I love you, mam, and so does my mam love you."

Then Redser let a bombshell drop, "I'm going away to Liverpool real soon."

My mother said, "Oh Redser, not for awhile yet."

"We'll see, Mrs. Smyth. Don't worry mam. I will let you and Jimmy know when."

I was sorry. It seemed now as if Redser and myself would be saying goodbye to each other.

"Thanks for the dinner, Mrs. Smyth."

"Sure you're welcome, son," my mother said.

With that Redser and myself and Terry left the mammy and we took off.

I said, "You know what, Redser?"

He said, "What, Jim?"

"I'm going to miss you." All those years ago and they are still so in my memories.

My mother always finished everything in good stead, giving Redser his dinner and also a few pounds in an envelope for his mother.

I was pleased with that, very pleased. Yes, mother, from those days till now you really taught us, your children, how to be decent people. I never forgot through all the years that my mother was a very special mother, God Bless you, my love.

This was to be the last time I was ever to see Redser. I never heard from him after he went over to his Uncle Tommy in Liverpool.

Chapter 13

The Clock Tower

The 40s were good punching days in the Liberties. I remember when Jim Monaghan out of St. Audeons House was to fight the great Joe Boy Collins. We all went up to the Stadium and our boy Jimmy took on the Irish Champion. He did us proud that night. He gave Joe Boy a boxing lesson that night. What a fight, it was magnificent. We carried him home on our shoulders. It was a great night. Jimmy never put a foot wrong.

At that time the Stadium was buzzing with fights two to three nights every week. It was the "in" thing.

I was coming into the flats one night when I met Marty Donegan coming out. He said, "Jim, I'm looking for you."

I said, "I'm doing great. I'm going over to the Hercules Club." I was getting involved in weight lifting, was putting on a bit of weight and liked the weight lifting to shape me up. I was boxing, doing quite well and tried not to miss a weight lifting session at the Hercules as a way to stay fit.

We walked and talked.

"What's up, Marty," I said.

Marty said, "Mikey's in trouble."

I said, "Mikey Dunne? I'm not getting involved," and I caught him by the hair and bit his ear.

He roared.

I laughed. I turned him around and gave him a kick in the arse. I said, "Now tell me all about it." I wasn't afraid of anyone in the flats, Marty was no exception.

He said, “You’re a fuck, Smyth.”

“I know, but then so are you, ‘comrade’. ”

Marty said, “He’s out the back on the waste ground.”

Now there’s a school where the waster ground used to be. Mikey was sitting there with his head in his hands. He looked up at me. “You look like shit,” I said.

He laughed and said, “I’m in trouble.”

“Tell me something new.”

“I got involved with a big job. There was a lot of heat.”

I said, “We’ll think of something. I won’t let you down, you’ll see.”

What was I to do.

Mrs. Wilson made apple cake for us. I took a slice of cake, put it in a piece of silver paper and brought it around to Mikey.

There was a guy who looked after the Clock Tower. I knew where he used to leave the key, in a little niche over the door. He used to come in once a week on Saturday to oil and wind the clock.

I went up to the top balcony. The Clock Tower was an extension up over the top balcony beside the Merriman’s flat next door to it. I still didn’t know what kind of trouble he was in. Marty told me it was some jewellers. You wouldn’t know who to believe. I’ll give him a dig out, I thought to myself, after that he was on his own.

I went up to the top balcony. I looked at the top of the door. I saw the key. It was there, a Yale key. I opened up the door and went in. It was a nice room. The back of the clock was huge. It ran by electricity. In one corner was a hand wash basin and a toilet. Nice one, Mikey.

I pulled the door closed after me and went over to Tom Keoghs.

"Tom, will you cut a key off this for me?"

"I will," he said, so he cut it and handed it to me.

I gave him six pence. He gave me three pence back. I said, "God, you're very dear Tom."

He said, "The next time you come in for a hair cut I'll do it for half price." He always charged you four pence and if he knew you he would give you back a penny.

I went out to Mikey, gave him the key and said, "You're in business. Saturday morning the corporation man checks it out."

"I'll be on the look out," he said.

We brought him up food a couple of times during the weeks he was there.

One day a squad car came into the flats. Mikey came down to meet them. He had told me the night before that he was getting pissed off with himself and his situation. So the police took him away and he went to jail. When Mikey went before the judge he told him that he was getting married. I couldn't believe that. He was married to his right hand. He was a character.

I was talking to my mother and she said, "Mikey is in trouble."

"The police were looking for him three or four weeks ago and couldn't find him," she said. "Now I wonder how many times did you go out to the top of the balcony. How many, Jim?"

I started to laugh. "You know yourself, mum." I put my arms around her neck and gave her a kiss on the cheek. "I love you dear old mum."

She said, "He'll get a sentence, Jim."

"Maybe not." I hoped he wouldn't.

I went over to Tom Keoghs and said, "Tom, I came over to see you about the news you might have."

"I've none," he said, "but if I hear anything I'll let you know."

I said, "I'm not pushed, Tom. I really don't want to know."

Then somebody said Mikey was getting married in three weeks time. So, that was it. That got a great laugh from me. The little girl herself who was getting married was keeping a low profile. Then the banns were read out in High Street St. Audeons Church.

Mikey was still inside. He wasn't allowed out on bail.

The Saturday before the Sunday of the wedding when he was to get married Mikey walked into the flats. A squad car pulled up with Lugs Brannigan in it, who walked Mikey into the flats.

There was a hooley in the flats. Duck as we called this man was involved with his accordion, and a drummer and Dixie Merrigan with his band. The craic was flying, it went on till late at night. Mikey went into his flat early.

The next morning he was getting married at noon. All were waiting to see Mikey. The Grushie had the money ready. The church was packed. Mikey, his best man and family were waiting in the church. It was a great atmosphere. Father Whelan was waiting. Mrs. Kelly the organist was waiting. Then she started playing, *Here Comes The Bride.* Lugs was there in his best pin stripe. I wondered at the time what he was doing there ... then thought ... then ... no need to ask.

The ceremony went off without a hitch. His brothers were there with his dear old mother. Just as he was leaving, Lugs wished them both the very best with a hand clasp to the bride, held for a few seconds.

Everyone adjourned back to the flats. The bride and groom got themselves arranged to meet their guests and we all started the celebrations. Murtagh threw open his door and the beer flowed freely. I and my mates were well looked after, Mikey saw to that. A great time was had by all.

There was plenty of *Wall of Limerick*, everyone sang.

At 8 o'clock the police car came into the flats. The policemen got out, stood at the corner and Lugs went up to Mikey who was giving his missus a goodbye kiss. They parted, he waved goodbye to the flats, and the lads took him into the squad car and he was gone. End of the story.

Those were the days when there was trust, as ... 'you get yourself married to that nice young lady, we will pick you up when you are finished at 8 o'clock and then you are our property'.

Mikey Dunne said it will be done and it was.

We said our goodbyes too. We will miss our old pal but it wouldn't be for long, eighteen months to be exact.

Chapter 14

An Ode to Danny

It was raining. It was a very cold Tuesday morning. I was living in St. Audoens. I had been out late the previous night, singing on a show and was feeling tired this morning. Besides, I was going to the funeral of an old neighbour who died of cancer. He had wasted away to nothing.

I liked him. Danny Adams was his name. He was only thirty four years of age with a wife and three children. I was sorry he had passed away. He was quiet, never spoke much. Usually he would never say, 'Good morning' to you, but I didn't mind this. Everyone has their little oddities.

I felt sorry for his wife. Josie was her name.

"You have a great colour," she said to me.

I was a bit taken aback by her remark. I put my arms around her to comfort her. She held on to me for what seemed like ages. I got embarrassed but I held her for awhile.

"Danny loved you, Jim" she said, "you know he had great times with you."

"I liked him very much, Josie, really I did," I said.

We said our goodbyes to each other and I went back to my seat. I only went to please my mother. I hardly knew the man.

My mother said to me, "Jimmy, listen to me. You don't have to know a person to show your respect. His death should never have happened." I asked questions, I got no answers. Mother said, "Josie is much younger than Danny."

I said, "Right, mother." I got the message. She was a

lovely girl and nice to talk to but something didn't gel together.

Danny was buried somewhere in the country.

My mother told me he had a blood disorder. He wasted away to nothing. It was so sad. He lived on Ushers Island most of his life.

The next day my mother gave me a note for Josie. I went around to the flat on Ushers Island but she had taken sick during the night and was taken to St. Stevens Hospital. She died soon after. God help her. They said she took her own life.

The children were taken into care. It was said they went to Golden Bridge Convent. Poor Danny and Josie. What a life!

The burial service for Danny was held in the High Street Church, next to St. Audoens. It was a simple service but very sad. Danny's mother became very emotional. She walked up to the coffin and said, "He was my first born, my very first." I fancied myself as a song writer at the time so I wrote this song for Danny's mother:

AN ODE TO DANNY

Of all the favours my God has given
To me, He's given more,
For He's given me you and you mean so much more,
For you were my first born,
My dreams came true.

You made my days on earth seem brighter,
Life's weary burdens light;
With your sweet little smile
You've made my life worthwhile,
For you were my first born and I love you.

And all those walks,
And talks we've had,
The fun and time together,

I recall them all as I sit here
And plan your distant future.

And when my time in life is finished,
I know I'll leave behind
One who is good, so loving and kind,
For you were my first born,
My dreams come true.

JS

A friend of my father's, Val Vousden, wrote out the poem in lovely writing to give to Danny's mother, who was delighted with it. She had it framed, where it sat on her mantelpiece until she died. When that happened, her daughter, who was living in England, took it back home with her where it now sits on her mantelpiece. I like relating this little story as it's very dear to me. This was a very sad time in the flats, for everyone liked Josie and her children, three lovely children.

But just as in life, there were good times as well in the flats.

Danny liked a drink or two but he never liked to be drunk in front of Josie. So, if he had had too much to drink as he came home to the flats, there was a big push cart in front of Mrs. Wilson's door. I would put him into the cart and push it up against the wall to let him sleep it off. That worked well. The drinking happened always on the weekend so, since I didn't have to go to school early in the mornings, I could stay up a little late to do this for Danny.

It was my mother who first spoke to Danny about his drinking. She and Mrs. Wilson did Therapy Classes. These Therapy Classes took care of many ailments, mostly a good number of the heavy drinkers. Dr. Hannigan joined in these classes and it seemed to be most successful with all the participants. Although meetings and classes were conducted in Mrs. Wilson's flat, it was very professionally organised and privately run. They took care of burials as well, mostly all the poor neighbours who had no insurance policies. They would organise a collection. Everybody subscribed to it. It wasn't charity. We all understood.

I especially remember a young mother out of our flats. Her name was Mary and her husband was Joe Harvey. They got behind in their rent and needed some money badly. My brothers and I were doing our *Three Smyth Bros.* singing act at the time so were in contact with a number of variety acts. We asked Adam and Eves Church if we could use their church hall. Tommy Poland, a comedian, was our friend so he got in on it, the priests said "Yes" and so was born St. Anthony's Theatre which is very famous to this day. Now occasionally there is entertainment on stage but it is most often used by TV crews filming in the atmosphere of the old St. Anthony's Theatre.

Our very first show was run for Mary Harvey and was a great success. The Hall opened its doors to the public in the 1940s with a presentation by Tommy Poland. All of the money went to the upkeep of the Church and to the missions abroad.

The cream of Irish talent appeared on its stage: Jack Cruise, Cecil Sheridan, *The Happy Gang*, Frankie Blowers, *The Karl Denver Trio* who had just made a number one hit in Great Britain at the time called, *Wim Oh Wey*. St. Anthony's Theatre was playing sold out performances most every night for years and years, from far back in the 1940s until the year 2003, and it all started with Tommy Poland, Jim Smyth and Fr. Oliver. There were great pantomimes, Kay Delaney, the MaePhelan Dance School, *The Bachelors* started here, singing first as the *Harmonicords*, "Butch" Moore, Sean Dunphy, Paddy Gaynor, the Singing Busboy from the Royal, Peggy Dell, Rose Tynan, I could go on and on.

One Sunday night we got a great treat. Ann Blyth, the American film star, came in to see the show and of course Tommy Poland asked her up to sing. She duly obliged, but she went on and on for hours. The crowd loved her and she loved them.

I used the Hall myself for lots of charity work, aided by Tommy Kay, my good friend, and also the Ringwood family and their young son Tommy. Crowds would begin to queue from seven o'clock for the show which started at eight. It was a packed to capacity house every night. A nice little gig.

Many young artists started their careers there. It was tough times in those days, and very hard work to gain recognition. Now, with pop idols and big talent shows, it's good to know that the public still likes the talent shows today just as always they have.

Chapter 15

The 3 Smyth Bros

Me and my two brothers, Frank and Des, were known as the *Three Smyth Bros.*. We were three good looking young lads in Dublin in the late 1940s, 1950s and early 1960s, up for anything, and had a good act with a very close knit sound. We enjoyed a considerable amount of fame and attention.

Fran, Des and I moved in big entertainment circles during those years. Top international acts doing their rounds at that time were *The Hilos, The Beach Boys,* and *The Ink Spots.* Locally, Dublin had the *Ambassadors*, the *Crescendos,* and later on came the *Batchelors.* They all did very well on the English circuit as well.

Con and Des McCluskey and John Stokes, all of the *Batchelors*, made some good recordings, although they broke up in the early 50s. Then they started up again as the *New Batchelors*, but died out. Sadly they never made it. They had nice songs, but nobody plays them now, although a few were recorded by others.

We three Smyth brothers were doing well in the early 50s. We were getting recognition, first played at The Theatre Royal at this time and were considered a smash hit. You know, if you played the Royal you were "made" as it was the number one entertainment venue in Dublin. Actually, it was not just true in Dublin but it was the number one venue in Europe as well. Through the years this was the Ireland venue for variety shows and major touring acts.

We played on the night when Bridie Gallagher went on with Billy Fury. Bridie didn't like Billy Fury's gyrations. Maybe it upset her, I don't know. I didn't see anything wrong with what he was doing, I put it down to moving with the times, but his boss, Larry Parnes, wasn't too pleased with the reception they received.

The Royal Theatre, as it was known, was on Hawkins Street where it housed many great performers over the years. One in particular was Danny Kaye. My brothers and I were booked to perform on the week after Danny left. One evening during the week before we were to go on I brought in some sheet music for our show to give to Jimmy Campbell, the Director of The Royal Theatre's resident orchestra. He asked if I would like to meet Danny before the show. Of course I would and did through Jimmy's thoughtful introduction that evening. Danny was a very kind and friendly man, the same on screen as off. The night I was there he went on and didn't leave the stage until nearly two hours after the scheduled end of his act. What a performance, "unforgettable", as the papers said.

Another great happening in the Royal involved one of the largest of the touring continental circuses. They took up residence at the Royal for they were a very popular act so had a long run. One of the big acts was a troupe of performing chimpanzees who were always an enormous hit with the crowds.

One night before the show a trumpet player called Tommy King fed the chimps some Brooklax tablets. They went into their routine, moving around so much that the tablets took effect early on into the act. They shit rings around themselves, it was flying in every direction! One of the cleaners remarked, after the show, "I heard of Epsom Salts, not somersaults". The management never found out who did this prank.

In the early 1950s the Royal organised a big Talent Night in partnership with the Eamon Andrews Agency and a guy called Fred O'Donovan. We *Three Smyth Bros.* worked for the Andrews Agency. For this particular show we were hired as a "guest artist", to do our own spot and also do some back-up singing for both the *Irish Dancing Troupe* and a comedian called Pascal Spellman. Other acts were a young band vocalist called Dickie Rock.

There had been a huge run-up in the competition heats, finally ending with eight Finalists, all of whom were given a good chance to win. There was coverage in the Herald and the Mail, great talk on the streets and Radio Eirann, and the town was buzzing. This was big stuff, being in a Final at the Royal.

On the night of the Final, Hawkins Street and Westmoreland Street were packed. Long lines queued up for hours before the doors opened. Most all seats had been previously booked but still the crowds came from Dublin and the country. The show was magnificent, professional entertainment. We were rooting for Dickie to win first place. He was outstanding, had great movement. The crowd loved his swinging of the mike. He could do no wrong. The atmosphere was electric.

The winner was the *Irish Dancing Troupe*, from the McCarthy School of Dancing. Second place went to Pascal Spellman and Dickie was placed third. This was "a great experience," we told him, and as it turned out he went on to great things, becoming a popular and much loved cabaret singer. He became one of Ireland's number one favourite entertainers of all time.

I always liked to listen to Frankie Blowers sing. He had a sweet style and was an out and out gentleman. The Royal was his second home, playing there often and Jimmy Campbell was always the orchestra leader when Frankie performed. Jimmy was a real old pro, you couldn't meet better. He and Frankie made a great combination and always had an outstanding show.

The *Three Smyth Bros.* got great media coverage from the show which went well for our future.

All in all the Royal Talent Show Competition was a great night's entertainment, and the *Irish Dancing Troupe* was a superb dancing troupe, one of the best in all Europe without a doubt.

Then there was the time, in the very early 1950s, when the Royal Orchestra went on strike. They were attached to the IFM musicians, so they all went out except one, Tommy Dando, who played the organ for all the Royal artists. The following week all the musicians on strike marched from

Gardiner Street all the way through town and up to St. Stephens Green. It was some sight. There were hundreds and what a sound they made, the cream of the crop of Irish musicians, marching and playing.

We Smyth brothers got great work after our stint in the Royal. We were included on a radio show with Maureen Potter, who was fun to work with and as well had made a big reputation for herself. Then the *Three Smyth Bros.* got our own show which we called *Odd Noises* and had a strong cast lined up, with Dennis Brennan and Pat Layde to play with us.

The *Three Smyth Bros.* did a season during the summer of 1958 for twelve weeks at Butlins Holiday Camp out in Balbriggan, County Meath. Danny Cummins was top of the bill, our "top banana", an awesome performer. He would always get six or more encores and that was every night. The performers were ourselves, Pat and Jean, Austin Gaffney, Gertie Wine, Phylis Power, Vernon Hayden. The late great guitar player and band leader, Jack Gregory was also there.

I feel honoured that the name of the *Three Smyth Bros.* was always included with the names of those great performers of the time at the Royal in the 1960s. I must list them to keep their memories together alive: Noel Purcell, Eamonn Andrews, Eddie Byrne, Jack Cruise, Pat Cahill, Cecil Sheridan, Mickser Reid, Joseph Locke, Danny Kaye, Frankie Lane, Barry Fitzgerald, Maureen O'Hara, Billy Ekstein, Nat King Cole, Denis Lotis, Dickie Valentine, Rose Brennan and the big band sound of Joe Loss, and all those big boxing contestants. I remember the songwriter Jimmy Kennedy who wrote *Red Sails in the Sunset*, Jimmy O'Dea, Maureen Potter, Danny Cummins, Jack Doyle and Movita.

The *Three Smyth Bros.* performed on the program at the Gresham Hotel in 1959 to celebrate the first night of television in Ireland. It was in its infancy of course but TV was just ready to explode and it certainly did. This was a mammoth, historic occasion for the Irish entertainment world as well as for we Smyth brothers.

Following the Gresham Hotel event, we got booked for the

Ed Sullivan Show in New York. While there we made a LP record for Westminister Recordings which sold quite well in the States.

We continued to make good strides in the Dublin entertainment scene throughout the 1960s. The story of the Royal did not continue to be as long lasting. It was announced quite suddenly that The Royal Theatre would be closing on 30 June1962. Everyone hated to see this happen as the theatre seemed as popular as ever.

Everyone asked, "Why did it close?"

The answer was simply, the people allowed it to close, to be sold.

Marian Finnucan asked on her show, "Why did it close?" It was a beautiful building with magic everywhere you looked, outside and in. Everyone had fond, loving memories of the Royal, it was a part of the culture of Ireland at the time, a living legend. Of course I enjoyed the many times we all had inside those walls. The Royal was being broken up, I was told, sold "due to overhead costs". But, with the advent of television in the homes, and more and more people going to the movie theatres, well ... the times were changing.

And our lives were changing, we Smyth brothers.

I was doing a bit of work with a pal of mine called Billy Burdock, son of the "Chips", who was the owner of Burdocks Fish & Chips. Our job was in a place called Trans Flash, a packer and shipper for goods coming in and going out of Ireland abroad. One day while working with Billy, we took time to go see the Royal one last time, just to say goodbye. The inimitable Mickser Reid was still working at the Royal. He was a famous dwarf, known by one and all at the theatre. His job was to run errands and make coffee. He was working with Cecil Sheridan. Mickser seemed a little sad, so Billy and myself waited until he finished with work and ran him home. This was while I was living on Frances Street.

People still ask the same question, "Why did they close the Royal, it is part of our history?" When the Royal closed its doors, I think the magic that was variety was finished. God be with Paddy Hanaway, Jimmy Campbell, *The Royalettes*, Alice Delgarno, Bob De Monte. No, we won't forget Tommy Dando.

People still mourn the Royal closing but life did go on just the same. Brother Des took a summer singing job in Butlins. I went with Peter Cusack and his band.

After the closing of the Royal, in the 1960s, I was still singing, still in show business, working mostly on my own and getting a lot of work. I joined the *Billy Brennan Trio* and then began with the *Laurel Park Orchestra.* Fran got married about this time, got a job and didn't stay in show business. Des did a television series with Hazel Yoemans. Then Des got his own band, a show band called the *College Men* and I occasionally worked with the band as well. He recorded some nice songs. One day in some town when he was on tour he came upon a pillow, so he wrote a song called *The Pillow That Whispered.* He recorded it, and it became a great hit for him! He also had a fantastic drummer in the band called George O'Reilly, a treat to watch. He was and still is Ireland's greatest percussion king. He was the man who gave the band its rhythm, its sound.

At about this time I got married, on 14 March 1959, during the time I was playing at the Royal. The girl I married was Essie whom I met at Marymount Hall, Harolds Cross, a good bus drive from St. Audeons. We were married at St. Bernadettes Church on Clogher Road off Crumlin Road in Crumlin, and moved into a flat on Francis Street. We had a son Michael the next year and so our family was beginning in the 1960s.

Chapter 16

Winetavern Street

Winetavern Street was a great street. It still is to this day. It remains very active with traffic leading on to the Quays. It goes right past Christ Church Cathedral and straight over the Liffey on Winetavern Bridge.

The Irish House was on Winetavern Street. It was a very well know public house with beautiful figures adorning the façade. Sure many a pint I drank in it.

Beside the Irish House was the pawnbrokers, Hector's Establishment.

In later years Hector's and the Irish House were sold to make way for the Dublin Corporation, who had extra offices to build. Oh it did cause an outcry from the people who wanted to keep the buildings as they were. But alas it was not to be. Fate had other ideas so the houses were all demolished. The Irish House had all the figures stripped off the walls and they were sold to a man in America. So they told us. It was a sad ending.

I loved that old street with its memories, those days were priceless to me. I very often frequented Hectors, the Pawn Office. To tell you the truth, it was a lifesaver. You know, a young buck rarin' to go and nothing to wear!

I remember one night I had a date but the funds were very much stinted, meaning I was absolutely penniless. What to do?

My pal John Chapman hit on a bright idea. "I'll get my Dad's suit, he won't be using it," said John.

I said, "Are you sure?"

John replied, "I am, Jimmy. If I had any money I would

lend it to you."

I said, "I never saw your Dad dressed in a suit and we would often go out with your Dad. Are you sure?"

"I'm sure Jimmy."

"Okay," I said, "let's get it and get moving on it."

John went home and came back with the suit. I checked it and it was the business. Perfect.

We only asked Hector one pound ten shillings.

Hector had a look at it and said, "Is it yours Jim?"

He knew me so it had to be. I said it was mine.

Taking it out of the paper Hector held up the coat. "Put it on," he said to me, giving me the coat. "Here," he said, "take off your overcoat and put it on."

My coat was off. I put John's father's coat on. Now at this time I was doing the weights. I was heavy and the coat was small. I turned around to Hector who took a fit of laughing.

He said, "You're like Norman Wisdom, here's a cap."

When I looked at myself I was indeed like Norman so I started to sing, *Don't Laugh At Me.*

Hector said to me, "How much do you need Jim?

"About a pound would see me alright."

"Here's one pound, pay me at the end of the week."

"Thanks Hector old buddy, nice one."

I didn't tell my mother about Hector's. Mother had told me not to go near the Pawn Office, but she found out and wasn't too pleased.

"It's no big deal," I said. 'I did it once, never again', I thought.

Paddy worked in the Pawn Office, a nice man. When I returned with the suit that I had worn and then parcelled up carefully I left it with Paddy.

"Here they are. Thanks Paddy, I will leave a pint in Quinn's or the Irish House, one or the other."

Then I brought the suit back to John for his father, all neatly parcelled, but what we didn't know was that Paddy had packed a girl's suit, a two-piece.

John's father worked in Jacobs. He hardly ever went out in mid-week, but this week he had an appointment. He went to get the suit in his wardrobe but the mistake was found out. Desolation.

But it so happened the coat was wearable by a man. It was black. Mr. Chapman saw no difference in the suits so believe it or not, he wore it the evening.

He was going to a whist game, where my father was attending. My father came in that night at about eleven o'clock. My mother and I were there having a cup of tea.

"Have a cup of tea, Terry," my Mom said, pouring it out.

"I will, Chrissie," my father said, smiling.

"Hello, Jim," he said. "You know, I went with John Chapman tonight and he was wearing a short black coat. I thought it was a lady's jacket, the cut of it. I said to him, 'Is that a new jacket, John?' "

'Yes it is Terry, first time, do you like it?'

I said, "'I do,' but, Chrissie, I wouldn't be caught dead in it."

We passed no comment on it.

Friday I went to pay Hector after work.

Hector said, "Jimmy, I'm missing a ladies suit and I still have your Norman Wisdom suit."

Why, then it made sense.

When I told John he laughed, I laughed, Hector laughed and Paddy nearly choked. Thinking about it in later years it is still funny.

I told my mother about it. "I like it, Jim" she said.

Quinn's Public House was a very popular place. Now let me tell you in the forties its attraction. It was known as a singing house. It had a piano and women were not afraid to be seen there alone. Ordinarily women would be very reluctant to be seen in any pub, but Quinn's provided a lounge in the pub which was known as The Snug and it became a very famous house, catering to the good and, of course, the bad.

A sing-song would of course, attract singers. A lady would fancy herself a singer so she would be allowed to sing, so that's how it all started.

I would sing a song on many occasions. I needn't tell you, I loved the singing and soon became well-known.

Liam Murphy played the piano and everyone knew him. Poor old Liam loved his drop of whiskey and often would end up his evening completely out of it. John Chapman and I would leave him home. He lived up in Inchicore so at the closing we would have to foot it up James Street with Liam. By the time he got home he would be near to being sober which wasn't too bad. I liked him, he was a nice man. I was to work with him in later years in Marymount Hall and the Plaza and some variety houses.

Liam never ate any food, only drank whiskey. I was singing in the pub one night with Liam when my mother passed by the window with Mrs. Wilson. I ducked my head down when she passed by, hopefully not seeing me. As I ducked my head, I hit against a girl with a tray. The tray was full with glasses of stout. A couple of women sitting at a table got the lot. They let out unmerciful screams, it was bedlam. We were thrown out of the pub, John and myself. It didn't matter to Liam, he was only there for the drink although he would always ask me to give a song.

I said to John, "Let's go."

He said, "Let's go, Jimmy, you know something, you're too good for them."

I didn't agree with him, but we went out.

It was a summer's night. Beside Quinn's was a big toy shop. There was a loud commotion inside. On a street facing the pub, (which is long gone) a fire had started downstairs in the two-storey shop. A lady was trapped on the first floor. We could see her screaming for help but nobody could get to her.

The fire Brigade was screaming down Winetavern Street. I knew the lady, she lived in Oliver Bond Flats. I used to mate around with her son, Tommy. Before help could get to her she was dead. It was a very sad happening. Tragic. She was a lovely lady. My mother knew her so well. They never re-opened the toy shop, it was just demolished. That would be on the street leading up to Christ Church. Quinn's was there for many years after. I did an odd few songs in Quinn's with my friend and manager, John Chapman. They were times to remember, good times.

My mother was very upset about the lady who died.

"By the way," she said to me many weeks later, "was that a Frankie Lane song you were singing? You should go in for a few competitions. There's one in the Kingsway Ballroom."

"I'm amazed, Mom, how did you find out?"

"I saw you in Quinn's Pub, you idiot."

"Nice one, Chrissie," I said.

"What about the Kingsway?" she said.

"Are you for real, I'd need to grow a little more."

She laughed, then said, "God rest that poor woman. I can still see her poor face looking out that window. Her loving son put those bars on the window, you know. They terrified me. Give us a kiss, Jim."

She put her arms around me and hugged me. We walked around a little like that, not saying anything, just holding on to each other. She was crying.

"Ah Jim," she said, "life can be cruel."

I said, "Don't cry, mother. What will happen to the boy, I know him? I often play ball with him."

"He will be alright," Mom said, "he will be alright."

Life was good to the young man. He did well.

My mother and Mrs. Wilson and Mrs. Kavanagh – Charlie's Angels – always came to the rescue with the children and all were saved by them. I feel so proud to have known them. They were always there to help the needy.

Time often takes me to Winetavern Street. When I look up towards Capel Street Bridge how the memories keep tumbling down. That disastrous burning once again comes into my thoughts. I shudder when I think of it. God rest her soul.

So these were my introductions to the sing-song living which started in Winetavern Street.

Chapter 17

Dixons

A new girl was coming to work in Dixons, a large paper manufacturer in Dublin who supplied all over Ireland

The girl leaving Dixons was going to have a baby. There was no such thing as maternity leave in those days. She was a well mannered girl and a beautiful girl. I heard in later years that she was related to Pierce Brosman, he being related to 007 James Bond, the nearest thing we had to a celebrity.

The new girl's arrival to Dixons was to be a big happening. Monday morning Ambrose and I were upstairs stacking bales of paper when the new girl walked up the stairs. A light was shining from the ceiling and shone on her head. She stopped, turned her head and looked straight at me. Ambrose took off. She wanted to know the way to the toilet. I said, "I'll show you, Miss. Follow me, please." The passage to the toilet was narrow and I had to press against the bales of paper stored up there to let her pass. She barely made it. 'Oh God,' I thought, 'where is Ambrose, or Barney!'

But help was near. Mr. Dixon came over to us and we sorted ourselves out as I went downstairs.

Her name was Penny. She was fun to talk with and was always chatting it up about the parties going on and men around. It was becoming pretty lively now as Christmas was just a few days coming.

It was John Allen at White's of Fleet Street who got me in to Dixons. Now his reason was this: when I was at White's I was next in line to go for the examination for my trade as an apprentice in the printing trade. I was longer at White's than the lad called Sammy Grumley but John Allen was a friend of Sammy's so he would naturally submit his name. It was simple, Allen turned the deal for his friend and I didn't get the job. It was a vicious thing to do but he was a vicious man. Then Sammy went for the apprentice job and failed the examination. A nice enough lad but a little dense and he failed to pass. The job finally went to a lad called Paddy. In the meantime I had gotten the job in Dixons, which turned out to be a good move for me with a bit more pay, so I moved on.

There was another lovely man working in White's called Mr. Monson, a good guy who was also poorly treated by Allen.

Allen had a massive nervous breakdown a few years later and ended up in a nursing home. I met him many years later outside a small Catholic Church in D'Olier Street. He was on a crutch and his legs were bad. I said, "You're John Allen aren't you?"

He said, "Yes."

"I worked with you in White's of Fleet Street. You were a bad bastard. Is this your crutch?" It was on the ground, he was trying to pick it up.

He said, "Yes, will you please give it to me?"

"Certainly," so I picked it up and said, "take my arm, John," so he did and we walked. I walked with him into the middle of D'Olier Street and left him in the middle of the street, walked to the other side and looked back at him. He looked so pathetic in the middle of the street. He shuffled along and at that moment in time looked to be a very sad old man. I turned away and made my peace with God. As far as John Allen was concerned I couldn't care less.

It was Christmas Eve, it was cold and I was going home. I got my Christmas bonus from Mr. Dixon and left. I bought a few cigarettes for Barney which pleased him, and bought Penny a scarf. I knew she had burned her old one in a fire and needed another one. We were finished with work. Mr. Dixon said, "It's time Jim, Barney, Ambrose." We stopped off at Mr. Shields, the butcher next door, to pick up our Christmas bonus turkey.

Penny was waiting for me outside. Barney and Ambrose took off together so Penny and I cycled off. It was cold but we soon warmed up with the cycling. I said "Goodnight dear Penny and happy Christmas," and cycled off home.

The old flats looked very cheerful. As I got into the centre of the flats I started to sing a carol, *Adeste Fidelis.* John Chapman ran over to me, Kitser, Marty Donegan, Paddy Monaghan appeared and John White started to play his accordion. It was magic. Before we knew it we had a singsong going. I ended up dancing with Sarah May, a good little dancer.

I loved Christmas time in the flats. They were hectic but fun times with family and friends. None of us had a lot of money, we could just get by but it didn't matter. We kept up appearances, managed something new now and again, it didn't much matter, just something to add to the wardrobe. Times were rough in my early years financially but the wealth was with the family and friends around

I had met this girl named Anne who lived in the flats and who had two children, two lovely little girls but no father. I played father and Santa Claus to give the two little ones a good Christmas.

It was a happy time in the flats. I made my rounds of the flats carrying a little orphan on my shoulders. Little Jimmy Cratchet we called him and we made music, went into most of the homes and sang for them.

After the holidays Dixons seemed considerably better.

I went out a few times with Penny although she was a bit moody. She told me she was keeping company with Mr. Ozzy. I couldn't believe her at first but Gracie and the girls next door stopped me one day and confirmed it.

One day soon after, I was heading over to the Hercules Club. I had just made the Irish Dead Lift record, lifting 650lbs with a body weight of 10 stone 30lb. The Club issued a challenge to Buster McShane, a body builder from Belfast. He was a great athlete who was called Mr. Ireland Body

Builder. Some years later he was to achieve fame by becoming the personal trainer of Mary Peters, who became Olympic Gold Medal Triathlon Champion. Unfortunately something happened and he couldn't travel to Dublin for our challenge. It was a pity, I would have loved to have met him, never did.

So, one night after the Hercules Club I stopped off at a dance in the Ballerina Ballroom. I saw Penny. She was dancing with an oldish man who was buried into her. It upset me a bit. She looked as if she had taken a lot of drink. He was holding on to her for dear life. I thought to myself, it's over now, just as well.

I was with Jimmy Cashin and Ritchie Shields.

"Let's go, lads," I said, "it's time for the last bus." I got my coat and we went outside. We passed a laneway where someone was hitting someone. I walked a little bit down the lane. I could make out two people. Now I made the form of a man hitting on a woman. She was crying and trying to get away from him.

I let out a shout. He threw her against the wall. He then told me to fuck off, threatening me with his fists. The girl came into the light. It was Penny. She was crying.

I made a run right up to him, smacking my shoulder into his chest hard. He spun over onto his back, shouting. I caught Penny. "Come on," I said, "let's go."

"No Jim."

I could barely understand her as she was quite drunk. Her nose was bleeding pretty heavy.

"I know this guy, don't get involved, please, Jim."

"Okay," I said, "I won't".

I was covered in blood at this stage. "I'll have to dump this overcoat," I said. "I might get it cleaned, not to worry."

I turned away from her. "Goodnight, Penny."

"Goodnight, Jim. You'll be okay, don't worry."

"I won't worry but will you be okay?" I never minded the guy. He was shouting, "I'll get you, you bastard."

The lad she was with came out at the top of the lane. Ritchie saw the man and woman. "That's a dangerous fucker, Jim, watch him very carefully."

She never came back to work in Dixons. There were a few comments from Barney. I didn't answer him. I asked Mr. Dixon about her leaving. He just said she got another job.

A couple weeks later, around twelve o'clock midnight, I was coming home from the Hercules Club. At this stage I was watching anything that moved. Ritchie Shields had warned me the low-rag was asking about me. When I came into the flats I would step into Number One where a lovely red haired lady called Carmel lived. I would wait there awhile and watch the proceedings, then I would move on home.

I was waiting and watching when the door behind me opened and a voice whispered, "There is a man. He was waiting at your block. He was talking to Mikey Dunne."

"Thank you Carmel." The door closed behind me.

Mine was S block. I waited awhile. Someone came down the stairs. I stopped at the end. The moon was beaming. It lit on a man. I didn't recognise him but it could have been the one. I wasn't sure. My foot hit against something. It was a tin of beans. Someone bringing in groceries must have lost it. I tossed it up in the air, catching it as it fell. I kept it in my hand, why I don't know. I moved along by the flats on the bottom level. In future, I thought, I'd bring a hammer in my bag. I still held on to the tin of beans. It might help me out if needed. I stopped outside Mr. Downey's and looked across. Mikey's head had come outside his bedroom window which looked out on to the flats. The man outside turned to Mikey. This surprised me. He raised his voice. I could hear him say, "You look after things Mikey, I'll look after you." He started to walk out of the flats. He waved to Mikey and was gone. I was about to walk over to my block.

I looked up. Kathleen Barker was looking over the balcony. She was a lovely lady, so quiet and gentle. She had an illness, tuberculosis, which was rampant at this time and she passed away a year or two later. The 1930s and 40s saw a lot of it, an awful lot of people died from it. Kathleen had it one day, she looked good but the very next day she looked very bad. She was an extremely attractive girl. I was fond of her and her sister, Bridie.

"Mind yourself, Jim," she said, "walk carefully."

I nodded and smiled at her.

She waved and I waved back to her.

As I walked towards my block I wasn't expecting anything. Suddenly somebody jumped out at me. It was Mikey.

"There was a bloke here just this minute looking for you and he happens to be a friend of mine."

At this stage he was becoming very aggressive. I was a bit taken back. I liked Mikey. He was a friend of mine. I could write a book on his early life. I could write about how I looked after him in the Clock Tower, feeding him from my mother's table.

He caught me by the coat and shook me a couple of times. This I didn't like so, as he swung me around first time and I came abreast of him, I whacked him in the mouth. He let me go and fell backwards on to the ground. I stood staring at him. He got up on his knees. He was spitting blood onto the pavement. He looked surprised.

"You little fucker," he said, "I'm bleeding, look at this." He spit on his hand and showed me the blood.

"It's red, isn't it," I said.

As he stood up I said, "You're a two faced prick aren't

you? Winnie doesn't want to know you, Tommy has left you, he got wise to you."

This hurt him. He had a go at me and then he stopped. He put his hand on his head.

I turned around. When I turned my head back he smacked me one. That's when we started to really mix it. He was still as good as the day in the back of Thomas Street when he took on Lugs Brannigan but I was better and I was faster and younger.

He caught me once for my two punches every time. We danced around each other and the flats swung around as well. I was bleeding from my cheek, there was a horrible gash on it. We were rolling around punching each other. He was kicking me. I caught his foot as I fell and twisted it. Then I stood on it twice till I heard his bones snap. I didn't give a fuck. I picked up the tin of beans and threw it at his door. I hit him on the back of the head.

Just then someone had me under the arms and was lifting me up. I looked up and it was lovely Kathleen Barker. Carmel was with her.

I was in a terrible state but all of a sudden I was stable. Strength came back in my body.

Kathleen said, "Bring him up to my flat, Carmel, I'll clean him up. I like him, he's a nice guy."

Carmel said, "I like him too, he was good to me when my fellow was inside. You know Kathleen he put life into my body and my kids."

"I know," Kathleen said, "he's a very generous man."

At this stage it was late. I was in the Barker's flat. Kathleen washed my face. I couldn't lift my arms up. She was gentle. She cleaned me up, took off my top and rubbed cream into my neck and shoulders. The skin was torn off my chest. It was sore, my head was sore.

I said, "What am I going to tell my mother and father?"

"I'll tell her, leave it to me."

She was gone for awhile and then came back in. "It's okay, you're staying with me because my father is sick."

"Where is your father, Kathleen?"

"He won't be back tonight."

I lay on the sofa. I felt like shit, looked in the mirror and looked like it as well. It was a dreadful night. I was out of it.

I heard someone getting sick. It was Kathleen. I got a wet cloth and rubbed her face and back of her neck. She seemed okay then. I held her and said, "You're a kind lady."

"I'm not," she said.

The moon was shining in the window, lighting up the kitchen. She was getting sick in the basin again. I washed her face and helped her back to bed. She went asleep right away. I don't know why, I just felt I had to sit there in the chair and watch her sleep. She looked very sick. I thought she was going to die.

She woke up the next morning, opened her eyes, lay very still, then looked over at me. But she smiled and said she was okay. We had tea together. She was a lovely person. Little did I realise she would soon pass away. I needn't tell you that was a very sad day.

All my life I was to include these lovely memories in my remembrances of this time of my life as well as my onslaughts with Mikey. The man I saw having a go at Penny, I never again came into contact with him, he just seemed to fade away.

I never spoke to Mikey till many years later. I was in Cleary's pub on Arran Quay. He was out of his mind on drink. He cried his eyes out. I can assure you it did nothing to me. He said, "Buy me a drink, Jimmy." I bought him a drink, said goodbye and never saw him again.

I was to see Kathleen many times after on many occasions. I spent many a happy hour in her company. I laughed so often with her till the day when the good Lord took her from us. You're gone dear friend but will never be forgotten. The flats were a very subdued place for a long time after she left.

And so that was the way my life went in the later 40s while working at Dixons. A lot of growing up was done there, there were happy times and there were the fights as well. I think I left there a stronger person. I had to be for shortly later I was to leave with my brothers for England and new and different adventures.

Chapter 18

Christmas Cheer

It was Christmas Eve in the late 1940s, a cold and frosty night, around four degrees Celsius. I was coming home to the flats from work at Dixons.

Barney was going to cycle up the Bridge Street hill but thought twice about it. He had a few drinks taken so I offered to walk with him up Bridgefoot Street instead. He declined but I insisted with a little force.

"It was a great day, Jimmy," he said, laughing a lot. I laughed with him. I guess it was because it was Christmas, you know, that magical feeling with a double week's wages in pocket and some more from regular customers.

The ground was icy in the flats and I slid a little, which pleased me. I looked up at the top balcony and saw mother was looking over the balcony. I can still see her figure now, waving to me. It is so definite in my mind's eye. I waved back to her. She said something, I didn't know what it was, but it didn't matter.

Next thing I know we are sliding down the square, having the time of our lives. All of a sudden it seemed all the flats were with us – Ginny O'Connor, the Barker sisters, Mrs. Kavanagh. Oh what a laugh, it was magic. Whenever I visit the flats the memories flood back. It was a great Christmas Eve.

My mother said, "Jim, I have to go up to Thomas Street, will you come with me?"

"Surely mam and why not," so we took off.

We started with the Maypole and Seezer's Black and White for food for the big fry-up on Christmas morning. Then we started to talk to Sarah May at her stall. It was nearly five o'clock when I saw him. It was Willie and he was staggering a little.

I went over to him. "Are you drunk, Willie?" I said.

"No, Jim," he said. "I have a dreadful pain in my side and I have to mind a friend's two children.

I said, "I'm with you," and I turned around to my mother and explained what was wrong. "Sorry, mam."

"Take him home, I'll be okay. By the way, Jim, is that the cripple who lives around on Usher's Quay?"

"It is, Mam, and you know, I pity him, I really do."

"I know you do," mother said, laughing, "you're all heart."

I pushed the pram Sarah May had over to Augustine Street. My mom took hold of it and they were off.

Somehow I got Willie down to his mobile house. The two children were waiting for him.

"Never a dull moment," I said loudly to myself.

I said, "Will you be alright Willie old son?" This Christmas Eve was not going too well for him. "No matter," I said to Willie, "tell me about the children."

"They will be picked up at ten o'clock."

I looked at Willie and said, "I hope so pal, because you don't look too good if I may say so."

"I will be alright Jim, don't worry about me."

A woman came into the yard and into the light. She was a little, fat lady with a coat two sizes too big for her. I was going to laugh but decided not to.

She said, "Willie," in a very well-spoken voice.

Willie gave a little jump. “Yes love,” he said, “hello.”

I looked at the girl and she looked at me and smiled.

I held my hand out to her. “Hello, I'm Jim,” I said.

“And I'm Abigail,” she said, “nice to meet you. Are you from around here, Jim, or just passing through?”

‘Cynical,’ I thought to myself but I will answer her. “I'm from around here, Abby.”

“That's nice, Jim,” she replied, “and the name is Abigail.”

I said, “I'm sorry, I will call you Abigail, that is for further reference, I do understand.”

I turned away and gave a little smile to myself.

“Do you find me amusing, Jim?” Abby asked

I turned around to confront her, taken aback. As a matter of fact she unnerved me quite a lot. As I looked into her face, she looked evil to me.

Willie looked at me apologetically, sort of. I felt sorry for him, he looked dreadful, his skin seemed to be bleeding, as his nose was. I thought to myself, ‘I have to get out of here.’

“See you Willie, you too Abby,” I said on purpose.

I can assure you it didn't go down well, but as a matter of fact it didn't cost me another thought. As I walked out the gate I said, “and fuck you too.” I didn't look back, just kept on walking. I was going to enjoy my Christmas no matter.

I walked into the flats. They looked real good after where I had been. I felt sorry for Willie but in what lucky bag did he find Abby. I'd say it was up in Woolworths.

We got a few of us together in the flats, as I remember, my old mates John Chapman, Eoin Finn and John Marty Donegan, my brother Fran and the singing was great. It was a fine night. Everybody joined in, Paddy Plummer and poor old Billy Willie Henry. Tony Branigan came down to lend a voice but I told him to take a hike which he did, and a great night was enjoyed by all n' sundry. I got a few bottles so we could drink a toast, as John said, "to absent friends, old mates." A night to remember and I needn't tell you a few tears were shed.

I made it up to the top floor #313 about ten thirty.

"That's early, Jim," my dad said to me, "nice going."

I gave him his usual supply of cigarettes.

"Thanks, Jim," he said, "you never forget do you?"

"Not for you, old timer," I said, "you're worth it."

My mother said to me, "How is that lad Willie?"

"He's good, mam – no, he's not," I said, "he is in bits."

"He's a very sick boy, Jim, God help him."

"I pity him," I said. "I think he has a girlfriend, mam."

Dessy, my brother was there in the room. "God help her," he said, "there is hope for me yet, isn't there mother?"

I said, "Good for you. I heard a story today. I heard you and Lizzie Stafford are getting together." This got a laugh out of us all, even my father.

My father said, "I'm delighted for you, Dessy," he said, "you'll make a great couple, God willing."

It was a great atmosphere, the love all around. Did you ever get that feeling, it's magic but you know that later you realise it only happens once. It never happens again, and when you realise that, that's when you miss it so much, that happy feeling of togetherness, as in a great family feeling when we share precious moments.

A thought came back to me. You meet someone you've known sometime before, where have we met? God, I can't remember, silly me. Mind you, I knew I had met her somewhere before. Where have we met? God, I can't remember, silly of me. Mind you, I knew I had met her somewhere, that's true. I never forget a face, or do I?

When I woke up on Christmas morning it was a good feeling I had. Six am it was but I got that feeling, something was not the best, this I knew, so I dressed myself.

I had to climb over many bodies everywhere. I slept in the back bedroom with Paddy, Des, Fran and myself.

I made my way to see if Willie was alright. Jesus but it was cold that Christmas morning. The flats had iced over. It was real slippery under foot. I made it out to the gates, just about.

Someone was looking over the balcony. It was a girl. She shouted down to me, "Jimmy, have you a cigarette please?" I had a few in a box. I took a couple and left the box on the steps with some in it.

"All for you, Mary," I said, "you owe me."

"Don't worry," she said, "I will pay you back, thank you." She was a lovely girl, we were good mates.

It was starting to snow. I was amazed I can tell you. I'd say this was a one-off, first time. There was a dead rat against Murtagh's wall. It was as stiff as a poker and black. It was actually smiling – a sly sort of grin. It reminded me of Tony Branigan.

I heard somebody calling my name and I looked back into the flats. It was John, he was running after me.

"You know, John," I said, "it's a wonder you have your shoes on."

"Look," I said, showing him the rat. I did my James Cagney routine, "You dirty rat, I'll blow your head off."

John started to laugh. “Stop, Jimmy, you know what, I would love to get Tony Branigan, and ram that rat up his arse.”

This I did laugh at. “I needn’t tell you, you wouldn’t wish that on any rat.”

Then I remembered the purpose of my excursion into this bitter cold Christmas Day. “I’m going around to see poor old Willie. I forgot, I have nothing for him, John.”

We were outside Mick Duffy’s shop where there was a crate outside with stuff in it. “You’ve something now,” John said to me. He opened the crate and took out a dozen eggs and three bottles of milk and handed them to me.

“Right,” I said, “thank you, John lad, no, better still, thank you Mick Duffy.”

I always remember the day I was buying cigarettes from Mr. Duffy and I said, “Will you put them on my mother’s account please, Mr. Duffy?”

He said, “No, there’s enough on it.” He was just being awkward, the bollix.

A neighbour in the shop told my mother. Mother went over to Mr. Duffy’s and said, “I want to speak to you. My account was paid two days ago, Mr. Duffy. I paid your wife the account owing. You’re out of order. I will never set foot in your shop ever again.” And do you know, my friend, she never did, although it meant travelling a goodly distance further. Respect, it doesn’t come as sweet as that. All my life she never let me down and how I loved her for it.

John and I brought the stuff around to Willie, only to be met by two little toddlers crying and Willie out of it, lying on the floor. He was ashen, in fact, sick all over, moaning, half crying with the pain.

I looked around for Abigail, calling her name, but she was gone, absconded or something.

We called an ambulance and got Willie moved. A woman came into the yard and took the children. It turned out they were Willie's sister's children.

Willie was minus his paltry savings. Abigail saw to that, the mealymouthed cow. I never saw her ever again, not that I wanted to.

Willie was lost to us for awhile after that. He often came into my thoughts. I felt so sorry for him, what a life he had. Then one day in a conversation I had with a bloke, I heard Willie had committed suicide. I never knew what way. Never asked.

What a Christmas that was. I enjoyed it and now I know what to think of it. It was magic time and, do you know, wasn't Willie a part of that Christmas? We all sang songs and got really happy because wasn't God a part of it all too? I rambled up to Mullinahack on Oliver Bond Street last week. Sure it's a posh place now with the flashy flats, but I remember when we sang *Silent Night* and the snow came tumbling down. Happy Christmas.

Chapter 19

To London, To London

Michael Wilson, his wife Maureen, with Maureen's friend Anne and myself made tracks one cold February Saturday for Dun Laoghaire. We were off to England!

Mikey, the son of Mrs. Wilson in the flats, was my old friend and buddy since we moved to St. Audoens. What an adventure this was to be for me, the first time ever outside Ireland, and me still a young eighteen year old lad and excited to be starting a new adventure to a foreign shore.

We all boarded the very famous *Princess Maud* full of high expectations. What a boat! It was an unbelievable replica of a boat, however I wasn't to know that on first sight. It was a bad sailing, the seas were very rough and everyone on board suffered. It was my first time to be seasick, really bad.

We eventually reached Holyhead, and got our connection train for Euston Station. I was wrecked and the others were not much better. We settled into a carriage. The train pulled off and was bound for London, the land of opportunity.

This was around 1950, and I was looking forward to London. I had never been away from home in all my born days. I was a little bit homesick at this point but no matter, I would pray things would be alright. 'Keep in touch with your God, Jimmy', my mother would say.

It was a sad parting. I loved my father and mother. "You're not too far away, Jim," my father said. "If you don't like it come on home". I was a lonely kind of guy and I wondered how I was going to cope. But Marie was up in London so I would have her nearby. We were always pretty close as sister and brother so I knew I could always go up to see her. It wouldn't be too bad.

We had a good trip up to Euston. Maureen said, "I told

your mother I would look after you."

"Maureen, I told my mother I was staying with you, so I'm staying with you. I like you and Mikey so that's that."

"You cheeky beggar, I love you too."

I knew I was going to like being with them. Little did I realise the time ahead.

We came into Euston about 7 o'clock in early evening. I was getting excited, a single man and feelin' good about his new adventure. A nice looking coloured girl let her bag fall on the ground. I picked it up and got a lovely smile and a "thank you". I hadn't seen many coloured people. I kept looking at her. She looked at me and gave me a smile. Nice.

I said to Mikey, "There are a lot of black people over here."

"I know, don't tell me about it."

We got the Tube to Angel Station where we got off. Maureen said to Anne, who was a quiet girl and had not had a lot to say on the trip, "I'm tired. I'm not going into work tonight."

We got the bus to Forston Street, number 130 to be exact. It was a long street with about forty small houses on each side of the street, and down at the end of the street, facing up the street, was a huge construction and engineering building with the name Aston Construction Company in big letters on the outside of the building. This is where I was to start work.

We went into the house, the place where I was to stay for some time. One large room was downstairs where two men and two women could sleep. That was us. The toilet was a bucket in the corner, to be used during the night. Mikey and the girls sometimes used it. Maureen's uncle soon came to live with us, so I needn't tell you this caused some stress. When he had been out for a celebration you could hear him all over London using the bucket a lot during the night.

The nights were cold. We had no central heating, in fact there was no heat at all. If Mikey was working late Maureen would get in bed beside me, saying, "I'm freezing, Jim." Then Anne got into the game. But I enjoyed it. Well, you know, mother always said, be nice to women. I never gave out to them. I think I just loved them both and for sure enjoyed being warm.

I was taking a lot of flack from the guys in the new job where I had just started to work. Mr. Birmingham was my boss, a nice enough man. He was the son of an Irish man so we didn't have any trouble between us. I worked there for most of the year or so and generally liked it. But it was the guys working there that I didn't like. They soon began to call me 'Paddy', or sometimes it would be 'Paddy the Irishman'. If they were going to show you a little respect it would be 'Pat'. I decided not to answer them when they called me 'Paddy'.

We Irish in England were more or less always called 'Paddy'. It was an Irish-English nickname that was taken to be an offensive term. It was a small little thing that was used to keep we Irish 'in our place', a term of derision, of pointing a finger at our differences. We Irish hated it and the English loved to use it at us to perhaps get a rise.

I started at first as a labourer, working with a big man called Slim, who was a good guy to work with. Then I was transferred to work with a guy called George, whom I didn't like at all. Every time I went home down Forston Street for a break I had to bring him back cigarette lighters. They were very scarce in the early fifties.

I said to him one day after smuggling in a load of lighters, "Just for 'pig iron', do you make much money on those lighters?"

"Yes, 'Paddy'. I sell them for double the price."

I took a couple breaks and after everyone had gone I came back with a big load of lighters. He never gave me a penny for myself. So I said, "Well, fuck you little George. I'm not bringing any more lighters back to you. And another thing, my name is not 'Paddy', it's Jim, you little prick." So I knew what to expect.

I saw him go up to the Foreman's office and began to talk to the Foreman, Clem Adams. That night as I was clocking out the Foreman said, "Smyth, you will be working with Slim on the riveting tomorrow."

I said, "Okay, Mr. Adams."

He said, "You will be okay, Smyth, you'll get on with Slim."

I said, "Okay, Mr. Adams. I'm dead easy. I'll do a good job for you."

"I know you will. Meantime, keep out of our friend's way," nodding his head in George's direction. "He made trouble for another Irish lad and made life tough for him, 'til one day the lad couldn't take it anymore. It was Friday night. They were having a few drinks. I was having a drink with Slim with whom I had become very friendly. George made a remark against the lad, who retaliated by slapping him hard in the mouth. George fell on the ground, got up quickly, took his handkerchief out of his pocket, wiped his mouth, glared at the young guy and walked out of the pub."

I was a young man, late teens. I wasn't looking for trouble. I wasn't far down Forston Street, so I walked home.

I got into the house and Maureen put her arms around me and said, "How did you get on, tonight?"

"Great. George got thumped," I said.

"I'm delighted," she said.

I told her about the cigarette lighters and she was hoping I gave him a good clout for herself. She was a good support for me.

"Marie is back after her holidays, you've to get in touch with her," Maureen said to me. "I'm so tired at night. By the way, I have to write to my mother but don't worry, I sent her on her money. I wouldn't miss that."

"Where is that smell coming from?"

"There's a new girl in, her name is Mary Hall. The landlord gave her a room. I suppose it's the room with the hole in the wall," said Maureen.

I started laughing. I said, "He's a pervert, you know that?"

"He is," said Maureen, "he tried to put his hand up my skirt the other day."

"Dirty bastard," I said. "What did Mikey say?"

"If I'm near you and he tries it, I'll go for him for sure," she said.

"This is a fucking mad house," I said, and eventually I would prove that to be true. I eventually got things sorted out and everything went on as usual, although I wasn't on good terms with the landlord, as said. He was just not a nice man, giving the new girl a hard time, walking into her room when he saw fit.

Mikey said to me, "Mind your own business, Jimmy." I did. I kept my mouth shut for the time.

Next day I was talking to Noreen, one of the girls at work.

She said, "It's a pity you're a man, Jimmy. I was looking for another person to live in my flat with me."

"No problem," I said to her, "I know a girl, Mary's her name. I finish at 5 o'clock. You wait for me outside the job. She goes in to work late, just at that time. I'll introduce her to you. She's a nice girl, you'll like her."

They hit it off like a storm. I met Mary a week later. She had moved in with Noreen and all was friendly.

Mary left our flat on the Friday that I introduced them. The landlord wasn't a happy man. He knew it was me who had upended his apple cart. He said to Mikey, 'I'll get that bastard Smyth.' He did get me afterwards but I weathered it.

London was a great place to be ... or not be at times.

I got in the habit of always being out, rambling on my own. I used to sing in all the singing houses and began to make a fairly good name for myself. I would sing a lot on Saturday and Sunday nights. I found out that there were quite a lot of my neighbours around from the flats in Dublin and they used to follow me to the pubs where I sang. Those were the good times.

I still remember the Nags Head and the pubs on Walworth Road. I used to love to go down to the West End and to The Windmill and the London Palladium. I knew the lads at the doors and would always get in free.

Soho was a great night spot. I was getting to know all the girls in Soho. The night life was magic.

Big John Bindon lived in Soho. He was one hell of a man with a massive and good reputation but that's another story. And I became very friendly with two prostitutes called May and Avril who lived down in Soho. They were two characters. They used to stand at the entrances to their 'house of Joy', as they put it. I was talking to them one night. May said to me, "You should get a job down here, Jim. All the boys and girls like you."

I would have loved to. Maybe, when I come back to London after Christmas at home that would be a possibility, but that was months away.

May gestured to a lovely looking girl, who came over to say hello, one thing led to another and she said her name was Lyola. May suggested I walk her home so we walked along. We passed the Palladium where Tommy Steel was on. I didn't like him too much. All my friends at the time were into Elvis and Cliffie Richards. Lyola and I made our way over to Tottenham Court Road and made for Lyons Tea Room. I ordered a pot of tea and some scones for us.

Just at that minute I noticed two well built guys standing beside me, one was holding Lyola's hand and easing her up on her feet and saying, "We've been looking for you all day. Where have you been?"

She said, "Let go of my arm, you're hurting me." He continued to push her toward the door.

I said,"We were just having a cup of tea." I was bigger than the guy who was ushering Lyola toward the door."

"Please don't hurt him, Tony, he is my friend," she said to the guy.

He said, "Get away from her," and was shouting loudly, laying it on heavy. I didn't know what he meant but was soon to find out. I got a bit nervous. Lyola was trying to calm Tony down but was not getting anywhere with him. Tony kept pushing his hand into his pocket.

The other guy Tony was trying to keep his arms at his side. Suddenly he made a lunge at me and caught me with a knuckle duster that he had pulled out from his pocket. He caught me at the right eye and blood poured into my mouth. I was fucking mad so I ran after him and smacked him in the mouth with my head. Twice.

I heard police cars coming so I moved real quickly. The police jumped out of their cars as they drew near the kerb outside the café. I stood beside a young coloured girl with a baby in a pram. She gave me a tissue.

"Wipe your face," she said, "there is blood on it."

I hurriedly got the blood off my face and said, "Thank you, Ma'am."

She said, "Miss," and smiled.

I put my hand on the handle of the pram and started to walk beside her. She said, "What's your name?"

"Jim. What's yours?"

"Betty."

We walked along the West End. I was bleeding a lot. She stopped the pram and took out a tissue. It was crumpled but looked clean. "Take it," she said, "and go into a toilet in the Tube station and clean yourself up."

I said, "Thank you. Will I see you again?"

"Okay, I'll see you outside Madame Tussauds at 7 o'clock tomorrow night."

I went into Tottenham Court tube station and washed myself. The cleaner said, "Were you involved in that row just now?"

"Yes."

"Be very careful of that guy, son, he's very dangerous. They say he carries a gun. The girl is his sister. If anyone as much as looks at her Tony goes for him. I can tell you, lad," the cleaner said, "he is dangerous, very dangerous."

I wasn't too happy with the things running around in my head. I began to think all sorts of things happening. All I wanted to do was to get out of here and back to the house and see Mikey.

When I got back to the house Mikey and Maureen were waiting for me. He tore into me. He said, "What in the name of God happened to you," he said, "I was worried sick about you."

I said, "Mikey, it's a long story, I'll tell you tomorrow," and that was that.

I was going to get into bed and realised I had no cigarettes so I went around to Jack's little late night store, just down and around the corner from Forston where I lived. Jack was a big man from Kerry who would always say to me, "When I die, 'Dub', I'll leave a great legacy behind". Everyone liked Jack. He would never see you stuck.

While I was strolling back to Islington I passed the Irish Club at Angel Station. One of the Casey brothers was standing outside. If you had never seen "The Krusher" it was an awesome experience. He was a massive, big, handsome man. You couldn't miss him. He stood around six foot six, and weighed around twenty two stone. Steve "The Krusher" Casey. He said, "What happened to you, 'Dub'?"

"I fell over a dog," I said.

"I hope you didn't hurt the dog."

"I didn't, Krusher."

"I'll see you down in the Nag's Head, you can give me a song."

I liked Krusher. He was a great wrestler and nobody messed with him or any of his friends when he was around. I waved to him, walked around the corner and got a smack in the head. I didn't know what had happened to me. I staggered, threw my arms in front of me to shield myself and couldn't see anybody. I thought I could make out a couple guys. I fell against the railings and held on. I was in trouble and knew my nose had started to bleed again, and my head ached. I was in trouble. I remember saying, "Jesus, help me".

I felt a pull at my coat and the other guy came at me. But just then I heard an unmerciful roar. It was "The Krusher" Casey in action. He had a big chain that had come off the door in his hand and he was mobile. He was swinging the chain around over his head. He caught all three of them and destroyed them. They ran screaming and "The Krusher" went after them.

I lay against the railing and stared. I couldn't believe my eyes as I watched. Krusher was poetry in motion. The guys ran from him and never stopped.

"Come here, you," he said, picking up my cigarettes off the ground where they had fallen. He put them in my pocket and said, "Home now, lad, you're too young to be out at this hour. Home with you, lad. You can sing me a song on Saturday night when I go down to the Nag's Head. Now you watch who you get involved with. Those boys are not nice lads at all."

He was a nice man, this Krusher. I don't know what way that melee would have ended without Krusher, I just don't know, but I don't want to think about it too often.

I sang him many songs in the Nag's Head, down on Walworth Road. Krusher's song was always, *I'll Take You Home Again, Kathleen.* I sang it many a time for him.

A year or so later I sang with my brothers, the *Three Smyth Bros*, in his Irish club called Blarney Tottenham Court Road, a widely popular of the many Irish clubs in London. Then a few years later when I was vocalist with the *Gallow Glass Ceilidh Band* we played again at the Blarney Tottenham Court Road. I made many appearances with the band in many halls, but through the years I was never again to meet Big Steve "The Krusher" - and I never again saw those guys whom he made bits of. But I was to learn later on that "The Krusher" Casey became World Heavyweight Champion, a worthy champion.

The sun has shone, the grass has risen,
I wonder where "The Krusher" is,
God rest his soul.

Chapter 20

Home for Christmas

I came home for Christmas early, weeks before the holidays started. I was tired with the struggles in London. Maureen wouldn't let me go and that was no way. I just couldn't hack it. It was sad for me to leave Mikey and Maureen but I knew it was best I get out. I was on the train from Euston, and was shouting out the window,

"I'll write ... I'll be back, don't worry."

I had been in some rough times and I had come home to 'lick my wounds'. Now I knew this was the beginning of another part of my life. I also knew I would go back but things would be different.

But it was nice to be at home and at Christmas time.

The flats and St. Audeons were the same. I looked around at the drab interiors and never saw such a warm homey place in all my life. Mr. Downey, the Caretaker, was standing at his door with a smile to greet me. Mrs. Wilson was anxiously waiting for all the news about Mikey and Maureen. I found out that no news had been sent home about my exploits in London and I got a great reception. It was nice to be home. Let's face it, the 'good lookin' Dublin kid' was back.

I wrote this song, *Christmas Bells* at the time when I had just come back home, in December 1950:

Christmas Bells, the sound of them always tell,
Of happy times when the family all home.
The fire will be burning bright and the
Christmas tree is all alight,
And the happy laughter rings out loud and clear.
And on Christmas morn we honour
Our Saviour's birth

And we thank Him for blessings He has bestowed on Earth.
Oh Christmas Bells, the happy times they tell
With the family all together at Christmas time.
So wherever you may roam on land or sea or foam
May Christmas bells ring out and bring good cheer.

The previous year was very prominent in my mind. I knew I would never forget the times, the places, the people, all the friends I had made. I was to meet many of them in later years.

But now to Dublin: Fran was home, Des was still up in Somerset but would come home close to Christmas and then we Smyths would all be together. Paddy was to be married the following year to his little girl from Whites Printers in Fleet Street. He was working in the Irish Times, had bad shifts and wasn't too happy with the arrangements.

It was good to be part of the scene again, to see my old friends Kay Delaney, Tommy Poland, George Walsh. We got into the swing of the shows again, and we three Smyth brothers now really began to sing together every chance we got.

I had a ramble up to Francis Street where it was nice to recap on all the old familiar places. Mr. Mushats, Johnny Rea and his sister, they were still in the shop. He'd gotten married and his wife was a nice looking girl, but his sister was something else, a beautiful woman if I may say so.

I met up with John Chapman and it was nice to see him again. He always was a quiet, nice guy. He married Annie Caroll, a wonderful girl, good for him. They made a great match together and soon had lovely kids. Unfortunately they had a little girl called Joyce who, in later years, was to die on the same week her dear father, John, passed away.

Anyway, our family was well and all together at Christmas – like the words by that famous song writer 'Jim Smyth' in his great *Christmas Bells* song! It was a great Christmas, a happy one for us all.

I kept my mouth shut. I didn't say much. I did tell my mother that Mickey and Maureen were in great form. I had bought a silver vase for my mother, but I decided to give it to Mrs. Wilson, and I gave my mother some money, and told her, and myself as well, that I would get home again next year.

There was a great get together one night at the Kevin Street Garda Station. I walked up to the guard at the front desk and said, "Could I see Sgt. Brannigan?"

"I think so. What have you done?"

I said, "Nothing, but I'll do you in in a minute if you don't shut up."

He laughed. He seemed to get a great kick out of it, suppose not many came in the front door and talked up like that to him.

Just then Lugs came out. "I heard your voice."

"I came up to give you a game of handball."

We stripped out of our clothes and away with us. It was a great game. I won the first 21-18. He won the next two games. Great sport, I enjoyed them. He was great, good to see him.

He looked at me and said, "Did you have a hard time over there?"

I said, "I never told you I was going."

"There's not much that goes on that I don't know about," he said. "Did you have a hard time?" he asked again.

"No, I enjoyed it. But I missed the Liberties."

"I bet you did."

I asked him, "How is Mikey Dunne?"

"He'll be out soon," he said. "Don't worry about him. You have a good life in front of you. I hope it's a happy one."

I liked Lugs, in fact I think I always liked him. You boxed fair with him and he boxed fair with you. "I'll go," I said.

He stood up and put his hand out. "Good luck, Jim," he said.

"Thank you, Mr. Brannigan," I replied. "I brought you this home." I gave it to him, it was a lighter.

He said, "At the end of the day when I go home at night I will sit down with my good wife and review the day. Tonight I'll show her this and I'll say, 'Mother, do you see this? This was given to me by one of the cutest little individuals I ever met, who knew when it was time to say, 'this is it'."

Then he said to me, standing up, "One day, Jim, when you think of me and talk about me, and then you will remember me?"

And here I am, sitting here, thinking, talking and writing about him.

I was proud to know Jim Brannigan. He came at a time when I was growing up and he was good for the Liberties. He was a fair man. He had many run-ins with the hard men, one with Mikey Dunne. Lugs confronted Mikey.

"You should not have done that, Dunne," he said, "you are out of order."

"Take me in then," Mikey said.

Lugs was standing at Jim Stanley's yard. It was a quiet time in the late afternoon, not many people around. "Let's see how good you are."

Mikey squared up.

Lugs had a cap on his head, his Burberry on but this time he had no cosh with him. 'Okay,' he said to himself, 'I'll have these gloves, they'll have to do.' They were brown, shiny leather. I think he used to polish them.

Mikey made his move first. A nice left hand. He just flicked it and it caught Lugs on the mouth. It drew blood and Lugs was not pleased. Mikey was dancing around and moving nicely and becoming very confident. He was leading with his left hand. Mikey was a well proportioned man and he moved in nicely on to Lugs' left hand. He shook it for a bit. Suddenly there was a look of terror on Mikey's face.

Lugs slammed him about three times. Mikey stood still, barely. Lugs let down his hand and went forward. I thought Mikey was going to fall down. His face had turned ashen. He was bleeding and was wet as it had started to rain.

Just as Lugs came up near him Mikey looked Lugs straight in the face and put his hand up to his face. As Lugs came nearer, Mikey crashed his fist into Lugs' private parts.

Lugs let out a shout. He crouched forward. He was in agony and at just that minute Mikey crashed his head into Lugs' face. Lugs moved back away from Mikey who ended up on his arse on the ground.

There was just the three of us, Mikey sitting on his arse, while Lugs looked impressive standing with his arms folded, and me. It was over. Mikey just couldn't stand back up.

Lugs looked at me. "You make sure he gets home."

"Right, Mr. Brannigan." But how the fuck was I going to get him home. I helped him up onto his feet. He opened the flap of Stanley's gate and sat himself down again.

I said, "Mikey, I'm going to get a car to take you home."

I went to Mrs. Higgins' yard where they had a box car. I took it and made my way up to Stanley's yard. We were in business. I got Mikey into the cart and started to wheel it down Lower Bridgefoot Street Hill and man, it's steep! I was half way down when I lost control of the cart and Mikey. I started to scream. There were not many cars in those days, thank God. Mikey Dunne and his cart took off and eventually stopped at Dirty Lane.

I think, when I said good-bye to Lugs after coming home from England, I said goodbye to a lot of my feelings. I was going to be away a long time this next time I left Dublin. I could see a lot of mileage ahead of me. But then there was a lot of mileage behind me too.

I would never forget those early days in London. I had some great memories.

But I was next going up to live in Bath, in Somerset. Maybe make it up to London to keep in touch with Marie, but will try my luck in Somerset, it seemed to be a nice place. All my mother's family were from up there, very wealthy people but a load of snobs I heard.

Chapter 21

Time in Somerset

Is this Somerset a part of "England's green and pleasant land", its "dark Satanic Mills"?

Taken from "The New Jerusalem", by William Blake

I stayed home through Christmas of 1950. The scene was good, we had lots of work and Des, Fran and I were all over the moon about going back to England together. We already had great recognition in Ireland. Maybe we would strike it lucky in England.

In early January we three Smyth brothers took off for English shores. Des had been over in Somerset about nine to eleven months the last year before he came home for Christmas. So he knew the ropes and had already fixed us up with digs.

Fran and myself were to stay with a couple called Mr. and Mrs. Offer who were in a way very mean people we discovered. Even the slices of bread were doled out at mealtimes. George and 'Dink' were their names. They had chickens and strawberry beds so I made sure we had plenty of eggs, although raw, and strawberries with cream which was lovely.

One night I came in from work a bit late and overheard George and Dink.

"Dink, I'm very worried about the hens."

"What's wrong, George," she said, putting the kettle on.

"There's been no eggs for two weeks now, I can't understand it, I'm baffled," he said.

"George, sing to them. I believe it's great," I said.

Later on, Fran came in from his work on the railroad.

"It's so cold out, Jim. Who the fuck is singing outside?"

I said, "It's probably George. I told him singing was good for the hens."

Fran started to laugh and what a laugh he had, on and on it went, in and out. We went out the back door and saw they were singing *Terry Dean*'s *A White Sport Coat.*

I said, "You won't get any eggs with your singing, George, you'll kill them!"

The girl next door came out to see what was going on.

I said, "The hens won't lay."

She looked at me and gave us a smile. Her name was Mary, a nice looking lady, coloured.

I said, "Dance with me," and held my arms out.

"Right, your move."

Oh, she felt lovely in my arms. I said, "You're lovely, Mary." I let my right arm drop down to her back-side. "You know what I noticed?"

"No, tell me, Jim."

"Your husband is home and he's looking out the window."

"Now," she said, "why is it that doesn't upset me."

We were good friends, Mary and me. What a good time we had that evening, brother Fran with his laugh and dancing with Dink, and Mary, a lovely woman, very kind and always in good humour. I liked that. She was black as ebony, so picturesque. She stood out.

My Uncle Clem had a couple of public houses in Bath. He was a nice man and his wife, Annie, was my mother's sister.

She and Clem were a great twosome, good business heads, both of them. I spent a lot of time in his pubs helping out.

Clem told me one day, “We are very fond of you, Jim.”

“I like you too,” I said, “but your son Fran is a pain in the arse.”

“I take it you don’t like him?”

“Sorry, Uncle Clem, did I say that? No.” And I didn’t say it but his son was a snob. Don’t know what happened to him.

I liked living in Bath. All the people were very friendly. My mother, in her early married years lived in Bath. The Roman Baths were a great attraction there. The streets were so clean, spotless. And you couldn’t raise your voice around town. It wasn’t allowed by city law. In Bath in the late forties, early fifties you couldn’t wear ‘teddy boy’ trousers or have an Elvis Presley ducktail haircut. And every night promptly at eight o’clock ‘bang on’ the police would herd all the tramps out of town for the night.

The most famous woman in the town of Bath was a prostitute who had the name of “Woodbine Lil”. Her pitch was on a big hill just outside town.

Our trio the *Three Smyth Bros* was really going down well with the crowds. We were working in the ballroom in town and also working in other towns around.

I was knocking around with a girl call Pat Wernham, a lovely girl whom Des had dated before I came over, and Fran was courting around with her girlfriend, Maggie Tolster. One night Pat and myself went into town to see a picture. We walked outside town and sat on a grassy hill for a time. Then we walked on up the hill and sat down again beside a wire fence. We were courting for awhile when suddenly my foot got caught in the fence somehow. I tried to dislodge it. ‘This is stupid’, I thought. I tried and tried but no way could I free it.

Then Pat looked at her watch. “Oh God, I have to go. Can

you manage Jim?"

I said, "Okay, you go on." I still couldn't get my leg out. I was in a terrible state. Pat ran off. I thought, 'To hell with this, and I had had great hopes for the evening'. I was panicking. It was turning into a nightmare and I was the victim. How did this happen?

I heard a sound and didn't know what to do.

A form jumped past my head. It was a huge rat.

So I chanced a shout. A movement. Then a woman appeared.

"Are you alright, love?" in an English accent.

I said, "Can you help me, please, my leg is caught!"

"I'll try sweetheart. I'm supposed to be working."

I said, putting my hand in my pocket, "I'll pay you".

"Alright, love, how much you got?"

"Let's see," I said, "I've got about four quid, I'll give you that." I had spent a lot on the meal with Pat so the pockets were light.

She said, "All right, darling."

I gave her the money. Then she took off her coat. She had some body on her. I tried to help her with the fence. She said, "Let me, love." So I let her. She pulled the fence up quite easily. I couldn't even budge it when I tried! I was knocked out. I slid down the bank on to the pavement. I put my head in my hands and could have cried with relief.

"Thank you very much, miss," I said, "I am very grateful to you. My name is Jim Smyth. You saved my life. I mean that".

She said, "Don't mention it. You're Irish, are you?"

I said, "I am. I was up at the pictures with my girl but she had to get off home for something."

She said, "Are you sure you were not looking for me? Don't let it worry you. I'll be seeing you."

"I hope so."

"Don't forget to come back and see me sometime. Just you ask for "Woodbine Lil". "

I was very impressed. 'Well now,' I thought, 'I've just met the diva who lives on the hill.'

I barely made it home, my leg was a mess. I was beholden to Lil, really I was. But for what she charged me for a helping hand, I doubt if you would get very far for a say at "Woodbine".

I later heard Pat had rung the digs and told Mrs. Offer to say she got home. I wasn't too worried whether she did or not.

The *Three Smyth Bros.* were doing very well in Somerset. We, as well as the *Terry Sisters,* were 'resident' with the *Ted Markham Big Band.* The *Terry Sisters* were beautiful girls and lovely to work with, very professional, a class act. The band worked seven nights, which was a very popular combination. Crowds came from as far away as Bristol and from all over Devon.

We were working with the band a couple of nights a week but we all three had to get day jobs. We needed to get a few Pounds together, and then we could go to London or branch out, do whatever to make something of our selves. Our mother and father were great to us, gave us a lot of help and encouragement so we were working in the right direction.

Des was working at *Stothard & Pitts,* the biggest factory in Bath. It employed about two-thirds of the population in town. So Des got me a job with his firm. It was a physically tough job but I didn't mind, I could handle it.

Fran and me were getting along great with Dink, our landlady. She fancied Fran a lot. "He's a lovely boy," she would always tell me.

I was great friends with lovely Mary from next door, and Des was with his girl, Maggie Tolstor, a great girl whom he was with for a great many years before they eventually split up. But as long as we three were in Bath he was with Maggie.

Summer was with us. It was warm, over-powering, stifling. In other words, it was hot! One evening I was sitting outside in the back, trying to stay cool and write a letter to home. I heard a sound, turned to see it was my next door neighbour.

I said, "Good evening, Mary. Glad you came out, nice to see you."

"And it's nice to see you, Jim," she said. "You were good last Saturday night when you sang."

"I went looking for you but couldn't find you," I said.

"I would have loved to dance with. John said you were very good, and thought you sang real well with the girls. Where's Fran?" she asked.

"George took him over to see Miriam. I like her, don't you?" I asked. "Mary, you're smiling, why?"

"I'm smiling at you. I think you strip down well."

"I do weights, that's when I have time," I said.

She came over and put her hand on my neck. It was a nice feeling.

"I'll sit beside you on your chair?" she said.

I moved over to let her sit down but she sat on my knee. I moved her in some more. And she sat and rubbed her fingers through my hair and we kissed that hot evening under the stars. I said, "Luv, lets go inside and get a shower to cool off" and we did. I heard Fran come in later and go to bed, and Mary and I kissed and stayed there most of the night. I liked being with her, let me tell you it was lovely. She said she had to go over to her mammy so I walked her to the bus. When the bus came, she got on and laid her head against the window looking out at me. Others got on the bus, and then it moved off. I was in a funny mood. I went back to the lodgings and sat outside the front door. George came and brought me a cup of tea and a sandwich. Then I fell asleep. I woke up about six o'clock, cold but refreshed.

After that evening, I saw Mary a lot. We became good friends.

One day she said to me, "Jim, do you know a man at work called Willoughby?"

"I do," I answered.

She said, "Beware of him. He doesn't like you."

"Gotcha. I don't care for him either. He carries too many stories and he hates the Irish."

"Now you have it right, Jim."

I always did ask questions and got answers. I remember my father saying to me one day, "Jim, always remember this, never forget it. If we could only see and hear ourselves as all the people around us can, there would be an awful lot of sad faces in the world today." I always remember it as it's so true in life.

I started to work in the foundry at *Stothard & Pitts*. Des worked there as well. It was a very large place, awesome in size, a couple of miles either way. I was working as a slinger with a crane. A guy called Jim drove the crane. He was one dogged man. I'd get a docket for a certain piece of machinery, sling my chain on it and lift my arm to take it away, which Jim dutifully did when it suited him. I would show him a clenched fist for him to hold it, and if I waved up to the sky it meant to take it away.

There were five men in my squad. I tolerated them to a certain extent. There were: Len Williams, Wally, Jim Mackell, Toby, Bomber. This man called Willoughby came in to do the overtime.

We were all together one day. I had just started. It was a cold day and we were in the hut. I was talking to Bomber, who was from Wales. He was a 'pro' boxer. I heard that at one time he was very good.

Just then Willoughby came in to the hut. We all said, "Hello, Mr. Willoughby."

I got the message.

"You the new man?" he said to me.

"I am, indeed."

"The nurse wants to see you. I hope you haven't got a dose."

He laughed. Someone else laughed as well. I wasn't impressed.

I looked at him and said, "I don't think so you thick bollix." The Bomber started to laugh. I had heard he didn't like Willoughby.

I walked outside. I was going over to see the nurse. Willoughby walked after me and shouted, "Hey Paddy".

I didn't answer. I didn't even look behind me.

He called out, "Paddy," again and added, "the Irishman".

I turned into a side lane, I was now real mad. I stopped. I knew he was behind me. Just as he turned the corner I cracked a right hand right into his stomach. I dropped him on the ground and said, "By the way," I said, "my name is Jim, not Paddy. Not that there is anything wrong with 'Paddy'. Sure, wasn't it a lad called Paddy who drove all the snakes from Ireland."

Now I thought he was going to hit me. "You hurt me, you Irish bastard, he said.

I said, "That was the general idea."

Just then I heard Des calling me. He was looking under a car, I could see him. He was in knots of laughing." At it again," he said.

I said, "You're late, it's all over, sorry."

Willoughby said, "I'll sort you out, you'll see."

I said, "You don't scare me, Buddy."

He said, "You think you're great."

I said, "Your missus tell you everything to do?"

"What did you say?" he asked. "Say it again."

I laughed.

I went to see the nurse. I was late. "I'll see you tonight, Des, at the gig."

"Okay," Des said, "and mind how you go, Jim."

I turned to Willoughby, "Hear that, Willow, Jim is my name."

He didn't answer. I didn't think he would. There was so much aggravation in our work crew. But I knew somehow Willoughby was trouble. It wasn't long in coming.

I went into the Medical. The nurse examined me and said the doctor wanted to see me. I said, "Thank you, will you want to see me?" Now I was looking for company, I guess I needed it badly.

I walked outside, looked back at the Surgery and the nurse was looking out the window. I smiled back at her and blew her a kiss. She lifted the window and said, "Pat

Wernham was asking for you."

A man was standing on the pavement, looking at me. "Are you Jim Smyth?" He held out his hand to me. "I'm Len Williams. I'm your Foreman."

"Nice to meet you, Mr. Williams."

"Did you meet all the men in your squad?"

"Yes, I did. All nice guys."

"Does that include Mr. Willoughby?"

"I've met him, I will tell you we had a few words."

"He's told me all about. He's a tough man."

I pointed to a mound of clay and said, "Is it there he buries his dead? Don't get me wrong, Mr. Williams, the way I talk to you. I don't mean any disrespect towards you, but I don't give two pennies for Mr. Willoughby and if I have to bow down to him, I'll leave your job."

He said, "Take it easy, I don't want you to leave. By the way, I heard from your Uncle Clem you are a boxer."

"I did a lot back home."

"He said, "I run a Club. I'd love you to join it."

"Great. I'll give it a go."

Just then the Bomber came over. "Your office wants you, Mr.Williams."

"I'll see you soon, Jim, and by the way my name is Len, right Jim?"

"Thanks, I will look forward to a few bouts with you, Len."

The Bomber said, "What happened today?"

I answered, “He asked for what he got.”

Bomber said, “You mind yourself at night. That Willoughby is a slimy pig.”

“Right Bomber, thanks a lot.”

“He said, “Okay lad, I will try and sort it out.”

I knew he was right. I did a foolish thing. When I joined the “Len Williams Club” I’d sort it out. I made myself clear that I was not afraid of anyone. They had all heard about what had happened but things would have to go under for awhile because we were all to go on strike.

The company was in dire straits, the job was in an upheaval. When I went home that night I met Mary at the door and her face said it all.

I said, “You look happy.”

“I’m sorry about the job, Jimmy, real sorry.”

“Thanks for your concern. It’s going to be a disaster to this town. When word gets around everyone will be knocked out. Most of the town worked at *Stothard & Pitts*. And there was no way I would pass the picket, any picket for that matter.”

George Offer said to me that night, “It’s alright for you to pass the picket, Jim.”

I said, “Now why is that George, tell me please.”

He said, “You are not in any union.”

“Well, I will join one then. I never passed a picket in my life and I’m not going to pass one now, so that was that.”

Fran, Des and I had some singing jobs in the ballroom, singing on Saturday night.

But the strike was the only topic of conversation, it was

big stuff. Since Des worked with me I asked him, "Are you going to work?"

"No way. My mate is a shop steward," he said.

"Suit yourself, I'm not passing any picket, end of story. Let's sleep on it."

Monday dawned bright, dry and cold, very cold. I had my suit on, was powdered and shaved and had breakfast with George, Fran and Dink.

I met Mary from next door going for the bus. There were quite a few men going to work. They had the 'work dress' on, brown gabardine overcoat, brown cap, bag over the arm, and about twelve to fourteen women were hanging onto the arms of their men, brushing their coats, mothering them like busy hens. Mary, Fran and myself couldn't believe it. This continued all the way down to the factory. I knew all the men. Most of them had their wives with them. Every time the bus stopped four or five more got on. The bus was packed. I got a seat and Mary sat on my knee. I could see no one from my own gang. I heard afterwards that they had all gone in early. Jim had picked them all up in his car.

I got a placard and took my place outside the factory.

It was a pitiful sight to see all those grown men being escorted to work by their wives. There were many workers standing around outside. The tension was rising by the hour. It was unbelievable. It was quite a demonstration, lots of police were present and it went on for some months. The women still continued to be with their men going to work. We on the picket line were singing and making a few shillings. We would do strike duty about two days a week.

During the strike time, I saw a lot of Mary and also did a few days in my Uncle Clem's public house so we were all able to send a few Pounds home.

I heard that most of the men who went in to work were treated like shit. I wasn't sorry. I said to George, "If your son had gone into work, what would you have done?"

"I would have put him out of my home," he said.

So, as you can imagine, it affected everybody. Those that passed the picket line were never spoken to for, in some cases, many years later. I never once passed the picket and eventually we all went back to work.

The crew I was with wouldn't talk to me.

So I thought, 'To hell with this, I'll see Len Williams,' which I did and we got it straightened out between us, but it wasn't finished, not by a long shot.

Willoughby, who passed the picket, was working with Jim Mackell. I heard they were great pals.

On Thursday of that week I went into the hut for my lunch. As I took it out I heard a few mutters, like, 'Hello, Paddy'. I said, "Let's get one thing straight, gentlemen. My name is not Paddy, it's Jim." They looked at me.

Bomber said, "That's okay by me, Jim." He then stood up, put his coat on and went back to work.

I saw him later and said, "Thanks, Bomber."

He said, "Okay, Jim. The ball is at your feet now. You started it, make sure you finish it. Be very careful and watch yourself."

"I will," I said. "I might be moving out in the summer."

"You will always make a few bob at your singing."

Len Williams came by. "Everything okay, Jim? By the way don't forget the boxing club."

"I won't Len. I'm looking forward to it." I went back in to the hut.

It was nearly time to go home. Just then Jim came in and said, "Are you off, Paddy?"

"Fuck you, Jim," from me.

This riled him. "Hey watch it now Paddy, watch it." He was getting red in the face, a bit too red I thought. I was sorry I had said it. I thought he was going to have a heart attack. So I said, "Steady on, taffe, you will sicken yourself."

He said, "... or I will sicken you, Jim."

"Stay where you are, Jim," I said, "your face is doing a great job."

This didn't go down well.

"Can I go now?" I said, "I've a date with a lovely coloured girl." I said that because he hated foreign people. Me, I loved everyone and I enjoyed Mary's company but I knew I had made an enemy. Jim was in trouble.

I went home that evening and drank a toast to Mary and me. But I knew there was an issue between us. That summer would see me in London. Bath and Somerset were played out for me, it had had its day. We did well musically, were getting rave notices in the papers. But the attitude between the workers at work was terrible. I got into work early next morning, feeling good but moving out soon, I hope. Too much hassle.

I went over to Des. "It was all arranged," he said. "We're going to London. I made a few contacts," Des said. "We have to go see Bill Henshaw on Charing Cross Road there."

I said to Des, "I'll miss Mary."

"Why?"

"Do you remember Pat Wernham?" I asked to him.

"Yes, I do. She was a lovely girl."

I said, "Would you know her again if you saw her?"

"Of course I would, but I mostly saw her in the dark."

I said, "Don't worry, you will still recognise her."

He looked at me. "Yeh," he said, "sure I will."

That satisfied him.

Des was looking at me with a bemused look on his face. "How are you getting on with that shower?"

I looked at him. I said, "Paddy, for the short time I can assure you."

Paddy said to me, "Those five guys you work with, they passed the picket and they won't be forgotten. You had a run-in with Willoughby, it's been said. You be careful of him, Jim, very careful."

"I will, Paddy, don't worry old son," I said. I knew Willoughby was a bad taste in the mouth.

"I'll see you, Paddy."

"See you, Des."

I went back to the graveyard. Jim was calling me. He pointed to a piece of metal on a fairy mound. It was a bit dubious. I didn't like it. I called to him, "It's too high. I can't reach it."

He got real angry, stood up in the crane, leaning out. This meant he was mad.

I picked up a small piece of metal and threw it at him. It hit the crane. He jumped back and shut up. Not another word. I looked up at him. We didn't speak. I looked at the pile of metal and thought, 'no way, dick-head'.

He jumped down out of the crane, picked up the chain on the white, marked piece and shouted to me,

I took the chain and threw it onto the pile of iron and let out a roar and said, "Me Tarzan ... You Cheetah". I said, "You get it now or I'm going home."

But I knew there was something going down. I was right. Bomber said, "You work with me, you are being set up".

I said, "Okay, that suits me Bomber." I was delighted to have a couple days with him. I liked him and enjoyed our time together. He was a rough diamond but was very straight. He said, "Jim, you are going to be done over."

I never told the brothers, I kept it to myself. After what the Bomber had said I carried a piece of iron with me to the bus stop, hid it behind a tree, then retrieved it on the way home. What I was doing did not suit me but it was a precaution which I knew was necessary.

I went a couple times to Len's Club. I had a few fights in the Club, did well, and Len was happy with me. "You did well, I'm sorry you are going."

"You heard?" I said.

"I did," Len said, "I did indeed. You could have done well. You move very well. By the way, I'm going to break up that crew you're in. I got Bomber a job driving for staff."

I said, "That's great news, Len, I'm delighted."

I went into work. The Bomber told me about the move. I never let on I knew, the other guys seemed shocked. They were all standing in a group and their faces told it all. I was nervous. I knew something wasn't right. One of the guys off the lorry came over to me and said, "I need someone to chain a piece of machine for me."

I saw the crane with the gib swinging in the breeze. I went to see where the chain was. I found it, slung it on the piece of machinery.

"Jim, will you put it on the crane?" Jim said to me. He sounded so polite, I said, "Okay".

I tied it on. It slipped so I tied it again. This time it held. Then I gave the hand signal, which was well known to Jim. First I showed him to take the strain, with my arm straight out. Instead he just took it straight up into the sky. As it was going up it hit against a huge steel 'cupboard', which toppled and fell against a road of girders and dislodged them. They fell all over the place and mostly on me.

I said to myself, 'Jim lad, you asked for this'.

One girder had fallen over my foot which hurt like mad. I was very lucky it wasn't worse. I was under the mound for awhile.

Des was sent for. Eventually I was got out from under. I had a very bad injury to my leg. I accepted it that there was nothing I could do.

Jim was the first over to me. "I'm sorry. I completely misjudged your signal."

"No way," I said, "you tried to wreck me."

The nurse and the Bomber came to my assistance. "Don't say anything," the Bomber said, "here's Len".

They bandaged me up and examined me. "Your foot is in a bad way but you will live."

"You are very reassuring, doctor," I said.

He said, "Jim, you are very lucky, it could have been much worse."

I simply walked into it, I knew it. I looked around for Jim. He was no where to be seen. Len was talking to the Bomber and they came over to me and helped me get up and home. Not a word was said between us on the way. When home I said, "Thanks Len, you can go now, I'm okay now."

Len said, "Jim, I'll sort this out, leave it to me. I'll look after your money for you," which he did. I got all the over-time as well.

One day during my recuperation Mary was sitting with me. Len met her and he instantly fell for her. I was delighted, I knew they would get on well together. She was good to Len and he was good to her. She was still coming in to me, looking after me, but when my brothers and I finally went up to London it was a sad parting.

Chapter 22

More London

London in the early 1950s was a huge, busy city with an underside of violence and terror, even though this was probably more or less true of all large international cities at the time.

London was rebuilding itself after the Second World War and there was massive construction work everywhere, especially in London but outside the City as well. As a result, powerful labour unions and gangs were a part of the fabric of society, especially working class society. London was a place to keep your nose out of trouble. We Irish living in London worked hard during the day and were together after work in our pubs where we could stay out of trouble. But it was out there.

Poor ol' Redser was a victim of the times and life in London. He deserved better in life. He was a talented boxer and kind person. But he was also a lad with a quick temper and that could get you in trouble in London. Trouble could come swift and with deadly effect.

So I learned early on to approach London carefully. There were far more opportunities in London for a young guy like me to get into trouble than I ever found in Dublin. I knew early on that I had to move carefully in London. I made good, loyal friends there, some of my family was over there as well and I stayed close to these people I knew. I stayed clean, worked in construction business during the day time and sang in the Irish pubs at night. I made good money there that helped the Smyth Bros get started when I went back to Dublin.

Mikey Wilson wasn't too pleased about me going down to the West End but I loved to walk down there and to the Greek Street in Soho. I wandered all over London and got to know The City well. It was about to get on her feet after the war years. I liked to walk my nights around London and feel the magic coming back.

The East End, now this place had a special feel all its own, unlike any other part of London. My beginnings started here with Mikey and Maureen and the house.

I remember one night I came into the house and Mikey made a gesture to me with his head that he wanted to see me.

"This guy Delaney upstairs has lost it, he's at the young girl."

I went upstairs to get something in the bathroom. When he saw me he said, "What do you want?"

I said, "Not a lot." He was very drunk and had his arms around the girl.

She said, "I want to talk to you, Jim".

I said, "Listen, Mister, the girl doesn't want your affections," and with that he pushed her aside and made a swing at me. It didn't land. I hit him and then his wife came out. She started shouting.

I took the girl downstairs and said to Mikey, "You better let her stay here."

"I think so," he said, so it was arranged.

Delaney upstairs roared down to me, "You get out of here, get digs somewhere else."

I said, "No problem."

Mikey asked me where I was going to go. I said, "I'll find somewhere." Delaney was an ignorant pig and I was the only one to stand up to him. I left.

I stopped by a couple friends, we talked and I realised I had to go back there to get my clothes. Delaney had the door locked, but fifteen seconds later the door opened. I went in, got my clothes and I was off, with Delaney shouting at me behind his door, "You're not welcome". I said nothing more, after all Maureen and Mikey were still living there. I found out the Delaneys moved to some other flat complex in London soon after. Don't know where and care less. I had to move on.

I loved being there with Maureen and Mikey, and Maureen was kissing my face off me as they weren't pleased at my leaving. We were going to see each other again, I knew, and I suppose if we had been quiet enough we could have got things sorted out and wouldn't have had to leave the digs. But no matter, it was over. I saw them years later in Dublin. Maureen came from Capel Street and Mikey from the flats so I knew we would connect up again, God love them.

I got new digs in London with a lad called Jim Hayde. He was going with a friend of my sister, Marie.

I was out walking in Greek Street and went into a burger bar. One of the waitresses came over and said, "May's in the corner. She wants to see you. By the way, do you see that coloured girl in the seat by the counter? She said you were to see her the other night at Madame Tussauds." I looked over. It was Betty.

Oh my God, I forgot all about it. I went over to her. "I'm so sorry," I said to her, "but I can explain."

She said, "I'm only joking. May told me about your troubles at the flat. Why didn't the two people you were staying with walk out with you and get the police?"

"It's over now, let's forget it," I said. To May I said, "Betty helped me. She got me away from the police."

"I know," said May, "I told her why you didn't turn up."

I said, "Thank you, Betty."

"By the way," Betty said, "May asked me to come up to dinner too. I think she wants to tell you something."

As it turned out, May told me she was pregnant, that April knew and she was going home to her fella, whose baby it was. Jeez the memories in London with May, Betty, Avril.

I walked Betty over to see her sister. We got a #30 bus, went about four stops and got off. Then we walked up about four flights of stairs, I waited outside on the balcony while she went in to see her sister. I was enjoying a bit of sunshine leaning over the balcony when a big, coloured guy came out of his door and looked at me. He punched his right hand into his left hand and said, “Hey man, can I help you? Would you be looking for someone?”

I said, “First, my fucking name is not ‘man’, and you couldn’t help me if I was dying.”

He said, “Man, this is my patch. I own this.”

At this stage I wasn’t too pleased with his behaviour. Betty came out just then and said, “Jim, I’m going to stay with my sister.”

I said, “Okay.”

She said, “Will I see you again?”

“Yes ... you will see me again.”

“I’ll see you on Tuesday,” she said. This suited me.

I turned to go down the stairs after saying goodbye to Betty when this bloke went up to the coloured guy and just smacked him in the mouth. I even felt it. “Don’t ever spit on my lovely daughter again. I won’t have it.”

And it was to be goodbye to Betty although I didn’t know it at the time.

I was going up to see my sister Marie and was looking forward to it. I got on well with Marie. She was a bit of a rebel like myself. A very attractive girl and a hell of a singer. I got the bus up to Whitechapel Road and found the pub where she worked, no bother. Marie had told me George, her boyfriend, would probably drop in to meet me. I was looking forward to this. I had met him before. He was one nice guy.

I walked in to *Blind Beggar*, a nice looking pub. I saw Marie right off. She was serving so I gave her a wave.

There were a lot of young guys drinking at the bar and a couple of them looked me up and down. I had learned not to return the stares for very long. No eye contact was the safest. My old pal, Lugs Brannigan would say, 'Don't be afraid of the man in front, it's the man behind you you want to watch'.

It was an impressive place. I found a little table in the corner.

Marie said, "I'll be over to you in a minute."

I took a paper out of my pocket and started to read it. I could see a few heads looking at me. I was hoping to get a drink. Just at that minute Marie brought me over some very nice sandwiches and a drink. We started to talk when just then a nice looking, well-dressed man said, "I've left money for that round, Irish."

I smiled.

"Thank you, Reg," she said, "by the way I'd like you to meet my brother, Jim. He's not long over here."

Reg put his hand out and said to me, "A pleasure to meet you Jim. My name is Reg Kray. Your sister is a great friend of mine. I'll see you around".

I said, "I hope so. Nice guy," I said to Marie.

He was a nice looking man, very well dressed, well tailored suit, blue and white shirt, nice tie, forgot the colour. But I remember saying to Marie, "Nice looking man."

Marie said, "He is. I get on very well with him. I like him, he's good to me. There was a drunk hassling me one night. Reg just tapped him on the shoulder and said, 'Shut up' and he did, and I haven't seen him since." She laughed. "Do you get the message?"

"I think so."

I liked the pub and anytime I went to see Marie I always got a friendly 'hello'. I remember Reg wishing me a happy Christmas and saying, 'Don't forget to come back now, won't you?' He would say, 'Have a drink on me', put a bottle of whiskey into my hand, pick up a glass and say, 'I drink to your health'.

And I said, "I drink to yous," and I did.

I remember those visits to the *Blind Beggar*. In later years it was Reggie and Ronnie, the Kray twins. They eventually received big status in the underworld of London. Reggie I knew very well, Ronnie to say hello to. All the other men they would be with were very friendly men. Little did you know though that if you crossed them what would happen. One wouldn't exactly know. Marie loved all the clientele in the *Blind Beggar* and I have a lot of memories of those times there, all good.

These were the good memories in London.

I was to go home to Dublin that Christmas of 1950. I got linked up with my brothers Des and Frank and we started singing again, this time as the *Three Smyth Bros.*.

Chapter 23

My Days in the Building Trade

I first worked in the building trade when I went over to London and Somerset in the late 1940s and early 1950s. On return to Ireland I quickly started again in the building trade but that was only for a short time, in the early fifties, for I got busy in the entertainment business with the *Three Smyth Bros.*.

When I first started to work in the building trade in London, it brought me into contact with great characters, some good and some, well, pretty awful. One awful man was a guy called Alfie.

I was working in Arbour Hill on some old folks' flats and, as luck had it, I was working with the plumbers. It was fairly straight forward work and little Georgie Elder was great to work with. His father ran the show with two other of his sons as well as George, and we all worked well together.

It was one o'clock and time for a break. As usual we were ready for one. I got my tea and made for the Hut with the lads. I sat down beside George. I noticed a new man in the Hut. I smiled over at him.

"Hello," I said. He never answered, just glared at me.

Finally he slowly stood up and said, "Who are you?" He was a tall, rangy fellow.

I said, "My name is Jim, I'm the mate."

Still not smiling he said, "You're the labourer."

"Yes," I said, "regular man about the job."

He said, opening the Hut door, "The labourers don't eat with the tradesmen."

I said, a bit taken aback, “You’ve got to be joking.”

He said, “I’m not laughing. My name’s not Jimmy O’Dea.”

George stood up and said, “I’ll go outside with you, Jim.”

I was not happy about what had happened, just a bit stunned. I had my food, looked at George and said, “What now?” There is flashing to be done, I thought.

“Ignore him, Jim, he’s from the old school.”

I said, “He doesn’t bother me.” But in a way he did.

George and I worked together the next week.

One day, Mr. Elder, my boss who was standing with Hughie O’Donnell the foreman, said to me, “Will you work with Alfie today, Jim?”

I said, “Okay Mr. Elder, I will indeed.”

I walked on to the site to look for Alfie. He was making his way towards me and Colm Wilkinson was with him.

“I have to work with you,” Alfie said to me. “Get a chisel and hammer.”

I got the tools and walked up to the site after him. I caught up to him. “Where are we working, mister?”

He said, “First of all you walk two steps behind me.”

I turned him around and said, “Mister you go blow it out your arse.” Then I said to Des Redmond, “Got a change, mister?”

Des was one of the best of the Foremen, great to his workers. I was with Des in the big building trade strike, the one concerning the cement, that turned very nasty. It went on for quite awhile. Des was always good to me and often changed me around to another and better little day or two of work. As he did this time with Alfie.

When I worked over in England, the building trade over there was much different than it was in Dublin. You got picked up in a van at a specific location every morning and brought to the job, and on that same night you got your day's pay into your hand. It worked out very well that way.

It was up to the ganger, if he liked you or not, as to whether he employed you the next day.

My building trade work in London didn't last too long although I was a great addition to a crew as I was a fairly well built young lad.

I was working on a job in Tottenham Court Road. There was to be two to three weeks work on the job, then I would be going home for the holidays. I would be getting together with the *Three Smyth Bros.* again, to sing in Ireland and was looking forward to that.

The boss on the Tottenham Court Road job was a chap named Tommy. He knew I was going home to get together with my brothers and said, "I'm delighted for you, Jim, you will do well." He gave me a right few quid which delighted me. At the end of the day I went to say goodbye to the boss. He said, "Everything all right back at the job, Jim?"

"I think so, would you like me to check for you?"

"If you would not mind, Jim."

"Okay."

I made it back to the job, opened the front door, walked into the back of the shop and made my way into where our bit of a canteen was. There was a crash like a window breaking. I took a run and crashed through the door, right into where we normally would be having our lunch at breaks. The scene knocked me out! There were three men and Lizzie, a young girl who worked on the job. She had little on but a tee shirt and had her hands to her face. Tosh was standing there looking pleased with himself.

I picked up a piece of scaffolding off the floor, smacked

him in the face with it and that took the smile off his face. I laid the other two guys out without too much difficulty as they were out of their minds with drink. I found out later that Tosh was the organiser of this affair.

I helped Lizzie up and got her dressed quickly. She was most upset, crying and holding on to me. I wanted to get an ambulance but she said, "No, take me back to the boss, he will know what to do." I knew she had been loyal to the boss. I washed her face and got her looking okay.

The boss Tommy was still in the restaurant, luckily. We had a cup of tea and she told him what had happened. He pacified her although I could see he was becoming very angry.

The girl, Lizzie, said, "It would have ended worse only for Jim."

"Leave it to me, let me sort it out please Lizzie," he said.

"Okay," she said. "I'm going home, bye Jim, thank you."

"No," the boss said. "I'll leave you home, you're not hurt in any way, are you?

They were very drunk and no rape occurred, but I wouldn't say the poor girl would forget it. I met her some months later. She looked nice and was back living with her parents again, but she never forgot that day, it would always be with her.

At the time I was singing with my brothers in the Blarney on the Tottenham Court Road when I saw her there. I said to Fran and Des when we were finished, "I'll see you back at the digs."

After we had finished our spot I went over to her and said, "I'll leave you home if you wish."

We were off, down to the West End, walking by the Palladium. "I'd love some Jellied eels," she said. We stopped at the stall, bought some and started to eat. I turned around and we were right outside our old job, only now it was a lovely shop.

I looked at her and she looked at me and said, "I know, I see it, but you know something, it doesn't bother me one bit."

I said, "How is Tommy the boss man? You know, I often think of him. I liked him."

"And do you know, Jim, he was very fond of you. He sorted Tosh out good and proper. He broke him up completely. I haven't seen him since that night. The boss is a big man now, Jim. He is very well known in London town. I see him fairly regularly now."

She was living in Highbury so we got the Tube together. The station was outside her house. I walked her to the door and told her good night.

She was a lovely person I met on my life's journey and what a journey I've had because somewhere along the way I always stop and meet some nice memory. I never saw her again. At all the dances we sang at in London she was never there.

But I met the boss man Tommy. Yeah, he was a big man in London.

It was a short time in my life that I spent in the building business. Did it have its good times? Not a lot. Its bad times? Plenty, yes, man, plenty. But to this day and I mean it sincerely, I'll never know why I went back to that building job in London and had that experience. Maybe if I hadn't, Lizzie would have died. It was a strange thing to happen to me ... and they're still happening to me.

St Audoens Tower

St Audoens Church

The Three Smyth Bros, Jim, Des, Frank (Fran)
1940's

The Five Smyth Brothers with their Father at Frank's wedding in the early 1960's. Left to right: Jim, Frank, Paddy, Father Fran Smyth, Terry, Des

Hal Roach and Jim Smyth

Jim Smyth, Gallow Glass in 1960's

Luke Kelly, Jim Smyth, Noel V. Ginnity, in Hitchin' Post 1976

Chapter 24

My Mother

My mother was a great force in my life.

She was a very attractive lady, always dressed exceptionally smart. As well, she was a great entertainer, a good singer, great dancer, both ballroom and Irish, a nifty tap dancer, and as well could play the harmonica. A lady knowledgeable in the ways of show business.

Do you need to be told who the Smyth boys got it from!

On thinking back, I'm reminded of so many things my mom told me and most all of them came through our experiences together during my early years. She was a wise lady, taught me invaluable lessons of life

Mrs. Brigid Conroy, a very nice lady, was a friend of my mom's. She and her husband George ran a café and B&B, situated up in Kingsbridge, not too far from the city.

One day my mother brought me and my brother Paddy up to see Mrs. Conroy, We had a great day, lovely food and lemonade. Later in the day we met Brigid's husband. He was an old man but nice to talk with. We all played lots of games outdoors in the afternoon.

We left about 8 o'clock in the evening and made our way home. On the way I said to my mom, "Mr. Conroy is old, isn't he, mom?"

"I think that is their business, isn't it, Jim? Every eye forms its own beauty," she smiled as she caught my ear in her hand, squeezed it and said, "you, my little beauty, you my little 'should-mind-your-own-business', isn't it Jim?" and she caught my face in her hand and kissed me.

Mom went on. "The truth was, when Mrs. Conroy was a

young girl her father said to her one day, 'Brigid, my daughter, there is a man I want you to meet.' So she met him and they got married. They may not love each other like dad and I do, Jimmy, but they have a lot of respect for each other."

I said, "Mom, Redser said the same thing to me."

"Well, bully for Redser," she replied, "I was beginning to wonder where he was. Just for that, I'll take another kiss."

"No way," I said and legged it down the Quays.

She caught up with me at the Brazen Head. Mr. O'Beirne was outside his public house.

"Good night, Mrs. Smyth," he said.

My mother replied, "Good night."

"I think," I said, "he was trying to get off with you, mom. Trust me, mother, I know."

My mother started to laugh and she couldn't stop. I liked to see her laugh. It felt good to me. There were tough times in the forties and fifties what with no work around and kids to feed and bills to pay, but we always managed to make it. No matter where she got it my mother always looked after us all.

Mom went on, "Bridget and Jim Conroy knew each other for about twelve months before they were married. He was in his late forties and she was just seventeen years old. Her father arranged the marriage for he knew he would easily be able to run the business if need be in the years ahead." In later years I found out the Conroys indeed had a very successful partnership, both in a business as well as in a personal way.

I met them in later years. My mother and I were on O'Connell Street. Bridget was the first one to recognise us. She said she had sold the business in Kingsbridge and went down to live in her native Kerry.

My mother said, “I’m glad you remembered them, Jim.”

“I’ve never forgotten, mother.” I said.

I also remembered my dear mother told me about Queen Street and Dick Clarke’s Dance Hall. “I learned to dance there,” my mother told me, “when I was a young slip of a girl.”

As she told it, “One evening two men were walking behind us going home from the Dance Hall”. Mother said they were walking us home from the dance, more or less chaperoning us. They each had a raincoat over their arms. It started to rain and quite suddenly it was pouring down. I grabbed the raincoat off one of the fella’s arms and threw it around my shoulders. It fell onto the ground! Mother of God, it was a raincoat cut in half down the middle in back, from top to bottom! It was quite the fashion in that day for men to carry a raincoat over their arm. Well, these two couldn’t afford a full raincoat a piece so they “shared” one, just so everyone would think they were fashionable. When the one raincoat fell apart on the ground the two of them legged it up the Quays in embarrassment. My mother said she did laugh and laugh at the funny sight of them on the run.”

My days with my mom in Benburb Street and the Phoenix Picture House for four penny admission were great fun, four penny each for admission and two penny each for a child. Sometimes we would stop by Keogh’s Public House, just next door to the Phoenix, to get a bag of broken biscuits which were sold for one penny, to eat during the picture.

One time my mother said to Mrs. Byrne and her husband and three kids to get ready, she would prepare dinner early on Sunday and they would all go to the Phoenix Picture House. They would have dinner in a big bowl! Mom would take five small bowls for each one of us and we would all eat our dinner while watching the big picture screen. I can hardly believe it now but it was the gospel truth.

Another of my mother’s adventures was with Aunt Annie, “my eldest sister, your Aunt Annie” mom explained to me. Aunt Annie was going steady with Clem, now her husband.

He was English and very wealthy. For Annie's birthday he had bought her a silver fox fur stole. Stoles were very popular, but especially the silver fox fur ones. Annie was so proud of it and would wear it out on Friday nights when she was out with Clem.

As my mom related, the night before Friday mom had a big date with my father. She just had to make an impression on my father, so it was essential that she borrow Annie's fur stole. She took it without telling Aunt Annie. My mom, being an attractive woman as she was, made a big hit that evening with my dad. When they returned home my father gave her a good night kiss and left her at the end of the street to the house where she lived. Suddenly it started to rain as she ran home but she made it into the house. As she was making her way up the stairs she heard Annie upstairs, laughing.

'God,' she thought, 'she is coming down.' My mother whipped the stole off her neck, looked around and the first thing she saw was the coal-bunker on the landing. She lifted up the lid, threw the stole into the box.

Next evening there was a knock on the door. It was Clem for Annie. My granny brought him into the room and told him that Annie wouldn't be long.

Annie really looked lovely but minus a silver fox fur stole! She couldn't find it anywhere, high up or low down. My gran said to Annie, "Chrissie will be in soon." At the time my mom was working at Creans, a big soap factory in King Street. She came up the stairs and stopped, remembering what she had to do. She opened the lid of the coal box, put her hand in and took out what looked like the remnants of a dead cat. It was black now, not silver grey. My granny looked shocked, Annie fainted. Clem took a fit of laughing and could not stop. Uncle Jim came in at that moment, picked up the black fur stole and coolly threw it out the window!

My mother's adventures continued wherever she lived. While we were living in the St. Audoens flats my mother became great friends with everyone, but one remembrance was with Mrs. Wilson. They became a great midwife partnership. In those days of the 1940s no one had money to go to a doctor to help with the birth of a baby so they would go to a midwife, who was cheaper. My mom and Mrs. Wilson delivered a lot of babies as midwives. God was good to them all.

When I came into the flats with a bundle that I had picked up on the Forty Steps, a baby boy, they were there to overtake the proceedings. As it turned out, Kate Wilson adopted him and christened him Finbar Wilson.

If a person died with no funds to bury them, the brown paper bag was passed around and the good neighbours contributed their shillings to the cause. It was a unique neighbourly act these people performed, and I think would be hard to find in this day and age. Perhaps there will never be such community kindness again.

My mother once invited a woman in to have some lunch with us. She wouldn't use the knife and fork my mother gave her. Instead she made a scoop with her fingers and scooped the potatoes into her mouth. I was amazed. My mother said to me, "Jim, don't ask questions about it, accept it. That's only minor to the question you'll ask yourself one day about life .... 'Will I accept it, stay still and move on or will I make an issue of it and get lost?' "

As I said, "my mother was a great force in my life". She was a great lady, she understood life and taught me most nearly everything I know.

Chapter 25

Brother Paddy

My brother Paddy was the first of the Smyth family siblings to be born. I was next born after Paddy, as you know.

Paddy grew up well. I noticed him a lot in his teenage years for I was a young lad at the time, five years his younger, and he began to amuse me quite a lot. Paddy palled around with Brian Donelly, who was a six foot tall blond guy. They both became involved in amateur boxing in which Brian was exceptionally good.

Brian would cycle over to see Paddy three times a week and I was delighted. Why not, I would get the opportunity to ride his bike! Brian's bike really belonged to his father and was made for a six foot man. I needn't tell you when I first rode the bike that it was hard going, but I mastered it somewhat and managed to get around and see quite a few places in the surrounding neighbourhoods. When it was time for me to stop the bike I would literally throw myself off it. Riding began to get easier as I got older and then it wasn't such a big deal, to jump off the bike. I improved so quickly that I began to give John Chapman a lift on the cross bar of the bike.

But Paddy wasn't too pleased with me taking the bike and he talked to my mother about it. So mother said to me, "Jimmy love, be careful with the bike. Remember it is not your property."

"I will, mother, I promise you."

Well now, I was riding it good by now with no problems maneuvering it around.

Jimmy "Dagger" Walsh said to me, "You won't ride it down the big hill on Thomas Street."

"I will, Dagger, you just watch me."

So I got up a bit early the next day and walked up the hill. As it happened, Sarah May was pushing her cart like she did every morning. I gave her a helping hand.

"Thanks, Jimmy."

"OK Sarah, so be it."

That evening Brian came up to the flats. So I borrowed the bike and started along.

"Nice bike, Jim," John Chapman said as he came up alongside.

I said, "My brother Paddy's friend owns it."

"It's a nice bike, Jim, although a bit big for you."

I said, "What's this, John, have you lost it? Weren't you on it with me?"

I turned slightly and saw that Paddy was behind me. "Do you want me, Paddy?" I asked.

"What would I want you for, what?"

I said, "Nothing, Paddy. I wasn't certain if you wanted to buy me an ice cream."

"I will not. I'm only just starting work."

I said, "Are you going to the Musical Society?"

He said, "I'm in the new musical, it's called *The Maid of the Mountain.*"

Chapman said, "Are you playing the Maid, Paddy?"

Paddy wasn't too pleased at Chapman, who started to laugh and said, "I'll get you a costume, Paddy."

I said, "Knock it off, John. Isn't the Maid pregnant in that play?"

Brian came into it and he made it worse. "I think you made the Maid pregnant, Paddy."

I gave Brian his bike back. "Thanks Brian," I said.

He winked at me and said, "Ok Jimmy boy, or is it 'the good lookin' Dublin kid' ?"

"Good looking Dublin kid me arce," Paddy replied to Brian.

"Paddy," Brian said, "now you have to give credit if it is deserved. Don't be so touchy, Paddy."

But Paddy was always very touchy. Growing up with him in those early years was none too easy. He was a prima donna.

I would be going to work with Paddy soon now. He had just at that time started work in Whites of Fleet Street who were in the printing business, printing such office items as head bills for personalised invoices, newspapers and in particular *The Stock Exchange*, a list for all stockbrokers. So it was decided to get me a job at Whites since Paddy was already there. Soon after I started, Paddy was offered a new position at Whites, as Compositor. I needn't tell you that this job was regarded as one of the best jobs in Dublin. He passed the exam in good style. My Uncle Bill, who was working in Whites, was married to my father's sister, our Aunt Maggie and a lovely lady if ever there was one. Uncle Bill was a fine man as well. I needn't tell you he got on well with Paddy. He got him into the trade, so Paddy was landed and he got everything handed on a platter.

"Don't wake Paddy up now, Jim," my mother would say if he was sleeping. "God love him".

But of course I was Jimmy Smyth and I was beginning to get a bit fed up with the adulation being showered on Paddy. I was beginning to pack on the weight now. What with all my training and exercising I was about a 45 inch chest and 16 inch upper arm. I could actually lean on Paddy which was a laugh to me, for a bit of craic. He played it up to the fullest by squealing and crying and calling for his "mammy". Eventually I would let him go. I would sob and say, "Help for my Mammy's boy."

Mother would say, "Jimmy, shame on you". Fran, little Terry and Des would all get a great laugh at this.

He worked with his hands on his printing job, setting the tiny type into place by hand. Delicate finger work so I was put outside the room till everyone got back to normal. But you know, it was great fun, our playing and teasing each other, I can tell you.

Paddy was keeping company with a nice little girl while at Whites. Her name, our mother said, was Maura McHugh, from the East Wall. Her father was in the shipping business. As it was explained by Paddy, he worked on the ships, he didn't own them,

It was great entertainment to watch Paddy getting himself ready for a date. He would get puffed and powdered and shaved. He used to use Gordon Moore's toothpaste. He would press a wave into the front of his hair with Brylcreem. It was well nourished. The process was something to see. What time he would put into it!

Then he would go somewhere with Maura. They always liked to sit at the seaside, any seaside as long as it sounded like a holiday resort.

Maura and Paddy became very close and of course they got engaged. Then the big day was set and we were off.

But I would like to say, before he got married, Paddy was very well respected by all our neighbours in the flats. They arranged a get together in the flats and every neighbour came to wish them well. Each one brought them a present as a token of their esteem and good wishes, and my mother was so thankful to them all.

Paddy told me he wanted me for his best man and I said I most certainly would be delighted to do so. He bought me a nice new suit and by God I looked real well if I do say so. The suit was a blue colour, well made in all ways and I had it measured to fit in Kings Store. I bought him a radio which he seemed to like.

The wedding reception was held in the Maples Hotel and a lovely time was had by all. Nick Eustace from the *Happy Gang* played the piano. Our mother and father were proud as punch, God love them. They looked so happy, and Paddy and Maura had a great day. I often have a wander back to that night when Paddy was going off to get himself married from our dear family abode. He said his thanks to all our neighbours and many friends who crammed into our flat with their presents clutched in their hands, smiles on their faces and their tender words of good luck to Paddy and his bride Maura.

I remember I said to my mum, "God love them, mother, all the lovely people who came to our flat with their great gifts, Some went back to work afterwards but they brought our family their love."

Paddy and Maura took up residency in Coolock, in Artane. I, with my old mate George Walsh, built a back yard concrete patio for them.

Paddy's on in years now, in his early 80s, well, healthy and happy. He and Maura have a lovely family and lead a quiet sheltered life. They have two lovely daughters, Brenda and Sarah and a son Raymond, who manages one of America's baseball teams.

I'd say they often think of those days, back in Whites of Fleet Street, and his pal Brian Donelly.

Maura had a lovely, singing voice. I remember her singing "De Ole De Aye" and that was before the aire came out and became popular.

Paddy did well for himself in life. He lives quite well and, as I said, leads a quiet life. He was the first "Mammy's Boy" to marry. He didn't stay in Whites all his life. He moved over to work for many years for the *Irish Times* newspaper and of course is now retired and living a happy life with his dear Maura.

Chapter 26

Brother Des

My brother Des, I must tell you about him.

Des was a great singer in his day and funnily enough he worked for a 'singer', for the Singer Sewing Machine Company. This was in his semipro days when we were often in contact with each other. This was in the growing up years of my life. Des would lay down the law a lot. I listened to him for awhile and sometimes I accepted it. Other times, as I grew older, I hadn't time to listen and I'd reply, "blow it out your arse Des," and usually it was accepted as it was intended.

Des went to Brunswick Street School in his early years for a short period of time. Then he decided to go to High Street School nearby, up near the Forty Steps. Mrs. Leonard was Head Principal, a big, jolly pleasant lady, fairly big in the buttocks area.

Des had a nimble mind and was the managing factor in our entering into show business. He taught us harmony singing as well. I liked singing with Frank and Des from the beginning and our singing together took off in the mid 1940s. We enjoyed our days together. They were a happy time, building upon our successes, always growing from big to bigger. We met many celebrities during this time, early on in the 1940s and more and more into the 1950s which was exciting to we young lads and often proved useful later on.

Those early days were good days. Des was a very professional artist from early on. Our trio worked well together and was a significant and necessary part of our young lives. My mother and father were quite proud of us. There was a great bond in our family. We spoke highly of each other and there was great love and affection between us. We *Three Smyth Bros.* travelled all over Ireland and England together and, as the saying goes, we lived out of our suitcases. Good times in my life, still remember them with fondness and respect. Respect for show business that is, not always show business people. Show business was a happy part of my life and it paid many of the bills. But you know it can be heartbreaking as well. When a singer is told they didn't register as a singer it can be heartbreaking as I'm sure you are aware. It's hard to accept when someone says, "no way" to your dreams.

We *Three Smyth Bros.* continued together for quite awhile, almost twenty years until in 1962 we went our separate ways. I went into a day job and also continued on as a part time professional singer and did some band work as well.

Des became quite active as a solo artist. He got a good number of television shows and paired off successfully with Hazel Yeomans. They had a good series on RTE called *The Hazel Yoemans & Des Smyth Show,* and became a popular double act. They had their own show for a couple years, then I think, let's say, Hazel went further afield to pick daisies. She is not around anymore. I think she got lost somehow in the traffic and you know London's a very busy little city. She was a classy lady but she did a runner from Dublin.

Des continued to prosper working as resident vocalist in many of the ballrooms around, like the Top Hat in Dun Laoghaire. Louie De Velici owned that ballroom and Des and George O'Reilly formed a show band. George, as said before, discovered Dickie Tappy Toes who became a famous man and I'm still coming to terms with that, Dickie.

Then Des came into contact with Val Doonican and Val had nothing but the highest of praise for Des. He "loved his singing", he would say. This came when Val sang with his own singers. So Des was gaining recognition, a nice one I say and it did his ego an enormous amount of good.

At that time in the 60s I was out and about singing. There was quite a lot of good work around at that time and the band gigs were okay for me. *The College Men Show Band* with Des was very popular.

About that time I went into the Hitchin Post for about ten

years and I lost track of Des. I know he continued to sing and always did well for himself. I always hoped he would do better and better, he was a great professional performer and highly deserved his success.

Among the many funny incidents we had together as a trio this one was memorable.

The *Three Smyth Bros.* were performing together in the town of Bath at a huge ballroom. The manager was an officious kind of man, as "I don't think you should include that song, you know the one you sing, *Begin the Beguine*."

Well, this was a showstopper! Anyway, we wouldn't chuck it and Des continued to sing it, well as he always did. We were not pleased with the manager and his decision, no way.

The bandleader introduced us on stage. There was a great roar from the crowd. They loved us. Between songs there was a request for *Begin the Beguine*. We continued with our act which was moving along real well. There were more requests for *Begin the Beguine*. We were going to have to sing it.

The manager came out on to the stage to bring us off.

The crowd shouted for more.

Des introduced the song. The crowd went mad but the manager said "no way". He was heading over to the microphone. I pulled him into a chair and got him into a headlock.

Des continued to sing the song.

The manager wasn't very impressed.

"My apologies," I said, "forgive me, darling."

He soon calmed down and we became great friends.

Terry Dean, the rock and roll singer, was also in the show. He thought the whole incident was very funny and thought we should keep it in the act. I can tell you it was the talk of the ballroom for many months after. It's funny now as I write it all down.

There were many funny incidents, the happy times were good times.

Collins Music Hall was a famous nude show in London, situated in Islington, It was a well known theatre, especially known for their nude shows. When the nudes were finished with their act the next show to go on was ours.

We had to walk down a long hall to the stage. I can tell you we were always waylaid on our way to go on by the exiting girls, not that we minded in the least. The girls made a point of wishing us well. We would insist on kissing them on the cheek, which cheek it didn't seem to matter to them. 'Take your pick' we were told. I can tell you we did just that. It's an awful pity it had to end. I guess time waits for no one, be it ever so humble and never overstay your welcome, as they all seem to say.

So that was my brother Des. He still sings a song. At this time he lives in Malahide. Des could blow warm and cold. The good side was great, the other side could be a pain in the arse. Sonny Knowles and Des were joined at the hip, the greatest of friends. The Bisto Kids they were called. Dickie Rock often said that if Des had gone over to Britain he would have become a star. Not to worry, Dickie.

Our years performing together were good times during the many shows we had in Dublin. Our highs and lows were from a good era. Des was a professional artist on and off stage. But Fran, Des and Jim, the *Three Smyth Bros.*, travelled many a long road together, were they not great times? By the good Lord they were the best.

Chapter 27

Brother Fran

I had heard that my brother Fran had been admitted to the Waterford Regional Hospital. I wasn't too worried. I presumed it was his prostate cancer. He probably just had a cold. I hoped. I wasn't feeling too well myself so probably it was the same kind of feeling. I hoped.

I needn't tell you I wasn't prepared for the phone call from my sister Rosie who told me, tearfully, that Fran had passed away. No my friend, I certainly was not prepared for this and absolutely couldn't accept it.

The memories came back.

I was thinking and hoping to make a comeback, we three Smyth brothers, but no chance now, none whatsoever. Our sound was gone forever, alive only in loving memories.

Great days we had together.

Brother Paddy was first born, then myself, Jim. Then our family moved from Queen Street to the Marshalsea Barracks. Soon after the move our brother Des was born and then the *Three Smyth Bros.* were truly born.

From his early days in the *St. Joseph's Boys Choir* that loving voice of Fran could hit the top octaves like no other. When John Flynn our choir director would shout, "Hit that top note again for me, Fran," he would duly oblige. Fran blended so well along with Des and me. What a combination we made, great if I may say so myself. Fran was a shy lad in his young days but always had a great voice and was a major part of our success as we went along in our professional life.

We *Three Smyth Bros.* played in Dublin and London, the Theatre Royal days, Radio Eireann, *The Ed Sullivan Show* in

New York, the American army camps in England. Fran was always the star.

Now he was to be laid to rest.

Fran and his wife moved down to Wexford, built a house, raised a lovely family and now was to be laid to rest in this little town. The church was to be opened for his burial as it was Holy Eastertide, so there was no ceremony. But we were all there, the brothers Des and me and Paddy and Terry and sister Rosie, our youngest. Sister Anna in Manchester England couldn't make it and dear sister Marie had left us a few years ago. Fran's sweet wife Anne greeted me with "I'm glad you could make it, Jim."

The morning in question was very cold and breezy with an abundance of rain. Mackens Undertakers were from that part of the country and they did the business, the funeral was impressive.

In the church the singing was excellent. The young men who sang were friends of Fran. I was asked to sing a hymn. As I looked around I recognised a man sitting by the altar. Why, it was my old friend, John Sheehan, the same John Sheehan of *The Dubliners.* It was a long time since I had seen him. He still had the grey beard around his chin and was still looking as distinguished as ever. Brother Des was by his side, looking well. We all said hello to each other.

The priest started the prayer. The singers started to sing the hymns. Then it was John's turn. He played the violin. The sound was sweet and lovely. There was not another sound to be heard. Beautiful. John was a masterful musician, a real pro.

It was Des's turn next. He stood tall and proud and sang a moving *Ava Maria.* Then I sang my hymn. It had to be *Sweet Heart of Jesus.* I got into it and it went very well. I looked across at the coffin and I just knew I had to say something. I didn't dare look at the coffin on the way up but it now looked different, there beside it. I don't know why but I just did. It seemed to say, 'you can do it, lad,' so I took off. The first words I said were, "Well, you're all boxed up now,

Fran, and I don't know where they will bury you. All I do know is that I will never forget you." I said other words, I now forget.

It's Sunday night in the Royal. Jimmy Campbell was there with a well nurtured smile on his face, impeccable in his white tuxedo.

"Ladies and Gentlemen," he said, "please welcome the fabulous *Three Smyth Bros!*"

The crowd gave a mighty cheer as Fran, Jimmy and Des lashed into *Down By The Riverside,* and then into the classic *Till Then.* What a thunderous round of applause they received at the finish. It was priceless.

A voice from the gods roars out from the days of the Royal. It was Paddy Hanaway himself. "Top o' the world lads, top o' the world."

In memory of my lovely brother Fran who will always remain close to my heart. May his wife Anne and his lovely sons and daughter enjoy the happiness they truly deserve.

Chapter 28

Sister Anne

My sister Anne was a very gentle soul. All those early years when we were growing up as brother and sister I remember her as always very quiet in herself, who led a normal and uneventful early life. She had pals she would go to dances with in later, teenage years, but by nature she was a quiet, sweet soul.

She became attached to Mai Phelan's Dance School when she was about ten years of age. She loved to perform on stage and was very good at the dance steps at an early age. Then came the stage performances and she loved that even more. She was a pretty young girl who had an instant appeal with the audiences.

At that time there was a famous theatre called The Queen's Theatre on Brunswick Street, now Pearse Street. Every Sunday night at eight o'clock they conducted *Talent Night* as it was called. During the week nights Queen's also ran a show called the *Happy Gang* which consisted of Mick Eustace, Gloria Green, Cecil Nash, Frank Tyrill, Bill Brady and a ventriloquist called Ben Bono. They were all great stage artists.

From the nineteenth century The Queen's Theatre was a famous and very popular variety house in Dublin. The Abbey Theatre company played at The Queen's Theatre from 1951, when they lost their own theatre building to fire, until 1966 when the new Abbey Theatre opened.

On Sunday nights in the 1940s the Queen's management promoted their *Talent Night*. The advertising was, "Come and be made happy," and many did just that It became a great night's entertainment for the audience and the atmosphere was electric for the entertainers. It got to me, my friend, and it has never left me to this day. I was hooked on the big time atmosphere. It's a difficult thing to describe in words but futures were made in show business on that stage. In good times, bad performances, it was still a "break a leg" atmosphere.

The Master of Ceremonies was Cecil Nash, a loud speaking, grey haired elderly gentleman.

On this particular night the first artist on was a young man who was a whistler. He was good, well liked by the audiences who always gave him excellent applause.

The next artist was Ben Bono, a ventriloquist who came out on stage and sat down in a chair. He had a little red-headed puppet named Buddy with him, who sat on his knee.

Ben said, "Hello dear friends, how are you? This is my friend Buddy," holding him up.

I roared up to him, "Hello Buddy, who washes your face?"

Buddy said, "My name is Ben Bono, what's your name," looking down at me.

And so I shouted back at him, "My name is Jimmy Smyth, nice to meet you sir."

He shouted back at me, "I hope you don't spell that 'sir' with a 'c'," which always got a laugh from the crowd.

Ben was a great ventriloquist. I was to meet with him a year or two later in the company of my brothers Des and Fran when the *Three Smyth Bros.* were in the audience for a *Talent Night* show he was in. He was just completing his act when he said, "Good bye dear friends, thank you and what about our young friend Jimmy!"

I stood up and got a big round of applause to which I replied with a big bow. The crowd gave me a cheer and I needn't tell you I was delighted. Ben Bono became a great ventriloquist artist in later years.

Next on the program was our Anne. She danced and sang *On Mother Kelly's Doorstep* with great feeling. She came over as a great trouper, a reliable, experienced person far beyond her years which went down real well with the crowd who loved her. She couldn't put a foot wrong.

Cecil came on stage after the last act and got a great round of applause. Then he brought all the acts back on to the stage together before the audience. He walked to the front of the stage, held his hand up, got the crowd quiet, then he said, "Ladies and gentlemen, I have great pleasure to announce the winner of this *Tonight Show.*"

There was a hush all around.

"The winner of this *Tonight Show*, ladies and gentlemen, is Anne Smyth!"

An enormous applause greeted his announcement.

Anne came forward and smiled ever so sweetly, just beamed from ear to ear as is said. She was so happy with herself and her award was well deserved.

My mum was crying, I was shouting and there it was. All the worry and time my mother took with her clothes seemed well worth it at that moment.

It was a great night all around for the Smyth family. We went home delighted with our selves.

Anne gave her winnings to our mother. Mum said to her, "No way, my love, this goes into the Post Office for you."

Show business had started to take over the Smyth family. "That's the start now, Jim," Mom said to me.

"I'm so pleased for Anne," I said to her. "Tell me, Mom, would you have liked to have taken part in show business?"

"Jim," she said, "who do you think taught Anne to dance!"

"Mother, you didn't!"

She looked at me and laughed and started to dance as we

came into the flats.

"Dear mother, how I love you. You always make everything so perfect."

"Well," my mother said, "I have something more precious than diamonds and pearls. I have my lovely boys and girls. Now what more could anyone want."

Mrs. Kavanagh and Mrs. Wilson came out to meet us and they showed their delight to Anne with many hugs and kind words. We all adjourned to our Flat #313 and had a good old knees up with all our friends

It went so well that night. It was beautiful

Anne became a lovely sister like Rosie and Marie. She brought her boyfriend home in her later years, a lovely lad. Tommy Hughes was his name who was in the Irish Navy. At the time they met, Anne was working in Donnelly's on Cork Street. They got married and soon after migrated to Manchester, England.

Anne and Tommy had two lovely children, a boy and girl, names of Chris and Tony. Tony became a famous man in body building circles, winning many titles. He was a tremendous athlete. Poor old Tommy met with an accident and unfortunately got himself laid up. He died some years ago, God rest him. Anne is still alive, so is Tony her son and daughter Chris and they stay in touch with each other and their mother Anne.

And I keep in touch with them all as well, but my thoughts always dwell on mother and how she manipulated the start of everything.

She would start with, "Let me see you do your dance, my love." Anne would do her dance. Mother would say, "No try it this way," and she proceeded to show her and so it started like that with us all.

I would say to Anne, "You're good," ...

"I know she is," mother would say.

So that's how Anne sang and danced and continued on to do so into her teen years, performing in most of Mae Phelan's shows. Then her job at Donnelly's began to take most of her time and she moved on from show business to the business world and then on again to a family of her own. All she ever did was a lovely success.

Chapter 29

Sister Marie

It was a sad day on Saturday, the 30th of October 2004. My brother Paddy rang to tell me his sorrow but I had this foreboding for some days prior. His voice was sad as he told me Marie had died. I didn't say a lot, just accepted the news. The cancer had finally won out. She had fought it all the years, never given in, always with the same determination. In the early hours of Saturday morning she went to sleep. She was never to wake.

How I shall miss you my dear, lovely sister, your sweet voice when you would ring me from England. It's in my head, I hear it now.

"Hello Jim, Marie here, alright darling? " and we would talk for hours on end. I would give you all the news of the neighbours, what was happening in the Liberties, all the comings and going in our family. Whatever it was it didn't matter, it was good to be talking to each other. We were close to each other once again, at that moment in time only you and me. We would recap the old memories.

On that Saturday I did cry. It had been a long time since I cried. Strange, I thought, so I was entitled to my tears.

I took the crucifix of my God off the wall. When I finished I tried to put it back up but just couldn't get it to stay. It wouldn't settle back. I held it in my arms. It seemed like I sat there for hours with the cross in my arms. I thought about my lovely sister and our lives together.

The times we were together in our early years, at the Blind Beggars Pub on Whitechapel Road in London where she worked, my trips up to see you, and your smile when you would see me. I'd give you a little wave and you would reply, "Alright Jim, I'll be with you now," and the greetings from the lads seated at the bar, "Okay Jim, nice to see you

... alright old chap." The pub regulars all had a special kind of greeting.

The two seats in the centre of the bar were Kray Territory, for the Kray twin brothers, Reg and Ronnie who pretty much ruled their part of town. They had big status in the underworld, and gave great respect to my sister, both of them. They were all a part of my life at the time, cherish those memories.

Then there was the time I was to meet your boyfriend George. It was a good meeting. What a blessing he was in your life. How your love together bloomed into a tender and sweet partnership which grew with your expanded family of lovely children you had together, Terry, Tracey and Denise and your lovely grandchildren they gave to you both.

When the cancer sickness took over your life you fought it for all those years with the help of your husband George. He was always to be at your side. You were an inspiration to everyone when your limb was taken from your body to allow you to live. You still continued to prosper and you lived all those years fighting for your life. You still did your charity work and still gave a good will smile for everyone that came your way. You spent your time, your life, giving to the poor and underprivileged. I am so proud to have been part of your life and have had you in mine.

The lovely little town of Delboy in Kent will be lonely this Christmas without you.

Your Mass was a beautiful memory with you singing your lovely songs on tape recorder. How touching and sad. Then I sang *Ava Maria* as you asked and wanted ever since you heard me sing it at our brother Terry's wedding years ago. It was in your memory ever since, and was your dying wish so George asked me to sing it for you. There was no accompaniment, the church was big but it went well and of course you were there with me. Hope it pleased you. It was a special occasion wasn't it? Your friends and family were all together to pay homage to you, the dear friend they loved so well. The journey to your resting place was quiet and peaceful. A sad hour, saying goodbye. Sleep peacefully with your God. We won't forget you easily.

I am sure a statue will be built to my sister for all the charity work she had done. How well she was known in lovely Delboy. She was such an inspiration to everyone. There is a large main street in Delboy with a colourful array of stalls. The stall holders were all at the funeral. They said to me and George that it wouldn't be the same without her. That I could relate to. George organised the funeral service which I say was magnificent.

We know we will miss you we already do,
The pain is so deep now, we're sad through and through.

Now it's all over, we'll all be strong
And we'll pick up the pieces and just carry on.

I will always remember the times that we had
The happy and peaceful times, it was sad.

You were always there for me, to help life along.
I would sing to Marie my love in a song.

I remember those evenings, the time was so slow,
You were soon to be leaving, how was I to know.

My dear sister I will finish on this amusing note to you. It happened in the Blind Beggars Pub on a Saturday night. You and I were talking to Reggie Kray, who was making shapes with his hands but then he was always making some kind of movement with his hands.

"I am making a definite statement, Jim," he said to me. "It's regarding Irish dancing. I think it's magic. What do you think, Marie?"

"I like it and Jim's mother-in-law is a champion Irish dancer."

"That's true," I said, "her name is Nellie Hall and she has medals to prove it," I said.

"I admire anyone who does a dance for their country," Reggie said. "I'm going home, goodnight Jim and Marie", he said.

We both said, "Goodnight".

"He did go on a bit about Irish dancing, didn't he?" said Marie, "but he amazes me with the knowledge he has of the dance. 'It's going to be very famous one day', he often said, and when I think about it he was right, it is very famous, now. You now have Riverdance, but how did he know then that this would happen?

"What do you think I should do?" asked Jim.

"Learn Irish dancing!" says Marie.

Chapter 30

Brother Terry

You know, in those young days of your life, your early school days, you are inclined to be a little too observant and often run into trouble by asking too many questions. I was inclined that way, believe me. I would ask older brother Paddy things but usually got no answer.

But this time I asked my mother.

I was around eight years old and I asked my mother, "Are you going to have another baby?" I said to her, putting my arms around her. "You're fat Mammy, are you having a baby?" and I put my arms around her.

She looked at me and said, "Jim, listen to me."

I said, "Sorry, I shouldn't have asked you that question".

"No," she said, "It's alright, really love. Listen, Jim, you like all your brothers don't you?"

I said, "I do, mother, very much."

She said, "Frank, Des and Paddy and you have a special little brother, right here," she said, taking my hand and putting it on her stomach. She smiled, looking at me. "Now Jim, nice?"

I said, "Mother dear I can feel it, it kicked me," and we both laughed and held each other and twirled around.

"I'm getting a little dizzy in my head," she said.

I caught her.

She said, "I'm good Jim, okay, I'm okay, everything will be okay. "

"I know," I said, looking at her and smiling. "I know you are, Mum, that's for sure," and she put her arm around me lovingly. I said, "Mom you are the greatest." I looked up at her, kissed her hand and a little smile lit up her face. I'll never forget those lovely smiles that my mother gave away while she was always on the go.

I met my pal John Chapman and called out to him, "John, my mother's having a baby!"

"That's great, Jimmy," so we journeyed on through the days and I tried to help my mother as much as I could till finally the fateful day arrived.

My mother went into labour and my little brother was born. He was christened Terry, after my Dad, and we were all such a happy family. I still remember that day he was born, it was special.

Mother had to be taken into hospital and Mrs. Wilson looked after us. I never tasted any potato cakes like Mrs. Wilson made and her homemade cake was lovely.

It was just a couple of weeks or so when mother was back home with little Terry and after only a short while I was allowed to change his nappy. Then I became a great friend to my mother and I needn't tell you she was delighted for the help and attention little Terry was getting.

Of course I got a lot of slagging off from John Chapman. He'd say to me, "Jimmy, did you change the baby's nappy?" and this of course would get a big laugh.

I said, "John, give up the jokes, please."

He continued until I got a little peeved. It was just after changing Terry. My mother was taking a rest because Terry had been cross all night so she had not gotten a lot of sleep. I said, "Go up to bed, I will look after Terry." I got him cleaned and powdered and he was purring at me. It was pleasant, I was getting a great laugh with little Terry. He was my number one pal. I loved him. Soon I began to take him out in his pram.

One day I got a bike. An old, worn out bike but a bike. So my Dad fixed it up for me and I was off. My little brother Terry came with me everywhere.

I was early on a big lad, in the Hercules Club and also boxing in Arbour Hill Boxing Club, and ever to the boxing matches. Terry came with me everywhere.

One Sunday my mother said to me, "Jim, Terry has a pair of swimming trunks on under his trousers. Is he going with you?"

I said, "I was going to cycle alone, out to Dollymount."

Then she started to laugh. Then I started to laugh with her.

"I get the message, Mum. He was going to go with me and go with his trunks already on so that there were no excuses."

Then I turned to Terry and said, "I'm going to Dollymount, are you coming, are you ready?" For sure he was ready so off we went.

I brought the bike down to the flats. I tied his clothes on the bike and we were off. Dollymount was a lovely, sandy beach located just a small way beyond Clontarf on the north side shore.

I said to myself, 'This is it, cycling out to the strand with my little brother on my bike. Now what more could you ask for!'

It was to be like that all those many years ahead and I needn't tell you, they were great times, the best I had. Terry, on the bike, would be chatting for all he was worth. I taught him the nature of the sea which was always of great interest to him.

Bill Reid was the Life Guard at the shore where we went at Dollymount. Bill was a huge guy, a well-trained athlete in track and boxing, muscular and in excellent condition so we couldn't be in better hands at the beach.

One day I discommoded him. It was simple enough. I simply said, "Bill, Mary was asking for you. Merry Christmas!"

This annoyed him to such an extent that it carried on and on till one day Bill was tired and he took a nap. Terry and me saw him lying on the sand. He was rather into a small hole or dip in the sand so we covered him over with sand from all around him.

He slept until about nine o'clock when he woke up covered in the sand and felt dodgey. A courting couple were out for a night stroll, heard him shouting and helped get him out of the sand. Oh man, it was something else! Nobody dared say anything about it, Bill never knew who had done it and, after a few months, the story finally pettered away. Luck was certainly enjoyed by all of us.

We were invited to Trinity College, to a big, international athletic meet between Ireland and America. All the Hercules Club members were invited to attend, and the American Athletic Club was in full attendance. It was quite an occasion. The hundred yard event was won by the Americans and Bill ran the distance event in his bare feet. Bill seemed to know it when I said he was the big man, he performed like one.

As well, the World Champion Discus Throw event was entered by none other than Bob Mathias. He had been training the discus event and was attracting most of the attention. Bill was watching him throw a couple. Then Bill decided he would show Bob how to throw a few discuses. Bob Mathias went along with it. I needn't tell you, it was good fun for Terry and me watching this event.

We had a ball. I told my Dad when I got home, "Dad, it was the funniest thing you ever saw, Bill in his long black shorts, down last to start and Bob Mathias who had been World Champion. Mathis never put a foot wrong, he did his job as a true professional. And of course Bill Reid had not yet connected into world rankings. This time he held his own though he did not win. As a matter of fact, he did not have a ghost of a chance but he came out of the games as a pretty popular man and heightened his popularity as a great character. It also said a lot about the character of someone like World champion Bob Mathias. I can tell you, he was a gentleman. Terry and I agreed, that was one prime day's enjoyment.

I loved having Terry with me at the boxing show. He would always sit in the front seat of the stalls which I loved, and yell and cheer me on. Once I was boxing Gunner McMahon from the Irish Army. The match was in Collins Barracks. Unfortunately he knocked me out.

Terry was sitting in my front seat and saw it all. He said to the referee, who was administering first aid to me on the ground, "He lay on the ropes, sir, and sprang at Jim Smyth sir. You know, sir, that's my brother who is knocked out. The Gunner should be disqualified, sir." And he was! Maybe that was thanks to Terry?

The men around him at ringside were enjoying Terry and so was my Dad. Terry was disgusted but the crowd gave Terry a big round of applause. It was another great night for Terry and me. If I remember rightly, we got a lift home and I needn't tell you my pals were waiting. "Did you win, Jim?" they roared

"No way," Terry said. "He was knocked out. But the other boxer was disqualified."

I said, "Terry that was noble of you."

"Don't worry, Jimmy," Terry said, "They will forget tomorrow, you will see."

"Bully for you, Terry, you're all heart, and I'm going to give you a piggy-back upstairs to the top balcony," which he loved to have.

My Dad would often go into Mr. O'Brien's Public House, just down the street. Terry sat on the first few steps at home but never walked all the way up our stairs. He would wait for me, or dad to come in from O'Brien's, to carry him up the stairs when one of us came in.

I said, "Terry, you are evil". At this stage he was about nine years old, but I don't remember to tell you the truth.

He was sitting head against the wall and fast asleep, snoring and waiting for one of us. I picked him up in my arms, and carried him up to our apartment # 313, top flat. I looked down at him, gave him a kiss on the cheek and said, "You little bum."

He groaned slightly. I held him a little tighter till I reached the top balcony.

Paddy Kavanage, our neighbour, often went for some fish and chips for he and his wife about this time of evening and would call up to me, "Okay, Jim?"

I said, "Great Paddy."

"That Terry fellow is drunk again?" Paddy would say. This got a laugh from us both.

I said, "Good night," opened my door, got Terry stripped and put him to bed. He woke up just as he was, so I covered him up again. He said, "Sorry you lost, Jimmy, sorry."

I said, "No bother my little mate Terry."

"Sure I have to box John Sweeney on Saturday."

He said, "Get in beside me, I'm cold."

I said, "I will first say good night to mam and dad, Terry," but he was asleep, out cold just like me as I was tonight at the fight. "No matter," I said.

My mother called me, "You okay Jim, you alright?"

I said, "I'm okay. Here's Dad," as I got over to open the door.

He came in to us and said, "Chrissie, I brought you home a bottle of stout. Knew you would like one."

My mother said, "I heard you lost, Jim. Sorry."

I said, "Little Terry had a ball. But I will be fighting on Saturday night. I will be boxing John Sweeney."

"Nice one, Jimmy. He is very good."

"I know, Dad. Terry told me." Our sister Anne left her school bag on the floor. I rummaged in it and found two pieces of coloured chalk. Terry was fast asleep so I put on the light, took the chalks and started to paint his face. As I began to finish I was starting to enjoy it. I looked at him and said, "Now, you look so comical."

I looked forward to tomorrow, to see his reaction. It was quite realistic and in some sort of way nice and peaceful. I was a messer, I will say that. This was a masterpiece. I looked in at Terry before I went to sleep. I started to laugh although I felt very tired. Then I was soon off to sleep. It wouldn't be long till I was away with the fairies.

Something woke me up. It was wet and sloppy on my face. I jumped up and into the "thing" and grappled with it. It turned out to be a dog and the smell of it licking on my face. Someone was looking in the window over my bed, laughing with make-up on his face.

It was Terry, the clown! I could not say a whisper. The dog had wet in the bed and, I think, on me. I was still. I couldn't move or think. I was freezing. I was full of dog snot. I was stinkin. I could do nothing. Just lie on the bed. If I could have gotten a hand on the dog I would have bitten his ear off.

It was Eddie Brennan's dog for sure and was called Lucky. I don't think it had had a wash in months.

I staggered to the washroom, got cleaned up, and sat down to the table for my breakfast. My mother said, with a smile, "What's that smell, Jim, do you get it?"

I said, "It's off me, mother, but the bed is destroyed with Brennan's dog. They call him Sparky. I sparked him, I needn't tell you, mother and little Terry. But I do say, fair play to you Terry, you got me."

I never mentioned it again nor did Terry.

But we proceeded through life together, he with me and me with him. We got a lot of laughs, I needn't tell you. Good times were always to follow each other. Terry was always part of my daily occurrences. They were great, I loved them as I always did him.

In his later years he got an offer to join a large Mexican Show Band and was with them very happily for a long time. He was a force to be reckoned with. He stayed with them for a number of years. Then he went into Jacobs Biscuit Factory on Bishop Street to work and it was there he finished his working years.

He got married to his Mexicali Rose "Brigid" and lived good years with his children Claudine, Eoin, Leyton and Craig. I still see him and he brings a lot of joy into my life. We still have all the old craic, never fail to still get good laughs together.

It's late, we are all in.

"Good night, Terry, my pal ... Night Jimmy, we're pals ?. ... Of course, Terry, always."

"Good night, Fran ... Night Jimmy."

"Night Des ....Night Mam"

Des did his impression of Mr. Fitspatrick, our neighbour,

"Night Paddy" I said ...

It was a roar like a dog. "What's that?" I said, "it's like a dog?

"It is," Terry said, "It's sleeping with Paddy. He's kissing

Paddy now, hear him Jim?" I will never forget that night. Just a simple phrase, "It was Priceless."

Eddie Brennan's dog and Paddy. He would never live this down.

Mother looked in to say, "Good night, boys. Is Paddy alright, Jim?"

I said, "He's sound, ma'am."

I hit Paddy on the arce. He just moaned.

Chapter 31

Sister Rosie

My lovely little sister Rosaleen was born on the 29th day of August, 1947. She was the last born of all my brothers and sisters.

Father was about a year out of the army with the end of the war and was suffering from poor health for the first couple years back home. No one knew what his illness was although all the other released soldiers were suffering from the same symptoms as well. But father slowly recuperated for the next couple years and then went back to work at Jacobs.

When our little sister was born into the Smyth family things just began to become better. Even my dad's health began to improve. We could see before our eyes his health was much better. My lovely little sister brought all the good luck back to our family. When the good Lord gave us little Rose she became the Smyth family's good luck charm.

She was as sweet and pretty as a perfect rose and we all showered her with our love. Her being with us just seemed to give us all a great incentive to sort our lives out.

Myself, I decided to give my mum a dig out by taking Rosie under my wing. I was like that with all my sisters and brothers, I made sure always to be able to know where they were, if they were in trouble or need of anything.

Rose began to grow up to become a lovely little yellow haired sister who loved to talk. I can tell you she had great listeners in us all. I think everyone of us wanted to baby-sit, just to listen to her little chatter talk. It would go on and on and I would love the listening part. As the months went by she became big in herself and I was finding it a great joy to be looking after this little kid sister.

It seemed that all of a sudden she was ready to be taken to school. Her school days started in the Georges Hill Convent National School, and Sister Regina was the Head Supervisor of the school. The smiles were great when I would pick up Rose, she seemed to love school.

Then there began to be times when my little darlin' would be in a very sad mood when I picked her up. I looked at her face and it held red eyes. She became a very quiet little girl.

One evening when I got her home my mother was getting the evening meal. She suddenly stopped when she saw her Rosie. Something was wrong so she would fix it.

She took Rosie into her arms, pulled her in close and enveloped her. Rocking with her she spoke softly, "What happened to my little angel," kissing her and cajoling her and soothing her down. Rosie dozed off for awhile. Then she woke up abruptly.

"Mam," she said, "mam, the Sister beat me and pulled my hair almost out. It hurt mam"

My mother started to cry then. I started to cry. I knelt on the ground with my arms around Rose and Mam. It was a good while before we could compose ourselves. Little Rosie was asleep, she had sobbed herself to sleep. In my mother's arms she was now safe.

I looked at my mother. Tears welled in her eyes. She stretched her hand to my face and wiped my tears away. "There you are, the good looking kid is back." She kidded me and said very firmly, "Dad and I will look after this business. That's for sure, that's for real sure. My blue eyed son God bless you."

I folded my arms across my chest and said, "Right mam, Okay." I kissed her and Rosie and I went up to bed.

My mum told me that this had happened before but the poor little dear was afraid to tell my mother.

A Sister Rita was the culprit. Rita was a young noviciate

and Sister Regina was the head nun at the school.

There were a lot of words spoken between my mother and my father when he came home. Then they both went together to Rosie's school where a meeting was held with the school authorities.

It ended when my mother and father took Rosie to another school, the St. Audoens School on High Street.

My mother never spoke about the incident after that.

But Rose never forgot it, she still remembers it until this very day.

Rosaleen continued to prosper after she changed schools. The years sped by quickly and they were good ones for us all.

I got involved with many talent agencies in variety, as the Eamonn Andrews Agency. The manager there was Fred O'Donovan who produced a radio show called *Odd Noises* which starred the *Three Smyth Bros.* as well as the lengendary Dennis Brennan, Pat Hayden, and *The Batchelors.*

Des, Fran and I decided that, as it was the Smyth family performing, we would introduce Rosie in with our Smyth brothers act. We found out, much to our joy, that Rosie had acquired a very sweet singing voice. So Des said, "Right Rosie, you're now in with us." Mam and dad were delighted and so was Rosie.

The song we began to sing for the show was a country and western song called *Big John.* It had a great sound from the four of us, Des, Fran, Jim and Rosie! It went out over RTE Radio. Fred O'Donovan went wild about it. When we heard it played back to us it sounded a knock out, we were blown away, so after that it was plain sailing for the four of us. Rosie sang with us on the *Odd Noises* show and many other shows which Fred was instrumental in getting us on. Fred booked all the big acts in town, including the twelve week show in the Gaiety every summer.

We were booked by Fred O'Donovan to appear on a barge on the River Liffey one summer in the early sixties and I can say it was quite a sensation for us all. The boat was moored at O'Connell Bridge, on the far side of the Liffey. This summer barge show was an extremely popular summer entertainment and we four Smyths were a smash hit. Rosie's sweet voice with our great harmony got terrific reviews.

One day Rosie surprised us all. She had met a young man and brought him home to meet my mum and dad and the family. He was a nice guy by the name of Tommy Stapelton. He pleased my mother and father very much and I liked him from the first time I met him. He and Rosie were a great combination, always together hand in hand. They got married and had a lovely family, Chris, Tanya, Mandy and Thomas. Poor old Tommy passed away some years ago.

Rosie I am happy to say is still a great friend in my life and we still keep in touch with each other.

We often reminisce about our singing and days with the legendary Fred O'Donovan and the Eamonn Andrews Agency, especially not forgetting Kay Andrews, a lovely lady whose job was as Fred's secretary. She never forgot gigs for the Smyth brothers. She organised our seasons together in lovely Butlins Holiday Camp down in Mosney town. Kay kept us all together at Butlins, together with the great lady Eileen Dixon, Maureen Potter and Jimmy O'Dea. Great times and success were had by us all. ...

God be with them all ... and my lovely sister Rosie.

Chapter 32

My Mother's Chips

My *mother's chips were famous*

Father Michael Cleary had a liking for them. He would always make his way to see my mother on a Friday around one o'clock. The bold Michael would knock on our No. 313 door, ah to be sure he was a familiar figure. I'm sure every time he visited St. Audeons House in his black garb followed by his two white Pyrennes dogs, he was always to be seen knocking on our door. My mother was fond of the Father and we never saw any wrong in him being there on a regular basis for chips.

Another priest was Father Whelan from *Michael and Johns Catholic Church.* This was a parish in the Liberties and he was also a good friend to my mother and loved her chips.

Mrs. Kavanagh, Mrs. Wilson and my mother had gained wide recognition for all the good they did. They always helped the poor young mothers who needed a hand-out. God love them. There were always collections going on. How I always remember them and their charity work. They worked tirelessly for others.

I remember the Lord Mayor of Dublin saying, "Ladies, if I had a medal with me I'd pin it onto you, you deserve it," he said. "I'm saying this to you as sure as my name is Alfie Byrne. " He was a great old chap and he always had a bag of my mother's chips in hand when he stopped by.

Des decided to go solo in show business. He was doing a season in *Butlin's Holiday Camp* in the 1940s His mate was Mick Purcell, son of Noel Purcell, who often stopped by to sample my mother's chips. As a matter of fact they sampled many other dishes as my mother was always generous with her food. She was a very charitable lady. That's why I always remember her with such love, because she gave a lot of love away.

When my sons, Michael and Dermot, were young they would never miss a Friday visit to my mother. 'We must have Granny Smyth's chips' they would say.

Ah, you know how I loved those days. There was such a magic about Audeons House. There was so much love around. Especially with Tommy and Kay Delaney around.

Tommy would say, "Mrs. Smyth, vinegar on mine".

Kay would say, "Tommy if you don't behave yourself I'll give you a crooked way of eating your chips." This would get a good laugh from my mother.

Mind you, sometimes "Burdocks Chips" were available around but it was funny that I never knew on any day who I would find eating my mother's chips when I came home from work. Often I would see Jim "Lugs" Brannigan outside our No. 313 on the top balcony, happily eating from his bag of chips.

To reminiscence, past times are my times. You know something, I love them, that says it all.

Chapter 33

The Grandfather

My mother's father fought in the First World War. His name was Patrick O'Grady, Ref No: 15400. His rank was Private in the Machine Gun Corps (Infantry) in the British Army.

I'm giving you all his particulars as I got them.

He was a hero and they classed him as such because of the bravery he displayed in battle, and to cap it all he was awarded the Victoria Cross, the British Commonwealth's highest military award for bravery in the field.

This military award has always been presented to soldiers who displayed outstanding courage on the battlefield. A commentary on my grandfather's exploits on the field of action was left with his Victoria Cross and my mother's family. It commented that he showed great strength on the battlefield, carried his machine gun on his shoulder and would run wherever the fighting would take him. He never showed any fear.

The VC was first introduced in 1856 by Queen Victoria and since then the medal has been awarded to only 1356 recipients. Needless to say it is highly prized to this day, and due to its rarity has fetched large sums of money at auction, often now reaching £400-500,000 at private auction.

My grandfather was known as a great fisticuff man. The 'bare knuckle Paddy' they called him. There weren't many who stood toe to toe for long with him. His name was legendary in the ranks.

Sadly, he was killed in action.

It happened in France on November 13 1916. He was never to see his wife and family, my mother, again.

He was a very handsome man. I saw a photo of him in his army uniform. I was very proud of him, very proud indeed.

My dear young grandfather was buried in France as were all fallen troops who died in battle in France.

There is a graveyard up on James Street for the graves of all the First World War fighters who made it back to Ireland so they could be buried in their home soil. I occasionally walk past it and am ashamed every time I do. Nothing has been done to the graveyard in years it seems. It's all overgrown, wild and forgotten looking. Most half of the graves are bunged into a corner of the courtyard. What an eyesore it is. Irish heroes buried in it - seems disrespectful of our heroes. It is a dreadful sight. It doesn't give me much joy when I pass by it, I can tell you.

Chapter 34

Aunt Maggie

I had great time for my Aunt Margaret.

She was my father's sister, a very saintly lady and we all loved her dearly. She was married to Bill Pidgeon who was just as nice as was she. He worked as a compositor in Whites Printers, a printing house of very high standing which was situated in Fleet Street. I was to work there in later years. It was classed as a very good job. So my Auntie and Uncle Bill were a pretty comfortable family.

They were generous to my mother and father but my father never took many hand outs. He was a proud man and proved it when he decided to join the British army. "It's to feed my family," and he said nothing more about the subject and no one gave him an argument.

After we moved to Marshalsea Barracks it was a treat to visit Auntie Margaret. We loved to see them. It would always be on a Sunday morning when we would get our lemonade and chocolate biscuits and of course a penny or maybe two pennies. If that happened, well, a man could make plans.

Aunt Margaret had a large family. She had three sons, Pat the eldest, then Liam and Terry. And there were two girls, Margaret and Mary. The girls were always nice to me and I liked them both. I remember I had Mary one night in her back yard. I enjoyed it and so did she. We kissed and cuddled till Mary said to me, "Jim we're cousins and not allowed to be with each other." So I said, "Is that right?" Well, what do you know, I didn't know but I was learning very fast. We didn't tell anyone of our liaison. It was our secret but we respected each other.

I respected her mother, my Aunt Maggie and Uncle Bill. Whenever I would meet Mary I would always kiss her. I liked her very much and she liked me as well. Margaret, Mary's sister, knew the score with me and Mary and it was her secret too. I admired her as well for this.

Liam and Terry entered the St. John of God College. They became very prominent members of the Order and are still attached to it to this day. Liam is known as Father James and Terry is known as Father Conrad. Their mother and father were so proud of them. All our family were invited to their inauguration. Father Conrad had his college in Cavan and Father James had his in Stillorgan. We never realised they would become such important figures in the Catholic Church. They both were kind and gentle in their young days and became famous in their fights for the underdog. Now they are part of a large charitable organisation.

The Pigeons were a lovely family, liked by all.

Margaret married a nice man called Danny and they had twin sons who also joined up with the St. John of God Church, wasn't that marvellous for both of them. I don't know where they are now, I lost track.

The last time I met up with the family was at Kit's funeral. Kit was my father's brother and a character if ever there was one. For awhile early on he worked in Jacobs with my dad but there was a lay off of workers at one time and it was 'last in, first out' as the saying goes. A mistake was made in the records and my dad was sacked when it should have been Kit but my dad accepted it and took the dole queue. My dad was always a kind and gentle man and Kit didn't put up any argument. I wonder why. Kit did a lot of work for Paddy Dowdall, the boxer. He used to massage him for his big fights.

Aunt Maggie was very generous to the poor and she helped out the needy on many occasions. She once hid an IRA man, which was carrying her good qualities almost a little too far I thought. One night he was being chased so she hid him in the coal bunker and got him away safely. Good on you, Maggie!

Aunt Maggie had two sisters, Jane and Brigid, living with her. They were all nice people, my close relations, very easy to get on with. Now they are all dead, Maggie, Bill, Kit, Jane and Brigid. Father James and Father Conrad are still working for God. I haven't seen Mary or Margaret for many years now.

And this was my father's beloved Irish family.

Chapter 35

My Old Man – He was the Greatest

My father worked in Jacob's biscuit factory from his early days till he finished his life. Never worked anywhere else – except when he was in the army in England in the '40s. In 1964 he retired from Jacob's on their pension which I can tell you was a laugh – for the pension amount of Irish 1£ 7shilling 6p a week. I wouldn't say that you could buy much with that, I'd say not a lot.

He worked over thirty years for Jacob's and my mother collected her couple of job-lot biscuits every Friday evening. Toward the end Jacob's got a bit catty and stopped the job-lot biscuits. This upset my mother and father. I suppose it was because the purchase of the biscuits kept my parents in contact with Jacòb's and when that contact was severed it caused a great deal of controversy.

I remember, it was one Friday that my mother asked for the biscuits. They refused her. "They were not available now" she was told. One of the workers heard it being said to her and he didn't like it. He told someone else, they in turn told another and a short while later it was all over the factory and I needn't tell you that it caused a great stir.

The issue went before the Jacob's Board and my mother, as usual, made a favourable impression with her speaking on behalf of the job-lot biscuits. As result my mother was reinstated with her biscuits and driven home in a lovely chauffeured limousine courtesy of Jacob's biscuit factory.

A little incident but it meant a lot.

Once again, Mrs. Smyth, you pulled it off and I loved you for it when I heard about it and you know, 'darlin', I still do.

It was no surprise that my father had many good friends in Jacob's, and why not, he was a lovely, gentle man who would never see you short a few bob.

Mr. Mushatts Chemist Shop. It was known all over Ireland. They would come in with their aches and pains. He would give them a touch of the relic. He had a cure for everything ... and what about baldness?

When my father came out of the army he had been serving overseas and was very ill when he came home. With this mysterious illness he had lost all his hair. He was very upset. As I remember him, his hair was his crowning glory.

I was in the Chemist one day for something. Mr Mushatt asked after my father. I told him about his hair. Mr. Mushatt was very concerned. He spoke to me about his treatment for baldness and my father listened to me and went with me to see Mr. Mushatt who attended to the bald condition. My mother was delighted and I will say we all were, because within six months the hair had all grown back again.

Mr. Mushatt was a great part of the Liberties.

Fond memories. When he finished work and was in retirement in the 60s and early 70s I always made sure my father had the price of a pint and a packet of cigarettes. It was a 'must' for me.

My dad and I never had a cross word between us, never except once, just this one time.

In the early 60s I was working in Campbell's Tea Merchants and Wine Importers on O'Connell Street. I had just come back from England, had gotten married, and was working at Campbell's on the delivery van with Paddy Robinson and Dillyer Delaney. Dillyer was a great character and well known in boxing circles. He was the man who dropped Charlie Henchikow with a magnificent right hook, a mighty punch!

There was also a man called Teddy who worked with us as well. One day he asked me to buy a pocket watch off him. It had been given to him as a present. I liked it so eventually I bought it off him.

I showed it to my father and he said it was nice. I carried it in my pocket for a year or two. One day I was short of money to pay a bill. I didn't sell the watch, I gave it to the man to whom I was in debt, Paddy Robinson at Jacob's, a worker with us. He was delighted with the transaction.

I was talking with my father one night after when he asked, "Where is your watch, Jimmy?"

I said, "I had to sell it, dad. Would you have liked it?"

He looked at me and folded his paper, the *Evening Mail.*

He replied, "Jimmy, you never gave it to me." I've never forgotten those words dear father because they were the saddest words I've ever heard in my life and I've never forgotten that time when you said them. He wanted the watch. I didn't know.

My dear father how kind you were to me all my life, you brought me into life, helped me along the way. When I was in trouble one time, serious trouble, your words were, "Jimmy if you committed murder, I'd still stand by you." After all those many years, it's still in my head. You were a special person in my life.

You were with me at my first fight, in the National Stadium. I was proud that night when I won. And the next time I fought I lost to John Sweeney. "He was a great fighter," you said, "wait till the next time." It came and I won.

I remember the time I was getting married. You said just to me, "I'll always be your friend," and you always were.

The day you passed away I remember it well. When we got the word that my father was sick, real sick, we knew it was the last time we would have him. We were ready to accept the worst and when it came it was the worst it could be, it was deeply hard to accept.

My father was the first to depart, in January 1974, then my mother a few years later. So now I had to go to Malahide to my mother, where she had been living in a retirement flat with my father, to tell her, to be with her.

I was let out of the car at the flats and my brothers drove away. I stood at the door for awhile, then sat down on the door step, had a cigarette and thought of and sang to him. Suppose I was getting ready to tell my mother, to be the bearer of the sad news. But I sat and cried and sang his favourite songs. Finally thought I heard mother so plucked up enough courage, pushed open the front door and saw her coming toward me down the small hallway.

She said, “He’s dead, isn’t he.”

“He is mom. He’s gone to his Maker.”

She was calm, so calm.

“I couldn’t go,” she said. “I just can’t accept it.”

“I understand mother. He will be hard to replace.”

“I knew he was going to die, I really knew,” she said.

We walked down the small hallway into her main room. The light was on. She had been waiting for me.

Our dear, sweet, lovable old pal was gone and how she and I cried together as we always did.

I wasn’t there to say good bye to you but I was there to be the one to tell my mother. I never will be able to pass the time with you again and know the love I have in my heart for you will grow and grow. The memories you gave to me will always be in my mind. We’re proud you were in our lives for you were a very special person. You touched many hearts and will always be remembered dearly by me.

I made a cup of tea for us. We sat together not saying a word. It was very quiet, no radio’s going, I was glad.

“I will stay with you, mother,” I said.

"Thank you. I'll get in touch with Marie and Anne," she said.

"Don't worry about that, mother."

"Okay, Jim. He was so gentle and quiet. He made an impression on everyone he met. He touched on everyone he met."

"He was part of my life," I said. "I won't forget him, never will." And now I never have.

It's been a long time since my young days, my growing up in Queen Street, the Cherry Steps. He introduced me to the ways of life and he always stood beside me. He was part of the folklore that surrounded my life. I miss my days with him. We have to die sometime, we know this, but the parting can be very sad for we who are left behind.

That was a part of my life I thought I'd never get over. He was very well loved by all. God be good to you, dear father, we'll meet again.

RIP 05 January 1974

Chapter 36

The Gallow Glass

I was doing well with the *Gallow Glass*. They were quite a famous celidhe band and made some popular Irish records.

In 1961 I began playing in Dublin with the *Gallow Glass*. At that time I sang top twenty songs yet always managing to sing pop tunes as well. We also did a bit of yodelling which was popular with the dancers. We took the band to London during the Lenten period because the Irish dance halls went slack during that time.

On one of those occasions over, I and the band went to Scotland. We worked the full eight weeks that we were there and feedback from the crowds was sensational. We did an evening show and then a dance afterwards, which would finish at 2 am in the morning. The crowds loved us, particularly the Irish songs like *Home to Mayo* and of course *Danny Boy*, a great favourite. But the most sought-after song was *Forty Shades of Green*. Every single night I was requested to sing it.

Bert Ewan was the promoter for our tour. He was the man who first introduced a famous group into Scotland called *The Beatles*. He had them when they were unknown and gave them their first start.

The first night that Bert heard me sing with the *Gallow Glass* he said, "That's great, Jim, you sing well, I like it". That was about 1962.

"We became great friends and, as the tour went on, even better ones. Into the third week of the tour, while having a meal with all the band together, Bert said to me, "Jim, I'm working on some television work for you."

I was delighted with this news. With Bert involved, this meant something good would come of it. I was on top with myself and during the show that night I could do nothing wrong. Everything was outstanding, perfect. Bert came backstage to congratulate me.

Toward the end of the week, as I was out walking alone, I met Bert who said to me, "I'm sorry, Jim, there's no television work. Your management doesn't like it. You would be working with my band and mine alone and your people objected to that. You do understand don't you Jim? "

"I do," I said and I did understand, no doubt about it. I knew Bert was discreet and wouldn't tread on anyone's toes. I didn't much mind, I could accept it.

"I'm not making any promises," Bert continued, "but when the tour is finished we'll keep in touch." And we did keep in touch for a good long time. Bert invited me to come back to Scotland. He said he would get me lots of work, but, sad to say, I didn't go. When we finished the tour and came home I had other ideas.

One thing I knew for sure, I would finish with the *Gallow Glass*. It had served its purpose in my life. It was time for me to move on. I had enjoyed the time spent with the band, composed of the brothers Jim Magarr, Paddy Magarr on accordion and Peggy, their sister, who played violin and her son Sean Keogh who played the organ. (It was almost their family band, the Magarrs and the Keoghs!) Besides, there were Paddy Dunne on drums, Brendan MacEnhill on accordion and, last but not least, towering above us all, was Mick Dempsey on the saxophone. All told there were the eight of us and we brought a very special something to Irish music.

It was said, the *Gallow Glass* did have a special kind of sound, quite different, quite unique, and this is why: Mick Dempsey. Mike was both a great character and also great sax player. His playing made the band different because, in the first place, a saxophone in a ceilidh band was unheard of at the time. Then, Mick's great playing produced a special kind of sound that was quite unusual and which made the *Gallow Glass* itself unique. Don't know where Mick ever got himself to. Would love to meet him again, he could tell a joke to top them all. He was a good comedian, very like Dean Martin to look at, with jet black hair, and could drink whiskey as well!

We had a week long list of dates on the Isle of Skye. While we were there it was a beautiful, sunny place to play. We were in the company of the "High Provost". He was the Judge and jury of the island, his word was law among his people and he was none other than the famous Bobby McCloud, one of Scotland's famous accordion players. He was known all over the world. But there was no one who could entertain Bobby like Mick Dempsey and his sax.

The parties would run into the early morning. Dances were held in a huge dining hall, and we played up at one end of the room. The only fault was that the loos were at the other end, a long trip to take while playing and dancing and drinking. You see, the Scottish people love the Irish and they especially loved the *Gallow Glass*. When you would come in contact with a happy Scotsman he would throw his arms around you and kiss your face. He'd tell you he loved you and he'd insist you have a wee "dram", and so it went on all night, wee drams, endless trips through the happy Scots to the loo. What magic music we made those nights, a magic sound.

On the last night of our stay on the Isle of Skye, where the craic had been mighty, Jimmy Shand had been playing but the night belonged to Bobby McCloud. It was his. The place throbbed to the rhythm of the band, all the musicians were in full flight. What a sound, but Bobby reigned supreme in Skye. You didn't dare step out of line there.

It was a great experience for me, I loved every minute of Scotland, Skye and our nights with the band. We made great friends during our time there. They wrote me for months after we left.

I left with the band shortly after we came back home, in 1963.

The *Gallow Glass* was going off on a tour of America and I decided I needed to stay at home in Dublin with the wife and kids. I agreed to go play with Paddy Magarr and didn't realise at the time it was a bad move for me, but such things are for another telling.

Chapter 37

Fist of Iron

One strong man in the Hercules Club was a man called Christy Sheridan. He was a handsome figure of a man. With me being attached to the club I knew him quite well and we became very good friends in the 1940s.

Christy and I both were Saturday night dance-goers. We mostly went to the Ballerina Ballroom in Parnell Square. This became our regular Saturday night get together and we went mostly to listen to Frankie Blowers. Frankie, who sang with the *Joe Coughlan Band*, had a great distinctive style all his own.

At this time Jimmy Cashin, Christy, Ritchie Shields and George Walsh were my mates and we would all go out together on Saturday night Usually before we went to the Ballerina we would drop in to the Ice Cream Parlour on O'Connell Street where our favourite dish was Melancholy Baby - or maybe two of them.

We were all into body building, always bulking up, putting on extra weight and then working with the weights. This was at the time the *Three Smyth Bros.* were just beginning to work around. Christy was developing a massive physique, much admired by all his club mates. He started to win a lot of competitions. Christy went big by winning the Mr. Universe title. In later years poor old Christy had to have an operation on his legs and sad to say he died shortly after coming out of hospital.

While we were together at the Hercules Club there was a birthday party in Christy's house in Cabra for his sister Nora. Nora's boyfriend was Butch Moore who was singing with a band called the *Blue Clavons.* Everyone liked him and Nora was madly in love with him. We all became great friends and saw a lot of each other. He would always turn up at our shows, and was mad about the *Three Smyth Bros.*. He was good looking and had a great voice but little did we realise he was going to become such a big star. Then his career took off with the *Capital Show Band.* He went from strength to strength. He married his Nora and was constantly 'walking the streets in the rain'.

Butch passed away in his later life, sometime in the early 90's as I remember, somewhere in America where he was living. He was very much missed by his family and friends. He had enormous adulation from his fans. When he would be performing on stage he would always tap at his right leg. It was fun to see all the would-be Butch Moores around town walking the streets, tapping at their right leg.

The *Capital Show Band* would always pick me up on the road when I would be out hitching a lift home from Naas when I was working with the Gallow Glass Band in the early sixties. I became a regular figure on the road outside Naas at that time.

After a few years I became restless pumping iron. I was getting big, singing with the brothers and making waves and enjoying life into the bargain. Life still continued to progress nicely in the flats. I was enjoying the years. They were good for me. I became good mates with the Hercules boys and the night life was becoming enjoyable.

I would often take a stroll up the South Circular Road on a summer's night and one could meet a lot of young ladies out for an evening stroll. They would mostly be in employment in doctor's houses, country lassies, mostly looking for company. If I was a loner I would get talking to them, invite them for a coffee and end up going out for a few weeks. I was a good talker, loved a lively conversation and made great friends among the girls. Then it was nice to come back into the flats where there was always a bit of fun going on. I got on with people and had many friends in the flats. But you know, they were good times in the forties and fifties. We were easily pleased in those days. I guess it was all eyes on the future which looked like a great future to us.

My father worked hard for us all his life, and most times work was very hard to come by. But he persevered. He joined the army in the Second World War; put his life on the line by getting sent overseas to produce a week's wage to feed his family back home. Then to return at the end of the War to his 'Homeland' a very sick man, but it didn't seem to bother him. He got his health back to form and returned to work again.

In my young married life, I was a lot like him. There was an old Irish saying, 'you didn't lick it off the stones', meaning you're a lot like your old man. I worked wherever I got it. Building work was in abundance. I worked in that. It was tough going to make the ends meet, but you were always trying to get ahead and you never gave in.

In the fifties my days in the Laurel Park Orchestra were good. The band leader was a man by the name of Roy Allen. He was a big man in size and he played the drums as well as conducted the band. He had a good speaking voice and good singing voice as well. He was quite powerful on the band stand. The sound from the band was always impressive. Then there was Rose Tynan, an excellent band vocalist and radio, television and recording artist, a very professional lady. I enjoyed working with her because she was a top singer in all ways. I worked with the band on Saturday and Sunday nights, at 9 pm and 1 am.

In the sixties I was working in Campbell's of O'Connell Street. Money wasn't great but by combining two jobs it worked out quite well. Campbell's were wine importers and also supplied altar wine all over Ireland. I worked on a bottle washing machine in Campbell's and also helped with wine deliveries in the Dublin area.

I had a flat in Frances Street at the time, with my wife Essie and two children, Michael and Dermot. I loved them and that part of my life. It was a happy time for me. My mother and father were alive and so was all my family. Marie and Anne were still in London. Des was doing well on the television scene. He had a show band called *The College Man* which did pretty well, made some good recordings. It was managed by Des and George O'Reilly. George played drums in the band and was one of the best in the country. I had a great time working with the band and still doing my day job.

The band was a bundle of talent. It had a great brass section, great musicians and at that time big bands were very popular. Hundreds of musicians in Dublin worked every weekend at all those dance halls like The Ballroom of Romance. The sixties were magical times in Ireland.

I saw a lot of my family during the sixties but we Smyth brothers were beginning to slowly drift apart. We were each doing our own thing, earning wages for our own families.

The owner of the Laurel Park Orchestra was Leo Neilan. He was a gentleman of the highest calibre. I was proud to have known him. One day he heard I was about to lose my job with the band. His answer to that was, "He stays," meaning me, Jimbo, "and you go," meaning the band. This was good news but in reality it was 'the kiss of death'.

He said to me, "It's my wish, Jim, you stay here." But the reality was the show bands had arrived and that was it. The man who sings, the vocalist, was the star, not the jazz heads, and I can assure you there were quite a few. The bully boys in the band made life hell for me but their life was to be short-lived. As for Leo Neilan he went on to great and respected heights. He went to America and became a high court judge there.

I was making a name for myself, singing really well, especially country music. I really liked it and felt good singing it. Frank Field was a big star in the sixties. I could sing all his songs and was going down well with the dancers. *I Remember You* was one of his greatest and very popular songs.

I had a big audition with Tommy James in Ulster Television for his show *Tommy Tea Time With Tommy.* It was a popular show in the sixties, going out five nights a week. I sang my songs and Tommy was delighted with my performance. "That was great, Jim," he said, "that will go down well on the show." But the producer said "No way, Not interested". Tommy said, "I'm upset with that Mr. Hunniford. I'm sorry Jim." I said, "Don't worry, Tommy." The bully boys got there before me I was to find out later on. It didn't matter to me, I was thriving and decided I should leave Laurel Park at that time. It was getting a bit too much.

The job in Campbell's had finished up for the day. I was in the lorry with Christy delivering some wine to a public house in Smithfield.

"I have to go in to see my mother-in-law," said Christy.

So we went in. His mother-in-law was Gypsy O'Brien, an old neighbour from my young days.

She was sitting on a chair at the end of the room when we walked in. It was dark in the room and I could just barely make out her form. I walked up to her. She caught my arm, put her other hand on my face and rubbed my face.

"Well now," she said to me with a smile on her face, "haven't we met before, young man, you are very familiar, you know, ah now, I know you, it's been a long time. Now would your name be Smyth? Now tell me."

I said, "It is, ma'am. I didn't think you would remember me."

"I remember your mom. Her name is Chrissie O'Grady isn't it?"

"It was but now it's Smyth."

"But it was O'Grady. It's nice to see you again. You're not long back from London are you?"

"A couple year's now, ma'am."

She said, "Come here to me. I have something to tell you." Putting her hand on my shoulder, she looked into my eyes and said, "You're a fine big man and here are two thoughts for you. First you will get bad news in the space of two. It will be severe for you but you will get over it. But in the later part of your life you will end your days a very wealthy man."

I have always thought she meant I would have the wealth of all my lovely family, and my health and those lovely grandchildren of mine, what more could one ask for. That was true wealth.

The bad news came to me two days later. Myself and two work mates, Mick Piggott and Mick Malone, were brought in to Mr. Semple, the manager's office and we were all sacked with a sincere apology. It was a bolt out of the blue. We were completely devastated. One of the men broke down crying. In those years work was very scarce. I had been working quite a long time in Campbell's and liked working there. I liked my work mates, they were nice people. But I was still singing in Laurel Park and would survive.

All those years since I had seen Gypsy O'Brien, she remembered me and foretold to me of this devastating event. She blew me away.

Mr. Semple said it was decided between Mrs. Kelly, Mr. Mac and himself.

I said, "It doesn't matter now, Mr. Semple. I wish you the very best sir and thank you."

When I last came back from England I got the job in Campbell's. I needn't tell you it was a godsend and you could have spent your life in it. But, that's life as people say, 'riding high in April and shot down in May'. It was a sad month in April but I got over it.

I still think of the times there in Campbell's. I never saw Mr. Semple after that day. I would have liked to meet up with him again in life. I met Willie Henderick who was the one who got me the job at Campbell's. He told me that Mr. Semple had separated from his wife. She was so upset she never left her bed until the day she passed away. Their parting broke her heart. How very sad. I had met her when she would come in to see her husband. I liked her, she was a lovely lady. She modelled with the Sadie Green Agency. It was quite an occasion when she would pay a visit to Campbell's. The girls would make sure to see her. She wore very attractive clothes. It saddens me when I think of those days. When you always expect the inevitable, the worse to happen, it always does.

Which leads me to another famous personality, Maureen Potter, whom I saw on occasion at Campbell's when I was working there.

On this day I came to the outside door of Campbell's to enter in and Maureen Potter was standing there talking to Mrs. Semple. It was nice to see Maureen. She began to talk to me so Maureen explained to Mrs. Semple how she knew me. I met with the famous Maureen Potter when we were both with the Eamon Andrews Agency. Maureen said her goodbyes to me.

"Goodbye Jim of the *Three Smyth Bros,* I think this little chat we had will go down well at the evening meal tonight, Jim lad."

"It will Maureen. Nice to see you and thank you."

She replied, "We'll meet again," and do you know, we did and she would always stop to say hello to me. I loved her for that. The bigger they come the nicer they are.

One day later on I met Maureen outside the lane leading backstage to the Gaiety. She said, "Hello Jim, how are you?" We spoke for awhile, then she said to me, "Would you like to see the show, Jim?"

"I would love to Maureen," so she brought me in and got me a seat. I saw the show and enjoyed her so much in it. She was such a professional artist and a lovely person to know.

Mrs. Semple always would make it her business to seek me out when she visited the job. When she came in she would always send a man called Jack to tell me she wanted to say hello to me. We would chat for awhile and I really did enjoy those long chats. She was lovely to talk to. If she had met Maureen lately she would tell me, with 'Maureen sends her best regards'.

I remember those days with a tinge of sadness: it was sad the way it ended but life is a sad playground anyway. The good must be taken with the bad.

Another person who used to call into Campbell's quite regular was a man called Ernie Smyth. He was no relation of mine. His reward for bidding us the time of the morning was a glass of whiskey, 'a ball of malt'. When Ernie was in his youth he was a great amateur boxer. They said he was the best in the world, but the old demon drink took hold of him. It was sad but we looked after him. We always put a glass of medicine into his fist. You know the old saying, I heard many a time, 'There but fortune go you and I'. How true.

Combining two jobs was good for me although it meant doing gigs on midweek nights. Often I would be late getting in from the gigs, then going to work early next morning but I managed. Such a person was called a semi-pro, meaning two jobs. I always took work whenever and wherever I got it.

To carry yourself through your life without getting involved in trouble was good. Being in the Hercules Club and staying fit as I grew stronger and bigger helped me stay on top of trouble. We, me and my brothers, managed to stay out of the worst things. We came from a tough neighbourhood in the Liberties. The people I became involved with were great influences, the priests, Boys Brigade, my friend Lugs. But you also had the bad element. We had to fight these people and just hope to win. I always managed to come out on top. Staying fit often helped me out of some close ones.

Chapter 38

The Children - Michael

My son Michael, my first child, was a popular boy in his young days and a handsome fellow as well. He received excellent marks in his school studies and grew up to be a learned man who could hold a conversation on any subject with anyone - as well as being a great comedian. He had a skill in starting businesses and soon proved his worth at anything he put his hand to. He early on took to sales and work was his forte. All he turned his hand to succeeded.

Michael has had a life long love affair with the beautiful Michelle that nearly ended early on when they were dating.

It happened when the Big Snow hit us and all of Ireland on the eighth of January 1982. We were living in Tallaght at the time.

It was an endless snow storm. It went on and on and no one could find an answer to it for, in the simple truth, we had not had a lot of snowy winters to give us experience in dealing with such a thing. The electricity went, also the television. We had a gas burner but we were not prepared for this storm, nobody was, we were all caught out. Roads were impassible, the food was running out in the markets. Some shops had groceries in stock but soon were sold out. Queues were everywhere, looking for food. Dermot and I would go out scouting for food, and we always did well so were more fortunate than most. But the shortage of food was bad and the snow never seemed to stop. We were practically cut off from civilisation.

The first night that it started I had a feeling it would be long and bad. It was snowing hard and heavy and there was no let up.

Michael was with us and Michelle was coming up later after work. Dermot was in from work early. Jackie and her close childhood friend Jude were also there. We had a big fire going so had plenty of heat, and we had a good stock of coal and firewood as well.

Essie was working in Tallaght with Hewlett-Packard. As the day wore on there was no sign of her coming home. I was ready to go out searching when she came in the door. How she made it home she still can't say to this day. She said she just kept walking and walking and then, through sheer instinct she made it home.

Michael said, "I hope Michelle gets home okay."

I asked, "You said, Michael, she is coming up here to you?"

"That's what I mean," Michael said, "home here with us."

I looked out the window. There was a full-scale blizzard outside and an easterly gale was blowing. Temperatures were freezing cold, way below zero, they said, -10C to -20C below. All buses had gone off the roads. Outside the front window our huge field stretched a long way down to the road and now it was covered in snow, I'd say a good few feet of it. And I knew that in the middle of the field there was a big ravine with a deep gully running through it. If you crossed the field and didn't know about the gully, you just dropped into it and were lost, gone. Now Michael tells me Michelle was coming up to us. She would probably only get a lift by bus or car to the end of the road. She shouldn't try and make it up tonight, no way I thought to myself.

It was six o'clock, then seven, eight, nine o'clock, no sign of her. She's not coming, I thought, not now, it's too late.

The storm raged on. We had our dinner. It was okay, I thought, we're all okay.

Then I heard someone shouting. I couldn't make it out but it definitely was someone calling. I had to see. I put on my coat, opened the front door, and I must tell you that was a job and a half but I made it.

I could just barely see anything. I finally made out a young man holding a woman in his arms. It was Michelle. I made my way to her. The young man was an itinerant who was camped along the road. Michelle had gotten a lift to the end of the road from a workmate. Then she started to walk up the road and lost her bearings. She was extremely lucky she didn't end up in Casualty. My wife, Jackie and Jude took a long time to get her stable. That was a dreadful night for Michelle and us, but she pulled out of it and was alright, thank the Lord.

I made sure after the storm to look up that young lad. He told me Michelle made it to his mother's caravan. He heard her shouting, came out and helped her in. He had to practically carry her over to our house. What a nightmare!

The snow fell and fell for days up in Tallaght. People broke into shops for food. I was outside a butcher's shop one morning with Dermot when a man broke the queue, skipped up from his place. Another man took offence at this and landed one on his chin and the man didn't stir. They called an ambulance to take him to hospital but they were told it was out of the question. In the end an air-bus was called in. I was not around when it landed some hours later but the lad in the butcher's shop told me the helicopter came down successfully to get the man and took him to St. James Hospital as his injury was serious.

So much for snow flakes falling on an open fire. This was the first of many incidents like this one. People broke into the supermarket in Springfield. The blizzard raged on for three to four days without stop. Eventually electricity came back. RTE didn't get back on for a few days after the blizzard subsided.

We were existing. Dermot and myself would go out early in the mornings to get the baby's milk powder. We would always bring home a lot of food. The shops in Dublin were sending out a large quantity of the basics of bread and milk to the shops in Tallaght. The helicopter also came to help carry out sick people, some women in labour. I suppose one would say their babies were called 'blizzard babies'.

A family living beside us were existing on crisps and bananas. We ended up providing them with some of our food. It was no big deal, we were glad to help. We helped most of the neighbours on our road. We gave great help to them, but when the snows melted away everyone got back to their 'real' lives.

It was sometime afterwards that Michael married the lovely Michelle. The wedding was a great occasion. I was asked to say a few words to the wedding party.

"I hope the bride and groom will be very happy, but if it doesn't work out, no blame on Michael and Michelle. Blame the young guy who carried her across the field in a wild snowstorm," which did get a laugh.

Michael and Michelle have had a love affair that started as childhood sweethearts and went through a truly stormy experience before finally getting married. They are happy to this day and have been blessed with two good looking sons, Adam and Alex. God be good to them. I pray they do well.

You never know what way life is going to work. Dermot still excels at his soccer, Michael is still good at his football and is an outstanding business man, and both my boys married lovely girls who settled in well with everyone of us and are a loved part of our family. God bless them all.

Chapter 39

The Children – Dermot

My son Dermot got the soccer bug into him.

This was in his young schooldays in the 1960s in Ballymun.

He was an excellent player into the bargain, fast and could use both feet. He first played for Ballymun United.

I was watching him play a match one day, enjoying his movements, when one of the local men tapped my arm. He told me a man was asking after my boy. This interested me. Who was this man? I was soon to find out, Big Surprise. A big man waved to me as he walked over and came up beside me. I recognised him at once.

It was Irish International Con Martin.

He stretched out his hand and said, “I’m Con Martin.”

“Jim Smyth, nice to meet you.”

We chatted together for awhile.

“Your boy Dermot is very good. He can move that ball, I’m very impressed.”

I was pleased with his interest in Dermot. He was playing good football every week and scoring every week as well.

“This is my job,” said Con, “I’m a scout for clubs in England.”

We walked for awhile. He took my home address. “I’ll keep in touch,” he said. “Something will come of this, I assure you.”

And, true to his word he kept in touch. He’d no phone,

as he said, but quite a number of cards. He wrote me many times, very interested.

Dermot played football and continued to impress. I used to go to all the matches and enjoyed everyone.

One evening my wife and myself and our neighbour Eileen went to a stage play in the school hall at Ballymun. It was a big show, many acts and performers, put on by the school. One of the scenes featured a young boy singing a song and he was magic. This was the first inkling that my son could sing. He had a great voice and brought down the house. They were talking about the blonde young lad for months after. Well the soccer was forgotten for now.

I never said anything to Con Martin so bit by bit we lost touch. I was upset but what could I do.

Dermot became involved in a musical called *Joseph and His Amazing Overcoat.* It was in Technicolor. He was good, very good indeed in this performance. He continued singing all through his life and still possesses a fine singing voice.

In his teenage years he got interested in karate and won many awards. He performed with the legendary Ed Parker who said Dermot was “terrific” which was an outstanding accolade.

Then Dermot formed his band called *Till September,* and made some popular recordings as, *Every Time I Close My Eyes, Where Are You Now?* It was a proud moment every time I walked up Grafton Street to hear his song, *Every Time I Close My Eyes*, being played in record shops. It was a popular song and sold well. He is still active in the music scene and does quite a good, polished cabaret act.

He has a great little son called Andrew and two lovely daughters, Rachel and Christine. Now you can’t do better than that.

Chapter 40

The Children – Jacqueline

My daughter Jacqueline is a kind, caring person and attractive lady and loving mother. This is what I had prayed she would grow into.

All those years ago, when I got word of her birth, I was working at Jennings of Dun Laoghaire as a brick labourer with a man called Johnny McCourt. I was talking to an apprentice lad called Tony Curtis, (not the film actor), and another lad called Colm Wilkinson, who later became very famous.

We three were having a cup of tea when John told me I just had a daughter. I was staggered.

"You've knocked me out, John," I said. "By the way, who told you it was a girl?

"Your wife rang me personally," John said. "She said it looks like you."

This got a great laugh, especially from Colm.

Tony said, "A few drinks tonight, Jim."

"Definitely."

I was still living in the Liberties, on Frances Street at the time and Michael and Dermot, my two young boys, were staying with their Granny Hall, my wife's mother Elsie.

There were a few drinks after work with all my work mates, Tony, Colm "The Terrier" Doyle, a GAA man, and Steve Kellet, a neighbour. All were with me to toast the arrival of my lovely daughter.

After that I went into the hospital to see her and it was

true. She was beautiful, when I first saw her and she still is. Do you know, Jackie became a very special part of my life and it started at an early age, when I was doing gigs with the Billy Brennan Group at the Hitchin' Post. So I saw a lot of her at night when I would come in late.

We moved from Frances Street to Ballymun and she and I became great pals from early on in her life. I remember I would include her in everything I did. I went to work in the Hitchin' Post about that time and she grew up with me being in the Hitchin' Post. We would meet every Tuesday night and go to the pictures together.

I remember one time in particular. I was to meet her off the 36A bus. The bus stopped in Parnell Square and my little daughter was not on it. I nearly had a heart attack. The bus driver said he had let her off a few stops back. Oh man! I took off, ran most of the way back the way the bus had come. I stopped at a small island between the Rotunda Hospital and the Ambassador Cinema. There she stood, a lonely little figure, waving to me. Oh how good it was to see her, she was a lovely sight. She ran to me and said,

"Now Dad, guess where we are going?"

I said the usual answer, "Can't but you will tell me."

"Bugsy Malone".

Then as she grew older she went with her pal Jude to work in Sligo. She did exceptionally well and was very happy there although I thought she would never come home. But she did and we rocked around like old times again.

We moved to Tallaght from Ballymun but I still met with her when she went to work in Brown Thomas. She would arrive home late on the bus and I would be there to meet her.

I was in the Hitchin' Post at this time and had come in contact with many promoters who would bring in the big shows. Mega acts would top the bill, all for charitable reasons. One of these I met was a man called Paddy

Maguire, who worked tirelessly for many charity causes. We became good friends He told me all about his family, his daughter Niamh, his sons Dominic, Aidan and Skippy, and of course his wife Lilly. He brought in The Wolfe Tones, Brendan Grace, Paddy Reilly, all the top liners. The famous Paddy Maguire from Saggart.

It was some months later that Jackie said to me, "Dad, can I see you? I'm bringing a boy up to meet you and mom."

I said, "I'd love to meet him," so that's how it went.

We met on a Sunday afternoon and I had to go to work at the Hitchin' Post Sunday evening.

"Dad, this is Dominic, Dominic Maguire."

"Any relation to Paddy Maguire from Saggart?" I asked.

"He's my father, Mr. Smyth."

"Well, you should be very proud of him because he's one of the best and I mean it."

I could not believe such a thing could happen. And all so unplanned. How ironic that my daughter Jacqueline would meet Dominic and only some months previous Paddy was telling me about his family.

Alas, Paddy was only to be with us for a short time after. He passed away some months after with motor neurone disease. It was a sad parting, so sadly missed. Father Brian Darcy said it all in his obituary column. He dedicated a full page to him, "to Paddy, a very generous and kind man who spent his life doing good for others".

A year or two after, Jacqueline and Dominic married. It was a great day with much happiness shared by all.

And now I have two lovely grandchildren from them, Jack who is a great little soccer player and hurler and Gaelic man, a Newcastle and Celtic supporter, a great little guy. And a daughter Ellen who takes after her mother: you don't mess her around, no way, a beautiful girl but knows what she wants and usually gets it. God bless her.

My lovely daughter, fine son-in-law, Jack and Ellen, how I thank God for their presence. Wish Paddy were around to enjoy these times when we all sit around together and enjoyed the company of each other.

We all miss our absent friends and loved ones who are no longer with us. All my lovely family of whom I'm so proud, Michael, Dermot and Jacqueline who have given me so much, Dominic, Lydia, Michelle and all my grandchildren. My wife Esther, she is my world because she made it all possible. God bless her.

Chapter 41

Dear Friend Kay Delaney

I met Kay Delaney and her husband Tommy in the 1940s and loved every hour we had together the rest of our lives. They were magical days, wonderful times with them. She was a dear sweet friend to me and Essie and my children. They all loved her. Her kindnesses, I could not talk enough about.

I met her on a Sunday in Marymount Hall in the forties. I was singing that night with my brothers, Fran and Des. It was the first big show for the *Three Smyth Bros.*. The show, run by Myles Breslin, happened every Sunday night in aid of Our Lady's Hospice of the Dying up in Harold's Cross. Although the Hall has gone with the times, the Hospice remains a landmark still, catering for all kinds of sicknesses. God bless them.

On this Sunday night Myles introduced us to Kay and Tommy. I liked them both immediately and we became great friends all our lives.

To tell the truth, variety work in Dublin at that time wasn't that great. There were not many theatres around for variety to perform in, so you made it in the church halls. But Marymount was something special. All the greats appeared in it. To mention a few, there was Cecil Sheridan, Jack Cruise, Danny Cummins, Hal Roach, Maureen Potter, Noel Purcell, Eddie Byrne. These were but some of the many thousand of artists who would offer their services for free to perform and nobody took any money for their performance. It all went towards the hospital. Myles Breslin ran these shows for many years.

When I went into the professional ranks, Tommy, Kay and me became close friends. We had great sessions in their home. It was a hearty place, located in one of the Rialto buildings in Barbizon Square in Bray. She changed her address a lot I might say but no matter where she was or when it was, there was always a special welcome in her home for you. The craic was fierce in the Poland House. She was born Kay Poland but her stage name was Kay Delaney, the Mammy Singer. She would black her face up and sing Al Jolson songs, black songs. One of her greatest was *Stay in Your Own Back Yard.* It went, *"... and honey never mind what the white chile do, ...".*

Kay and Tommy were a great act, she was a knock out, got great write ups in the papers and Tommy always remained a funny, inventive character who never failed to entertain.

Myles Breslin was running Marymount Hall for many years. Tommy Nolan, a singer who performed at Marymount, married Myles' daughter and the two went to live in Blackpool. They had a family of four girls. When the girls were still young the family all sang together and were called *The Blackpool Sound.* Then the four girls grew older, went on singing on their own, and were known as *The Nolan Sisters.* In a few years they became internationally famous all over the world.

Kay continued to impress her many fans wherever she went. She became exceedingly popular. We came in contact with the *Harmonichords.* They were made up of Con and Dec McCluskey and John Stokes who were just starting their careers. They too started at Marymount. Tommy opened up St. Anthony's Theatre and the *Harmonichords* started to sing there where they got great support from Tommy and Kay. They weren't great at first but they soon developed real well. They were struggling to get recognised and Kay gave them help in those early years. They were rough years, money was scarce, but we helped each other.

My brothers and I continued to prosper, things were getting good in the fifties and sixties and Kay and Tommy were also doing real well. She continued to get better as the years went on and she did more and more appearances. We continued to come in contact with each other. Then we slowly drifted in different directions. I worked with my cabaret trio and then in the seventies went into the Hitchin'

Post. During this time in the seventies it happened, poor old Tommy died. I was at his funeral. It was a sad time and Kay took it very sadly.

The *Harmonichords* went on to become the *Bachelors* in 1962, who had great number one hits in the 1960s. Then they broke up their trio. John Stokes went his own way and the trio just never made it after that. Sadly, they never got back to see Kay who loved them no matter what.

I met up with Kay again in the 1990s when I got in to see her in the K.C.R., a great cabaret lounge in Terenure where she was singing with Ritchie Glynn, a drummer boy as I remember. I stayed in touch with her after that and soon after she got sick. She wasn't able to get around at this time and it bothered her. She was housebound and found that difficult to take. Her friends held a function in the hope that they could purchase a moped to help her move around. She became a well known sight in her little red moped, driving around Ballyfermot where everybody knew her. She continued to sing in her old cabaret spot as before and loved every minute of it. It was sheer determination that kept her going. Never say die. She was a much loved character by many.

I remember one night in particular, sometime back in the 1950s. We were all in Kay's house. There was a knock at the front door. Tommy went out to answer it and came back in to us.

"A young man is outside and wants to see you, Kay."

"Bring him in Tommy," said Kay. "I'm sure he is very cold."

I threw a few more logs on the fire.

The lad came in. He was well dressed, nice suit, collar and tie.

"How are you, Kay?" he said. "I told you I would come. I want to stay for awhile, please."

Kay said, "Of course you can stay, you're welcome Pat O'Donnell." He did stay. He stayed for over fifty years. He became a great benefactor to Tommy and Kay and little Joe. In the latter part of Kay's life Pat was always there to give her a helping hand and to be there for her. I took a liking to Pat that first night. He was part of the magic of the fifties, the craic and good times in Kay's house.

"What are you looking for, Tommy?" Kay said.

"I'm looking for my old razor blades, I want to give them to Pat to play with." I laughed but then I would have laughed at anything Tommy said. He was one funny man, no matter what the occasion.

Kay continued to do very well for herself. She appeared in every major theatre, the summer seasons in Butlins, in England, Great Yarmouth with the Morecambe and Wise shows and in those old time music halls. In those shows she was queen.

In the end she took very ill and was confined to her bed. Eventually she was admitted to St. James's Hospital and it was there she was to end her days.

I saw her the morning before she passed away. She wasn't in good spirits, her stomach pained her.

"I'll be in tomorrow," I said to her, "I'll see you then."

But it wasn't to be, she died in the early hours of the next morning.

She will never be forgotten. I will always remember her and the great laughs for her Tommy. Great nights when the laughs were for free and the nights ended too quickly. She helped a lot of struggling young beginners in her life.

I'm sure she enjoyed the singing at the Mass. Her old cabaret pal Sonny Knowles dropped by to show her a bit of respect. I said, "Good for you, old timer, nice to see you," and we all took off to Redford Cemetery in Greystones where she was laid to rest beside her beloved Tommy.

What a legacy of great memories she left behind. She gave great joy to everyone, her loving son Joe, Nora, her grandchildren, all her kind neighbours and friends. All her eighty years on this earth.

'And we will stay in our own backyard ...'

16 July 2004, St. James's Hospital

Catherine (Kay) Delaney Poland

RIP, star of Stage, Radio and Television

The sun has shone,
The grass has risen,
Now you know, Kay,
Where your Tommy is.

Chapter 42

Sonny Knowles

Just listening to Sonny Knowles on television telling Shay Healy about his coming into show time made it seem like he was stealing apples from an orchard. In other words, he was 'Boxing the Fox'.

It's no crime, Sonny, we all did this in our young days.

How and ever, as Sonny was embarking, to be exact, into his life of crime he was rumbled. Sonny took off with the owners in hot pursuit, up the streets, over the fields, over hedges as well. Young Sonny was running for all he was worth. The crowd had become much larger so Sonny was holding his own against much higher odds but he knew he couldn't hold out much longer.

He turned a corner of the road and there was a large house in front of him. 'I'll try it,' he sobbed to himself.

The door was open. He pushed on it, went in and closed the door after him. He went up a flight of stairs and through the first door he saw, conveniently for Sonny, a load of young people and some elderly ladies, two to be exact, who held their arms out to him saying, "Welcome. Oh blond stranger, please tell us who you are?"

"Don't you know me, ladies? My name is Sonny as in funny, you know, like 'I've walked a million miles for one of your smiles dear lady,' sorry ladies'."

"My name is Molly Coolahan," the lady said, "and this is my sister Babsy. Have you come to train as a stage artist?"

"I have indeed kind lady," Sonny replied, smiling.

All the boys and girls that were there gathered around him and said, "Join us stranger. Be our 'top of the bill'."

One tall, skinny boy said, "Be my friend, will you, boy? My name is Dickey Tappy Toes. Have you heard of me? I'm a drummer."

So Sonny and Dickey Tappy Toes became great friends. And he said, "Thank you, all my friends."

He started to sing for them and Molly said, "I'll take care of your cares for you. I'll be there when you're feeling blue," and they were all in such a happy mood.

The people who were chasing him were all looking in the window. They were shouting to him, "We'll get you, Sonny."

Sonny waved back at them and then all the boys and girls waved back at them as well.

Molly said, "Oh my God, this will be his trademark," and they all waved their hands to him and they were happy.

Molly's sister Babsy said, "The Badger has arrived."

That's exactly how Sonny Knowles started his career. He didn't have to steal apples anymore. He became a singer and a cabaret artist.

His mother and father were very proud of him and also his brother Harry. Molly bought him a lovely white jacket and a bow tie, a nice black one. He looked lovely. He met a nice girl called Sheila and they got married. He became famous and they all lived happily ever after.

The house where it all started is now a shrine. They all group around it at Christmas time and sing Christmas carols.

Good old Dickey Tappy Toes went out. It being the Feast of St. Stephen. It was a very happy Christmas to everyone and all. How our hearts beat with gladness when we think of that day many years ago as this all happened to be near Christmas time.

The little white haired lad had a lot of soul. Molly said he came from another planet and I can tell you, if you knew Sonny like I know Sonny I can tell you straight, he is from another planet.

This time I might get that drink he promised me.

Chapter 43

The Hitchin' Post in 70's

The cabaret scene was in full swing in the 1970s. There were hundreds of cabaret lounges all over Dublin and the talent was excellent with great singers who all wanted to be the next Tom Jones or Roy Orbison.

I left the *Gallow Glass* in 1963 and spent most of the rest of the '60s with what was left of the big bands. By the late 60s I was working seven nights a week getting into the cabaret scene. The big show bands were still around, but just barely, as they were being squeezed out by the cabarets and the sing-alongs, the up and coming new thing. So, when we were offered a residency at the Hitchin' Post in Leixlip in 1970 we accepted with alacrity. It was the worst mistake I ever made, we discovered in years later.

The 'punters', as we called the general public, loved to sing on stage so the sing-alongs were becoming more and more popular. They would put their names on a piece of paper and send it up to me. I was the Host and the punters would be highly offended if their name wasn't called out that evening.

Some nights, time just ran out and I couldn't get them all up on stage, although I tried to get as many singers up as I could because I knew how much it meant to them.

Just think, the kids around the breakfast table next morning saying, "Mammy did you sing a song last night?"

"Yes, darling I did and I went a bomb."

On going to Mass on Sunday morning you would be pointed out: "Oh you sang great last night Letty, you were bleeding great."

This was life itself to so many. It rapidly became a

highly popular bit of entertainment for the punters.

At the Hitchin' Post I had a good backing band called *The Tree Tops Trio*, made up of Anne Malloy on organ, Billy Brennan on drums, and Big Joe Fitzmaurice on guitar. I worked with them a couple years before coming to the Hitchin' Post. They were a good trio who gave the Hitchin' Post the professional sound it needed. Sorry to see them go, they left us about 1976.

As I said, when I moved into the Hitchin' Post there was nothing sensational about it. The owners were Matt Ryan, a Tipperary man, and his wife Maureen. The building had just been extended but was not yet fully finished. They were still working on it when we started. In the beginning, for the first couple weeks, we helped get things organised and all was going down well when Maureen approached me to start a sing-along. It was to happen every Sunday night and became a huge success. I was there for eleven years and packed about eight hundred people in every Sunday night. Come hail, rain or snow, we opened at 7:30 pm and by 8:00 pm we had a full house, every Sunday for eleven years. I handpicked everyone and it became a famous sing-along for miles around, with terrific singers every night. It always remained just that, no trouble, just a nice pleasant night's entertainment.

The mid-week nights also became highly popular, as the show bands were still good draws. The Hitchin' Post booked big bands the likes of Dickie Rock and Fran O'Toole, Joe Dolan, Red Hurley and Brendan Boyer, and Eileen Reid. These were all big show business performers, widely known, and drew in big crowds. Every mid-week night they were booked with us.

Early on, just after opening in the early 1970s, Matt Ryan came up to us and said the Hitchin' Post had hired a girl singer who was coming from Belfast, Dana by name.

"She sits on a stool and sings," he said.

When she arrived she came with her mother, father, a manager and his wife. They had travelled straight from

Belfast to us, no stops and were starving. We had chicken roasting on the spit and we gave them a good and proper welcome.

The entertainment evening was organised by Big Allo Kelly who was a great character, liked by all. Dana did her act and it went well with the crowd. She was a nice little singer, nothing sensational. For the encore I lifted her up on a stool and lifted her down again with a little slap on the bum which always brought a big roar from the crowd. She appeared many times with us and became very popular.

Then came the evening of the EuroVision competition and our Dana was chosen to represent Ireland in the competition. She sang *All Kinds of Everything.* And lo and behold, Dana from Ireland won the entire EuroVision title for 1971. All Ireland went mad! When she returned to the Hitchin' Post it was an enormous big night not to be believed. Cars were lined up on the roads for miles in all directions trying to get to the Hitchin' Post. What a great crowd and night of celebration for us and for all Ireland. Everyone wished her well and then soon after she went from the Hitchin' Post on to other horizons in Northern Ireland politics.

This was truly the decade of the cabarets in Dublin, they were springing up all over town:

A class act in Dublin was Maxie, Dick and Twink with ***'The Jimmy Conway Band'***. That is: Maxine, Aubrey Dickson and Barbara, (names they never used) a terrific trio of girls. Jimmy Conway was their band leader. Then they went on to Canada and America and made a big name for themselves there. Through the years Maxie still works in radio and is quite successful. Dick made a name for herself in films in the US. and Twink is successful as a pantomime name in the Gaiety and on radio with the Mike Murphy Show.

The Clare Manor: This was a big cabaret, located in the Clare Manor Hotel in Malahide. Sadly the Hotel burned to the ground the night of fifth of November 1980 following a disco that evening. In the Clare Manor Lounge, Joe Cuddy was an outstanding singer with the band, and his brother Noel was their manager. They did very well in the Clare Manor Lounge and then began singing all over Ireland and Europe as well. Of course they were often booked into the Hitchin' Post and were always received very well. Joe Cuddy sang and recorded records and he did so well for himself that in 1987 he was awarded the VAT Award, a big honour to show business people.

Country music was very big. Ray Lynam, who sang on his own and was top dog, and the ***Smokey Mountain Ramblers*** with Big Pat Ely who were right up there at the top as well. The *Smokey Mountain Ramblers* had George Kaye on fiddle, a good-looking lad called Steve Morrissey, and a master genius of a manager called Des Kelly who was an ex-showband manager and a gentleman if ever there was one. Steve had a great singing voice and was highly popular but he met with a bad car accident early on that cut short his promising career.

I especially liked the style of the ***Recordites***, a mime act which was quite professional and well liked by the crowd, made up of Syd Evans and George Martin. We hit it off at once and became good friends and remained so for many years. We three were travelling home together one night, as I was living in Ballymun at the time, when we were passing the Skylon Hotel.

George said to me, "Will you come in with us, I want you to meet someone?" so I followed them in.

George led me through the hotel lobby and into the Main Ballroom. There was a stage at one end where quite a crowd had gathered around one person. George moved the crowd slightly and I got a glimpse of the man in the centre. It turned out to be **George Best**. He looked great, tanned and loving every minute of all the attention. I'll never forget all the beautiful women around him, some actually feeling his arse. He seemed to get a great kick out of it all.

Ian Hendry, the film actor, and Jim Dale from Carry On Films were there taking it all in.

We all became good friends immediately. George Best was delighted to see his old friends and meet me. He immediately pulled us all three up on stage and organised it all that we sing *Forty Shades of Green*. What a sound we made. The crowd loved all the hype going on. It was quite a gathering. I had a great time with George Best, and met him many more times after for good occasions

Syd turned to me and said, "I think we'll make a move."

I said, "Good idea, Syd, but I think Bestie wants you."

Bestie roared over to us, "night Syd, night Jim, George. I'm not retiring, I'm permanently retired." He was a great looking handsome man, Bestie. He drank a lot but that was his business. The way his life progressed in later years was not all it could have been but it was his life and his choices.

Syd and George let me off at my home and Syd said to me, "Jim, what did you think of Bestie? You know, if Bestie had farted he would have got a round of applause."

I agreed with him. "It was a massive experience."

Bestie was a charismatic, magic personality, never to be forgotten.

Many times I introduced ***Gloria Hunniford*** on stage. She was a great singer with a large voice and easy going style that went down well with the crowds. She later went to London and got into BBC with the Terry Wogan shows although she never sang in any of the performances.

Fr. Michael Cleary, known as our Singing Priest, came to the Hitchin' Post and was the darlin' of the crowd. He did his Elvis impression and told the same jokes every time he came but he could do no wrong with the crowd.

I knew him from early days in St. Audoens House in the Liberties. When he was a curate he would call to our house on Friday for a visit and a plate of my mother's chips and fish. He was a great friend of my mother so I saw a lot of him when we met again in the Hitchin' Post. I never spoke anything but good of him, to me he was always "my Catholic Priest". He would come to see me and bring his two dogs with him. They were lovely dogs, snow white Pyrenees mountain dogs. He always packed the house and never lost his popularity over the years. Always known as *the Singing Priest.*

The tale of ***Joseph Locke and Luke Kelly*** was a memorable and difficult time for me on stage at the Hitchin' Post*:*

It all started with Joseph Locke, a great voice and a tempermental man. I was on a lot of shows with him and he never changed, always a pain in the arse. It was on a Sunday sing-along night, I was singing good in those days. I called his name out. The man I called was a midget. This got a great laugh with the audience. He had a lot to drink and was abusive and I knew he was trouble, all three ft. of him. I eventually got him finished and off stage but he kept coming back to me, shouting remarks at me. Eventually he was put outside and told he was barred. We would see him on an odd night but he wasn't allowed into the cabaret room.

A couple months later there was a big night on. Top of the bill was Luke Kelly of *The Dubliners*. I liked Luke's singing and was looking forward to see him perform. Luke was one famous man in town. The crowd started coming. There were hundreds. The house was full to the rafters, a real 'full house'.

Who comes to the door but our little friend.

"You are not getting in," he was told.

This didn't please him at all, he was not impressed "I want to see Luke Kelly, he's a friend of mine," he said.

Luke arrived and he told Luke about being barred.

Luke said, "If he doesn't go in, I don't go in."

This caused a major upset that went on for a bit of time, taking us to the opening time. The crowd was becoming restless.

Boss man Ryan said to me, "Fix it quickly".

Eight hundred people were waiting for Luke to go on and were very uneasy knowing something was wrong yet not knowing what it was.

Luke pushed in the stage door, said, "Luke Kelly."

I said, "Nice to meet you. You have a great crowd here just waiting for you," and taking his hand in mine led him onto the stage.

"Ladies and gentlemen, the King of Ballad Singers in person, Luke Kelly," and Luke was on!

Luke gave a great performance and nobody was the wiser about the turmoil backstage. He gave about four encores and the audience loved him.

When he finished he came up to me, smiling. "You're a cute man, Jim," he said, "let's have a pint. Everything worked out well. I was happy about it. I didn't know what was happening. You fixed it well, Jim," he said. "We'll go out for a pint some night."

I said, "We will, Luke," and we did.

"Right," he said, "I'll drop in some day this week." We used to go out regularly during the weeks ahead.

And that turned into Luke Kelly and Jim Smyth from the Hitchin' Post, working sessions at the Spa Hotel many times for a wedding party, singing for the guests and Bride and Groom.

I remember well Luke with a bottle of malt in one hand and the other arm around my shoulder and us singing those Irish ballads together. We got into some sessions together!

The Miami Showband with Dickie Rock and another nice lad, Fran O'Toole, who had a tragic ending to his life. Shot to death on a lonely night on a road so far from their families and loved ones. A tragic ending. I remember their performances, Fran had a great voice and they were both popular with the crowd. “Don’t lean too much on Fran,” Dickie would say to me. Fran was a thoroughly professional man, never smoked or drank. I liked that in a performer. They had two ‘roadies’, lads they took with them on road trips, one was Joe Thomas and the other was Vick Smith. Joe used Brut aftershave lotion – liberally! You could smell him before you could see him. You got the smell of Brut and you would say, “Here’s Joe”. Vick was a nice, gentle old guy, always gave me a £ when he was with me, why I still can’t make out.

Eileen Reid was a great performer with outfits that were magic. I remember she came to do a spot at the Hitchin’ Post. It was after Abba from Sweden won the EuroVision Song Contest in 1975 for singing *Waterloo*. Eileen came dressed to look like the blonde girl Abba with a little skull cap, tight trousers, long boots up to her arse. She moved like a storm, a great act to watch, a great mover.

Brendan Grace started his career with *The Ginger Men*, a fairly good ballad group. They played the Hitchin’ Post and very soon after that, broke up. Brendan began to do a bit of solo work. Then he was riding a motor bike, had a crash, and broke his leg. He hobbled into the Hitchin’ Post to do a spot for me. I always liked his singing voice, liked the way he carried a vocal.

I bought him a pint, he was not doing so well at this time. One night he was doing two gigs with a half hour between each gig. He had about thirty minutes to get from the Hitchin’ Post gig in Leixlip to his gig in Blackrock. His father drove an ambulance for a living, so it was decided to use it. If he worked the siren all the way from Leixlip to Blackrock he could just make the gig. He worked very hard at the performances he gave. One night he came to do a spot and he had a tape recorder with him. Some voice was on the tape to introduce Brendan. When he finished his act there was no voice to bring him back on stage. The whole idea didn’t work, it was a shambles but inventive. That was Brendan.

Colm Wilkinson. I met Colm when I worked in the building trade and he worked in his father's asphalt business. Some of his family were in show business, his Uncle Bobby, a very good drummer, and his sister Rebecca, a very good actress and nice looking girl. Colm was knocking around with the band scene. I saw him performing in a coffee bar in Rathmines and thought he was great. He came to do a spot in the Hitchin' Post. It was a Ladies Club that night. I suggested he play *Tambourine Man* and Colm was a great hit, the girls loved him. He was good that night but he made it so big on the world stage that he moved on. It was nice to know I knew him on his way up.

Of course you have to have a Talent Manager: there was a young looking guy called **Louie Walsh** who was doing just that. Louie would come up to see me at the Hitchin' Post. He'd stick his head around the door and ask for me.

"Jim it would be, how the hell are you?"

"I'm great, Louie," I'd say, "come on in."

He was one nice lad. I always liked to see him. He was attached to the Tommy Haydens Agency. I'm delighted to see him doing so well. I always had great time for him because he took some stick I can tell you but was a good man at his job. The fruit of the pudding is in the making and Louie was always a fan of Daniel O'Donnell, the great Belfast singer. Good luck to you, Louie, Daniel loves you.

I was good pals with **Pat McGeegan**. Pat represented Ireland in the 1968 EuroVision Song Contest. He was an out and out great singer with a tremendous voice. He played the Hitchin' Post on many occasions and had a large following. I liked his company, he used to tell me many a tale.

He told me a marvelous story of when he was playing the London Palladium with a well-known group called *The Big Four*. In Pat's act he would stand front centre of the audience, put a simple little tin whistle in his mouth and put his arms behind his back. Someone from *The Big Four* would come up behind him, put his arms around Pat and finger the holes in the whistle while Pat would continue to blow.

When Pat was playing the London Palladium, the host, a top comedian named Des O'Connor, called a musician out of the Palladium Big Band who happened to have a tin whistle on him and they proceeded to do the same act as Pat had been doing in his act. Pat just couldn't believe it, he was shattered. Someone had taken his act away.

One day when Pat wasn't working he stopped by, picked me up and we went for a drive. He had his young son, Barry, with him.

Pat said to me, "This is my son, Jim, he's a great little boxer."

"Nice to meet you, Barry. I did boxing as well when I was your age."

"I heard you were very good, Jim," said Pat.

"Not bad, Pat. Just made out okay," I said, "You're a great little guy, Barry. I hope one day you'll be World Champion and that's the gospel truth." Those were the words I used.

I met Pat many times after through the years. One night he rang me at home and said, "I still remember what you said to young Barry, that you hoped he would become World Champion. Well, he just became one, thought you would like to know. Barry has just won the World Featherweight Champion title for 1985."

"It all worked out as I said it would, Pat."

I did enjoy hearing Pat sing at the fights. It brought back a nice old memory to me of a great singing man who had wonderful rhythm and was loved by the crowds

Pat McGeegan passed away some years ago and he's missed by me and many. He was one straight talking man. If he said it was black and crooked you could bet your last penny he was right.

Noel V. Ginnity, a very funny man and great entertainer and singer. He was very tempermental and would always fight for the underdog. Noel was in full flight one night on stage at the Hitchin' Post. As always, the house was packed, not an empty seat. Noel wasn't making it with one party in the audience. They laughed when they weren't supposed to laugh, clapped in between jokes and not at jokes. Eventually, Noel leaped off the stage down to the crowd to explain his jokes. When they saw him coming towards them they got off their seats and surged around him, kissing him. They tore his clothes off him, he was full of lipstick. Eventually management sorted it out. It seemed the party were Chinese and hadn't a word of English. I told Noel and we did see the funny side.

Sonny Knowles was known as "Mr. Cabaret". The crowds loved him, especially his sing-along songs. He'd give everyone a wave with his hand and from it got the nickname 'the window cleaner'. The last I knew he was still going strong, now for many years. Good luck to him and wife Sheila. He gave a good show in the Hitchin' Post, off and on, for the eleven years that I was there.

***Red Hurley and His Band*:** Red Hurley was a very polished singer with a lovely style. He had a great band in the1970s, himself with Jim O'Connor and, through Manager Louie Walsh, he had a guy with him called Tommy Hayden. These three exceptionally good singers were a top class sound. Still to this day Red Hurley has a fine singing voice. I enjoy his talent on television.

Brendan Boyer was a hard working entertainer and he always pleased the fans. I remember, he was to do the Hitchin' Post one Friday evening so he left his gear in early in the day. I went into the dressing room to check it out. His shoes were on the dressing table. I couldn't believe my eyes, they were size 16! Brendan sang with a group called the *Big 8,* with Tom Dunphy, a great country music voice. I'd seen the *Big 8* when they were at the Royal Theatre, and I was with the *Laurel Park Orchestra.* The *Big 8* were just starting their show band business then. They did many splendid nights in the Hitchin' Post.

Brian Donnelly was a multi talented man. And a big man. Six foot tall. Brian was a close pal of my brother Paddy. They went to school together and became members of a musical society. Brian was a versatile man in the society, possessing a very fine singing voice. He was also well known in boxing circles. He boxed many a good fight contest. I liked him. As I was growing up in the early years we were both attached to Arbour Hill Boxing Club, home of the black and gold colours, and they shone real good when we were there. We kept in touch and then Brian took over the Plaza Cinema, promoting great variety shows there. I was working with the *Ray Allen Band* in Laurel Park. It was great to work the Plaza on Saturday nights. We packed it in every night, Liam Hefferman on the piano, you just couldn't go wrong. I loved my times there, the crowds were great. They loved variety and you could not go wrong with them.

Brian was a tough man in his heyday. He was called upon many a time to lend aid in a heavy handed way which he did with much grace. He also took over the Pearse Street Cinema, sorting out a few unruly people in his own way. He can still produce a fine singing voice, can be heard singing with the Boxers Choir. The roll call would read like a roll call of honour and achievement in boxing circles: Brian Donnelly, Gerry Coleman, Harry Perry, Val Harris.

Frank Mangan I worked with him in the Hitchin' Post. He was a weird man and a very good organist. Not weird like the "Elephant Man" but a bit like Marty Feldman, mental. He made many appearances on television and made some good records with Earl Gill, who worked with Gerry Doyle on bass, George the Schomez Plunkett on drums, Eamon the Young on sax and whistle.

The Hitchin' Post was a great theatre because of the fabulous entertainment that came across the stage: country music giants Slim Whitman, Carl Denver, Johnny Cash. All added to the outstanding variety and top class entertainment that came across the stage.

They were good days, the 1970s. Life was a cabaret! Then you could get drunk on a ten shilling note and still have enough left for fish and chips. One of the good ones here and there have either been killed or died by now. May the drums roar and trumpets blare for them all. 'It was on a summer's night but the sun wasn't shining'.

Chapter 44

A Night in Jail

I finished work early in the Hitchin' Post one night, then took the 6G bus outside on the road to go up to the Liberties to see my old pal John Chapman.

I was in good form, always looked forward to seeing the lads from the flats. Got off the bus and headed direct ahead into O'Brien's Pub where right off saw John O'Brien working as lounge supervisor. He was good at his job, a good mate of mine. We finished our drinks, I had a few, then made for outside and spoke with him for awhile longer. We bid each other good night and made our separate ways. John headed over to Smithfield where he had a new house with his wife and family.

I pulled the collar of my coat up around my neck. I felt cool after being in the pub and all the warmth around there. Then I was off.

I said to myself, 'Jim, you drank a little too much ... but no matter, you enjoyed yourself ... tho' you shouldn't drink so much.'

After a long moment of contemplation and walking, I continued, 'I won't,' I said to myself, 'I won't.'

I walked towards the Adam and Eves Church and the Forty Steps. As I approached the Church I saw the redhead prostitute on her way up the Steps.

"Nice one," I said.

"Well, now," she turned and said, "it's the good looking Dublin kid," she said and threw up the back of her skirt, showing a brief white 'arse.

"Oh you girl, you." I had a wee noggin of brandy in my

coat pocket. I took a dollop of it, put the cap back on and threw it to her. "Here," I said, "darlin', have a ball."

She looked at me, "Nothin' upsets you does it?"

"No, why should it? I've lived in this district all my life. Good night, love, have a good night."

She gave a little twitch with her 'arse, looked around to see if I was looking, saw I was and gave a little laugh. "I knew you would be," she said.

In case you were wondering how I knew her, some years ago when Christmas trees were tall I ran across her. She hadn't been a prostitute in the early days, only recently. She had a short life, unfortunately. A couple years after this meeting on the Steps she met with her death. I attended her funeral to pay my respects. It was a sad day, she left four children.

Continuing on, I crossed over Winetavern Bridge that crosses to Ormond Quay, then around the corner into Capel Street, then crossed the road into Jervis Street.

I had had too much to drink, I knew it, and I needed to relieve myself badly. I walked down a little lane. Just when I finished and readied to go I heard a noise like a shuffle. I looked to my right. There was a man just standing there. He was smoothing back his hair with his right hand.

I got a little nervous.

Then I saw another figure move away from the wall and I knew I was in trouble. Said to myself, 'if you've ever been in trouble before, you are now'.

I was wearing boots that came up to the calves of my legs, because I carried a cosh down inside my boot. One day in town I was with my wife when a guy went for me, knocking over my wife. I managed to ward him off with the cosh which I always carried ever since an incident at the Hitchin Post when a guy was mad because I didn't call him up to sing a song, and the cosh has been my protection ever since. Now I was grateful for the lesson.

Slowly I took out the cosh, watching them.

I waited. They were some distance away.

The tall one was looking me up and down.

The other one said, in a country accent, “Hey boy have you something for me now, you look like a distant relative. Bringing something home for me? I’m fucking telling you this, if you haven’t anything for me I’m going to have you.”

I didn’t have a lot of money on me, a few pounds, but I wasn’t worried, a few pounds or a lot, I wasn’t givin’ any.

I waited.

He slowly came within an arms length of me.

I didn’t move.

He said, “Now, sunshine, what have you got for me?”

He was fat, very fat and I knew him. He lived in the Oliver Bond Flats and I think he recognised me.

I said, “I’ve nothing for you, Fatso”.

“What did you call me?

“He said ‘Fatso’,” the other tall one said.

The fat guy said, “Let him answer me, will you.”

“I said ‘Fatso’”.

He made for me at that moment and I quick wacked him across the mouth with the cosh. I knew he had something in his hand when I hit him. The cosh went into his mouth. I’d say he was spitting out ivory for months. He let out an unmerciful roar. He threw his hand up to his face and turned away, shouting to his mate to get me.

I could see a knife on the ground.

I wasn't too near it but the tall fellow made for it. I made for him. I kicked him. I hit him hard on the side of his leg and than I ran. The two of them were on the ground and I felt sick.

Just then a squad car came into the lane.

I looked around and the two guys were on their feet, one of them was holding his head, the other was leaning against the wall. I had been lucky.

When I spoke to the two guys in the beginning I had taken them unawares. It seemed they had been attacking people constantly. They were two hardened criminals at it.

The policeman took the cosh off me. I didn't see where the two guys went. I never saw them again.

"Will you come with me," the policeman said to me.

"I was very lucky. If I hadn't had the cosh I would have been dead," I said to them.

They brought me to the Bridewell Police Station.

"You'll be alright, sir," they said and I believed them. They were nice guys.

"Will you look after the cosh for me?"

"Don't worry, I'll make sure no one goes near you," he said laughing.

It was a lonely night.

Carrying a dangerous weapon was all I had had on me but it was all I needed. At the Station, the room I was left in had a little window at the top of the wall and a light outside was shining in.

How would I tell the family. My mother, she would be out

of her mind. Anyway, I would do time if necessary. I thought for awhile. I knocked on the door.

A voice answered, “Go to sleep, sir.”

I found out afterwards the door was open.

They let me go home about six o’clock the next morning. They said I had been charged with “Disorderly Conduct”.

I went home, got a shower, changed my clothes and thought, just in case, I had better get myself a solicitor. So I did. And I went to court and the cosh was never mentioned in the trial. The solicitor defended me well I think. He said the matter went okay, that all was settled and I thanked him.

As I was going out of the courts I said to give my apologies to the two policemen. One of the lads said, “Lugs Brannigan told me to tell you he was asking after you”.

“Thank you and thank him”, I said and I really meant it.

I went over to Adam and Eves Church and was on my knees praying a long while. I was grateful, very grateful. The Lord had been with me, I knew. I often think of that light shining in through the window up high. It was a lovely sight. I will never in my life forget that experience.

I gave up the drink sometime not long after that. I haven’t touched it now for many years. I never really drank to a great excess but now I enjoy great solitude and beautiful peace of mind not partaking o’ the drink.

Chapter 45

Mum home to Dad

For me, when my Dad died it was hell. He was my hero, my very best pal. I would always look to him, mostly to intervene to get me out of the trouble I was in. He always came up with trumps for me. I loved him for this.

His dying in the hospital put me in a state of shock. I was with Paddy, Des and Frank. We all were in tears watching him lying there in bed, so helpless. He was trying to breathe and trying to talk and not able to do either well. He wanted to tell us something but he just couldn't get anything out. He tried and tried and nothing came. So he just died there in the bed, he just stopped breathing.

A nurse came in, examined him, turned to us and said, "I'm so sorry."

My father had just passed away.

There was no sound from us. Just silence.

He looked so at rest. I went up to him in the bed, took him into my arms and held him to me. I kissed him on the face and said, "My dear kind, gentle father, thanks for all the good times you gave to me and one day old buddy I will tell everybody what a great father you really were."

I went outside the hospital and gave a Morris Miner a couple of whacks. I guess I just lost it. Then let out a roar with *Top o' the World DA*!

Frank put his arms around me and said, "Come on Jimmy, we'll have to tell Ma."

"Frank, you know he was the greatest. He knew things about me from years back."

"Don't take it out on the car, Jimmy."

"No, I won't. I was upset, okay Frank? We were good pals, you and I Fran, weren't we."

We got into someone's car, I don't know whose. It doesn't matter.

We drove right across to mom. We looked at each other, they all looked at me. It seemed to be a foregone conclusion. I was the one to go in. We arrived outside 24 Rosevale Court.

Paddy asked me, "Alright Jimmy?"

I said, "Okay Paddy I'll be okay. Go on, take off, I'll see you tomorrow."

I sat down alone on the step outside mom's door and smoked a cigarette. I was smoking at the time. About eighty cigarettes a day. Then, I gave them up later on. Now I needed one.

I wasn't worried about telling my mother. I started to think about dad and then started to sing *Dublin in The Rare Old Times,* one of dad's all time favourites. He always sang it to me, he loved it, sometimes we sang it together.

Then I thought about him singing *...the one-eyed yellow idol* ... and how he would sing it to us kids for as long as I can remember. He would love to get us into singing it with him ... oh, yes, he loved it, the words were funny, the rhythm of the music and the way he sang it was great ... and so it went ...

There's a one-eyed yellow idol to the north of Khatmandu,
There's a little marble cross below the town;
There's a broken-hearted woman tends the grave of Mad Carew,
And the Yellow God forever gazes down.

This lyric parody was written about the turn of the century and was a musical hall staple in the early twentieth century. *The little yellow idol* was influenced by the parodied ballads of Rudyard Kipling. This was the music of my father's childhood, he loved to sing it, and our family loved to hear him sing it. It was our fun song together with dad.

I was crying, trying to sing it now and wasn't making a good job of it.

Mom was coming down the hall to me, I could hear her step. I pushed opened the door and saw her coming. "Hello dear Chrissie ..."

She said, "Hello, Jim." She walked toward me, put her arms around me and gave me a kiss.

"He's dead isn't he, Jim."

"Yes, Mother. He's gone. I'm going to miss him."

"I will too Jim, I will too and God help me." Then, "Come on in, we'll have a cup of tea. Will you have a drink?"

"No thanks, Mum."

I had the tea. We were talking. "Stay tonight, Jim."

"Okay, Mum," So I stayed a few nights during the week.

I looked at his chair where he would be sitting. He would have to turn his head to see me. I sat down in it and it was comfortable. He had a pair of slippers beside the chair. I looked at them and thought to myself, 'there is no one who would ever fill them in my mind'.

On one night just after the Academy Awards, in the early 1940s, we were all sitting in our top floor flat. We had just moved into St. Audoens and were all together listening to our Crosby Radio that we had paid for at the costly sum of 2/6 per week. Then the next day you took off to join the army and now you're leaving me again. It will be a long time till I see you this time. When I do, then I will run to meet you.

The funeral took place and all arrangements were looked

after by Paddy and Maura. God bless them.

And now I swore I would look after Mum and I did to the best of my ability.

Mother said to me one day, "I hope Essie is alright with this."

I said, "It's no bother, Mother, no bother whatsoever."

Time passed for mother and all of us. Things were going well. Marie would come home often which pleased Mother no end. She came over from England on the holidays. Some friends of mine, Anne O'Flynn, Annie and Catherine Rodgers would often give me a lift over to see mother. You could tell she was delighted with all the company. She was in her element. One time we were having a cup of tea together when my mother produced a deck of playing cards and proceeded to tell the girls' fortunes from the cards. She was right on a good number of times and you could tell she had a great time. The girls became constant visitors to my mother after that. They said, "We love your Mum, Jim."

I said, "I'm glad, real happy about that." So we had good times, Mum and me and the ladies.

I was working in the Hitchin' Post. It was the 5th of April 1978.

It was on a Monday night. I was on my way home. Paddy, my brother, phoned me with the news.

My mother had suffered a heart attack and had passed away.

I think it was a relief to her. She was becoming very lonely and would often say it to me. I tried to get to see her as often as I could but I knew she was missing my dad. So you know she had found true happiness at the last.

She was buried in Balgriffen Cemetery next to the love of her life, my dear father and may they both rest in peace, in the love and kindness of almighty God. To me, they were both a constant help through life's troubles and strife, especially in the growing up years when I so needed their guidance through the dark nights. So it was my brother Paddy who told me my dear old mom had passed away. You know, in a way I rejoiced in the fact that my dear mom had at last found her happiness. She was buried beside her true love.

God bless them both, may they forever find the happiness they truly deserve. May they rest in Peace.

Chapter 46

Stardust Remembered

The Stardust fire was a fatal fire at the Stardust nightclub in Artane, north of Dublin in the early hours of 14 February 1981.

Forty eight persons died as a result of the fire. Cause of the fire is still unknown.

The Stardust ... what a chill it conjures up to this day. The name sends a shiver up your body. I dread the sound of it. I really do. It has never left my memory and now it is over twenty five years later. It reaps the winds of time again and the voices go screaming into the night. It is a tragedy that will never be forgotten.

I still remember the morning after, and all that day till nightime. I was working on stage at McGeowans of Stonybatter, Manor Street in Arbour Hill on the North Side. It was a nice little cabaret lounge. I liked it and the customers were great. It was owned by Big Con Tracy, his manager was his brother Danny. Liam was the doorman, what a character!

I knew quite well some of the people that died. The lovely Keegan sisters, their father John was an old friend of mine. The sorrow I felt, knowing John and how he idolised his daughters, was deep. When I spoke to him some hours later he was inconsolable. Con Tracy and I held him in our arms. My heart went out to him but I had no answer to his sorrow. He knew that. He just said to me, "Stay with me, Jim." Myself, Con and Liam Coughlan did stay with him.

I got many calls from quite a few lounges.

A lad called Hughie Hynes, who worked as a singer in Bridget Burke's Lounge, went to a few places and asked them to have a remembrance in each lounge, carried out in respect for the boys and girls who died.

The hurt that everyone felt will never be forgotten. Families still mourn and always will.

Balgriffin is the main burial ground. My parents are buried in Balgriffin. When I visit their graves it gives me time to pray for the Stardust victims.

This tragedy became a personal remembrance in our family.

Brother Des and his family were living in Coolock on the North Side, not too far from Malahide and Artane. Des had two teen age daughters who used to walk every Friday evening up to the Stardust for a night of fun out with their friends. They always went every Friday evening. They didn't go on the evening of 13 February 1981. For no real reason. They just didn't go.

I and my family mourn in a deep, private way for the Stardust victims.

Chapter 47

Mascot on Amiens Street

I finished in the Hitchin' Post in 1981. It was the best thing ever to happen to me.

After leaving the Hitchin' Post I did some singing jobs around town and then began to work with Equity in films. I also went to work in McKeowns of Stoneybatter. All my old neighbours from St. Audoens House drank there. We had great sing-songs goin on there.

I met a man in McKeowns called Liam Coughlan. He had a shop in Amiens Street called The Mascot. One evening he said, "I heard you're leaving here, would you like to work for me?"

I said, "I would. I'm working in the films so anything goes."

He was a nice enough bloke, somewhat a shaper, and I was soon to find out his good and bad points. He loved his cigarettes and brandy and his wild, wild women. He was living with a nice lady called Anne, and had a sweet little chick housed in a flat in Baggot Street and a wife and family in Limerick town. Busy man.

The shop was a hive of activity. There was a great clientele, mostly from the flats.

I was on my own one night when my old pal Fergal Quinn came into the shop. Great to see him. It had been some years since I had come into contact with him, since our days in Red Island Holiday Camp. He was working with his father, Bob, who owned the Camp and I was working as vocalist with Roy Allen's band. We became good friends. It was nice to recall old times. He made it a habit of coming in for his paper each night. We had some good old chats, reminiscing. He was still the same old Fergal, never changed. Maybe that's the reason he is so successful.

The people from the inner city were just like my people from the Liberties. I made many friends with all the customers. They were very friendly and most of the goods sold were on the tick. Their husbands got paid on a Friday so it was easy for us to give groceries on the slate.

There was one girl I became very friendly with. Her name was Kay. We had some good conversations, great craic. I liked to chat with her, we talked about everything. Music and stage. I heard her singing one night at a sing-song in a pub and she impressed Liam and myself with her great voice.

She came into the shop this particular night. I knew what she would take home with her. As she was reading the paper I was getting her groceries and had them all ready on the counter.

"What would I do only for you," she said.

I said good night to her and she left.

I watched her go up the street. She waved back at me, then she was gone.

The light came on in the pub. It cast a funny glow where she had been. Maybe I was in a peculiar mood, maybe it was the night. Whatever it was, I wasn't in the best of form.

I had a long way to go home. I lay awake that night when I got into my house. I was living on Drumcairn Avenue in Tallaght. I said goodnight to my next door neighbour, Mick McGraile, a real nice man and thought about my dear friend Kay as she left me.

I got to sleep eventually. Just crashed out. Woke up next morning, out of it. I got to work at about 10 am. Liam was waiting for me at the front door. The minute I saw him I knew something was wrong. He caught my arm and said to me, "Kay committed suicide last night."

I lay across the counter and nearly passed out.

Liam said to me, "Come on, we'll go into Clearys, get a drink."

I said, "Good idea," and it was.

I went home and didn't go back for a week. We were all so upset, what a tragedy. She was a lovely girl, such a sad loss.

One night shortly after two young boys came into the shop. I gave them some sweets.

"Thank you, sir," one of them said to me.

The other lad said, "Mister, I have something to say to you."

I said, "Right, lad, tell me then."

He said, "We heard these boys talking about your girl in the shop."

We had a girl called Anne who worked in the shop, a young, nice looking girl.

One of the lads said, "The boys we heard talking said they were going to rape her one night."

I wasn't going to believe them. Then I thought, well, it could be true. Better sure than sorry so I got Liam down and he asked the two lads for more details. It so transpired there were three guys who had it in mind to follow her when she was going home one night.

We got the police who sorted it out. It could have gone the wrong way.

This shop was really getting to me. The work in the films and *Glenroe* was great. I was going to give up the shop. Far, far too morbid now.

The 1980s were a changin'. Sometimes too fast for me.

Chapter 48

My Dear Wife Essie

In the eighties I was working a lot in Equity, getting plenty of work in the film business, and worked for years in *Glenroe.* They were good days in the eighties.

Suddenly things started to go badly.

My wife's health started to fail her. She started to lose power in her legs. She was unable to move around freely. Jackie, our daughter, and myself cared for her. It grieved me to see her so helpless.

She was such a nice, kind mother. I couldn't take work too far from home as I had to be within walking distance so I could get home quickly.

When the doctors examined her they couldn't find the source of the trouble, but she was failing rapidly. I will always remember those days, the fear, the anxiety of not knowing what we were dealing with and for the future.

Every week our lovely next door neighbour, Mick McGraile, who drove a taxi, would drive us to St. James's Hospital, then pick us up again and drive us back home. The poor man had his own troubles. He had two children diagnosed with cystic fibrosis. He truly gave of himself and his time to help us. They were dreadful times for us. We had to be with Essie at all times. She was slowly losing her hold on life, we could tell. She was attending the hospital weekly and they could still not find a cure.

I was always at home with her. My religion was Catholic and I have always practiced it. All my years across the water in England or here in Ireland or Scotland my religion came first, I loved it. I started to pray to Saint Padre Pio. He was always in my thoughts and prayers. There was a Padre Pio Prayer Group two nights a week. I was part of it and we all prayed together for her recovery.

My good friend Valerie from Springfield, and Mick McGraile remained true, helpful loving friends throughout these times. God be with you both and all the people in the prayer group who prayed night after night for my wife's recovery.

One day my wife's sister Mary came home from England. She said she would take my wife back to England with her, so I said nothing. Then I said, "God willing".

We wheeled her out in a wheelchair. An air stewardess took her off us and wheeled her on.

She was gone from me. Would she ever come back?

I got back to where I lived on Fettercairn Avenue in Tallaght. I stayed there with Jackie and waited.

Mary and my wife got to London. She never moved out of her wheelchair. They arrived on a Tuesday. On Wednesday morning they made their way to St. Thomas' Hospital. The hospital said, "Sorry, we can't see her, she's not English," so Mary left her address at the hospital. Maybe they would change their mind.

"Sorry," they said, "there is a very long waiting list."

It was to be understood, and they were very upset.

Essie retired to bed at Mary's house, tired and discouraged.

At 10:30 pm that very same night the door bell rang. It was a medic from the hospital to say, "We will admit you, we have a bed for you."

"This is most unusual,“ Mary said, "but we are so happy to accept."

They took Essie in an ambulance. Mary rang me the next day and told me. I was delighted with the news.

Mary said to me, "I just can't get over this, I can tell you Jim it has knocked me out. They are bringing her into the theatre at three o'clock today, this afternoon."

She was taken to the St. Thomas' National Hospital in London. A Doctor Trent examined her and said, "What did your doctor find wrong?"

Essie said, "They said it was a nerve disorder."

Doctor Trent said, "It's a tumour on your spine and you are a very sick woman. We will operate as soon as possible," so they got her ready for theatre right away.

It was an extraordinarily traumatic time for us back home. All we could do was pray and pray.

During the course of the operation she woke up. She turned to Doctor Trent, who was performing the operation and said to him, "There is a lovely smell of flowers in here".

"There are no flowers in here, now please go back to sleep for me," Doctor Trent answered.

When the operation was over Doctor Trent spoke to Mary. "Your sister," he said, "is very ill. I can tell you I never thought she would make it. I'm going out on a limb by saying it was a miracle, but if you want my opinion that's exactly what it was."

I agreed when Mary told me.

It was a malignant tumour which had been there for months. Well, my thanks to you dear Saint Padre Pio. Thanks to my dear friend Valerie and our prayer group, for all those endless nights of prayer. I hope you all continue to enjoy good health in your life as do I for my dear wife Essie.

Essie continued to gain in good health and eventually she went back to work in her management position in Hewlitt Packard Electric.

I still just can not believe the happy ending to our days

and hours of agony and worry and endless prayer, An awesome thing indeed is the power of prayer.

Chapter 49

Tallaght to Perrystown

My move in 1994 from Drumcairn Avenue in Tallaght to Perrystown was a good move.

In 1990 I began working for Hewlett Packard while living in Tallaght and worked there for six years, so part of the early time at Hewlett Packard we were living in Tallaght and then, in 1994, we moved to Perrystown while still working at Packard. There was a great buzz in Packard and I enjoyed every minute working there but unfortunately they closed this plant in 1996.

To leave Tallaght was sad but drugs had begun to move into the district. The move was there so I took it and me and my wife moved on.

The years in Tallaght were happy ones. Leaving our next door neighbours, Mick and Bernie McGraile was a bit upsetting with their lovely lot of young children who were so mannerly. One of our neighbours was a single mother called Maura who had two sons, one of whom, Lee, was to die tragically. A big blond handsome lad. Yes, I would miss my old neighbours, the walks, St. Marks Church and Sister Hannah, my good friend

The move to Perrystown brought new neighbours into our lives. On one side of our house our neighbours were Mary and Martin Brown and three children. On the other side of us lived Emily whose husband had passed away many years earlier, and her brother Mick, who were a great twosome.

I was there for a few months when I found out that Mick had worked in Hewlett Packard. This amused me so we had something in common. He was retired now. Every evening he would go for his walk to the Submarine Bar.

“It was just to partake of the black liquid, Jim, “he said.

"And why not, old timer, why not," I would say. "Barry Fitzgerald will never be dead while you're alive."

He would never miss a night. You could set your watch by his coming and going. He was always the same, a kind and gentle man who would always stop to exchange a greeting with you.

He would always have a lift from the pub to his door. Then it was a goodnight to you and a good night to him.

One night Emily heard a sound at the door. She came out to find him dead at the door. Sorry I couldn't say goodbye to you, old friend. A lovely neighbour and nice guy up to the end. I miss him asking me, in the mornings, if there are any letters for him. Or his smile and hand wave.

Emily in her young days was a fine country singer and still is very much in demand at musical functions. She has a daughter, Karen, who is married and a very attractive lady with brains to burn. She is a legal eagle. A great girl to have a conversation with. Always enjoy she and her husband when they stop and we have a great chat.

Tony and Margaret live across the road from me. Their last few years have been traumatic and so tragic, when they said goodbye to their son when he left to go to America to work and was never to return. He got lost in a forest and was never to be found again. This I find very sad, so touching, and perhaps a bit strange to leave behind a beautiful wife and children, a doting mother and father who idolised him. No one could ever give the family an answer about his disappearance.

Tony was a Liberty boy. "I'm from New Row in the Coombes," he said to me one day. "I worked in Jacobs Biscuit Factory."

"Well," I said, "it's a small world, Tony. Did you ever know Terry Smyth, my father?" I asked him.

"I did," he said. "One nice man," he said to me.

I remember shortly after his son went missing poor old Tony went into himself, became quiet within himself. He would never speak to anyone. He became a silent figure. I have great pity for him because he and his wife were two lovely people.

Their missing son Paul's wife is a very pretty girl and they have lovely children. One day I'm sure the children will ask questions. I hope the family can answer them. I sincerely hope so.

Then there is a nice old guy named Mick who lives a couple doors from me and who has multitudes of little utensils in his garden. They are really in quite good condition, the utensils, a miniature pan, a kettle and a pot.

He confided in me one night that "something must happen".

I said, "Something must happen? Tell me about it, Mick."

He tipped his nose with his finger and winked his eye at me. "The little people, Jim," he said to me.

I thought he was flipping his top but he was quite in earnest. I said, "Right you be, lad." I did the next best thing, I legged it.

The ornaments are still in his garden and are looking nice and polished. I met him the other day and what a conversation we had. It was about Mary McAleese getting re-elected.

"Poor old Dana," I said, "didn't she try hard though."

We both agreed she had but Mary was in for a good time, is a lovely woman and good president.

Mary and Martin Brown who live next door to me were picked up for Mass by a lady called Mary in a red Toyota car, and since I am just on my way out with the same Mass in mind I hop in for a ride.

"A life saver," I say to her, "you're an angel, Mary.

Which brings me to the church. The Holy Spirit here in Perrystown is a nice church, very majestic in appearance. Father Harrison and Father Ryan are nice and deserve a mention. I talk to Father Harrison a lot.

I remember in my young days I knew a lot of priests, Father "Flash" Kavanagh from High Street Church, and Father Whelan from St. Michaels, who was called John "Stew", because he always served a delicious stew to guests. He was a great friend to my mother and Mrs. Wilson and of course Mrs. Kavanagh. Father Michael Cleary was a good man. I liked him. He would never be stuck when he visited our flat in St. Audeons, my mother would always have a welcome for him. In later years I came into contact with him and he was doing well. During his cabaret days I always had a great time for him.

Father Feeney from Leixlip is still there. He put in some great years, a nice man. Father Colm from Fettercairn in Tallaght in later years left the order and got married. He is now enjoying great happiness so it can work either way and great joy can be achieved.

I met another great character of a priest by name of Father McLoughlin from the army. His parish was situated in Collin's Barracks. He was their "Padre", a lovely character. Father Gilbert who managed the choir in Merchants Quay where I was attached at one time, was very famous in his time. Father Oliver stared in St. Anthony's Theatre and made a lot of money for the church, as well as for the foreign mission. I was the one, along with Tommy Poland, who started in Father Oliver's shows.

It has been a great sadness to me that my Catholic Church has been tarnished by the filthy alien men who should not have worn the black. But don't get me wrong, some are good and some are bad. That's to be found in every walk of life. In all my lifetime I've known a great number of the good ones. I've met good men in the priesthood through the cabaret work, so I cannot say otherwise. I don't have the education to pass judgement. My life has been full of hassle and I've enjoyed it. Perrystown has been a good time in my life. Good happy times with my wife and family and grandchildren who mean the world and all its oysters to me.

I keep forgetting I'm well into my seventies now but I'm soon reminded by someone to 'take it easy' as they say and I do. I'm up in the morning and out into the streets. Little did I realise on that Friday night in the Hitchin Post in Leixlip, as I lifted Dana up on her stool for her song and put her guitar into her arms and gave her a pack on the cheek that one day this wee little lassie from Belfast would contest against Mary McAleese herself for presidency of Ireland. Do you ever wonder what way it will all end up.

As for my little move to Perrystown, the move was a change in our home and neighbours, but it was more than that. I discover once again that neighbours have their own tales of life and woes and joyful experiences, just as did our neighbours in Tallaght and even further back, in the Liberties.

To wax a bit philosophical, life is the same the world over for we're all here by the grace of God to walk our own paths through the mishaps of life. And, furthermore, by and large people are a kindly lot, loving and helpful of their neighbours in whatever ways come to them. That is one thing I've found out in life.

Or so it seems to me.
May God bless us all.

Chapter 50

Bang Band and Liberties

When I was living away from the Liberties in the later years, in Tallaght and Perrystown, I would get to thinking of the old days in the Liberties, then I would get on the bus and ride up to the Liberties to visit and look at the changes. Although some of the memories were not changes, they were just re-visiting the old times and places.

I would often walk down from James Street. The famous Catherine's Bakery building is still there, but the business has long gone, sorely missed as is Thompson's, on the other side on Bridgefoot Street, who always catered for the poor in the Liberties.

Woolworth's was on the left side now. Blanchester Mills is still there and, not to be forgotten, for Seezers black & white pudding, a regular Sunday morning treat not to be missed. They would queue all the day Friday and Saturday for it.

The stalls on both sides of Meath and Thomas Streets offered lovely ripe fruit.

It was great to walk down from James Street right to High Street, passing by O'Hora's shop, a huge complex, where you were never short of a munch. The Maypole stores, always in a beautiful, clean state.

In the sixties and seventies "The Cosmo Hair Saloon", run by "Olly" George Robinson and little Jimmy, catered for all the showband stars. As Jimmy said, they were the "Brut" force, you could smell them before you would see them.

The first time I met "Bang Bang", I remember it well. He was on the platform of the No. 21 bus. This bus ran all the way from town, right on up all the way to Inchicore. He was a very strange looking man, pale face, jet black hair, a very quiet man. That is, when he wasn't Bang Bang.

He was a great talker. If you asked him a question, he'd shy away from you and give a little smile. Yet little did he realise, as did his mother think, that he would become a cult figure in the Liberties. Anyone you would ask about the Liberties would always bring Bang Bang into the conversation.

I was with my mother one day in Thomas Street. She got into a conversation with a woman when she turned her head and then said, "Oh this is my son, Jim."

The woman said, "Hello, son, you're a great looking boy. Oh, here's my fella, will you listen to him?"

It was Bang Bang and he was travelling on foot. The bullets were flying in every direction.

My mother took a fit of laughing.

The woman said good-bye to my mother, "Good-bye Mrs. Smyth, I'm off."

"Goodbye Mrs. Dudley, I'll see you again please God."

I was watching Bang Bang ride into the sunset with his mother.

My mother said, "His name is Tommy Dudley."

I said, "Mam, he's a great character."

"Jim, you never said a more true word." And when they mention the Liberties they will always remember Bang Bang and his trusty steed, the No. 21 bus.

There were other great names from the era in the Liberties, Lugs Brannigan who was a fighter, not a boxer. But still he went down well with the stadium crowd.

Just thinking of Lord Mayor Alfie Byrne, just thinking of the characters in the Liberties. He used to ride around the Liberties on his bike. He was a great figure of a man with his top hat and his waxed moustache. He'd be waving to everyone either side of the road. He was extremely popular. I never saw him in a car. He always used to cycle to St. Audeons House, to see us all I guess. He always had time to talk to you no matter when he would meet. All the neighbours loved him in St. Audeons House. He would go out of his way to talk to people. "How are things progressing Mrs. Smyth," he'd say to my mother. My mother and Mrs. Wilson would tell him all the news. He was a great mixer and everybody loved him.

In my years in the Arbour Hill Boxing Club I met a lad there called Benny Briscoe, whose father became our Lord Mayor. Benny was a good boxer, a quite tall lad. We had great punch-ups together. He always came out on top. I didn't like this so I decided to nail him before he went to college. We were to do three minute rounds. Big Jim Crystal was Time Keeper. First and second rounds I let him get on top. It was coming up to the last minute of the third round. He was very tired. I was the same but I was ready. Just at that minute his father came into the club. I nodded at Benny, "Your father," I said. He turned his head, smiled at his father and then I hit him. I knocked him out. Sweet smell of success after all those other times when he had knocked me around. It was nice to get one up on him. He never forgave me for it, though.

Ah a walk down Memory Lane in the Liberties.

Chapter 51

Santa in the 1990's

My wife Esther was working in Hewlett Packard, situated on the Airton Road in Tallaght.

In the early 1990s over 1,600 men and women were working there at the time. This facility was where they build component parts for car interiors. There were three shifts in motion every day, 8:00 am to 4:45 pm, 4:45 to midnight, and the night shift, from midnight to 8:00 am. Essie was forever asking me to apply for a job there.

It was coming up towards the Christmas holiday time when she came in from work and said to me, "Jim dear, do you know what my boss Nuala is looking for?"

I said, "No Essie, tell me, and here's a cup of tea for you."

"She is looking for someone to play Santa Claus in Bewleys, someone to collect for the itinerant children in the community. Nuala said she couldn't get anyone to help her out and asked me to ask you, Jim. Would you?"

I said, "Tell her I most certainly would be happy to do it."

Hewlett Packard Management Catering was supporting it so they were in charge of all arrangements. In no time I was outfitted in my Santa suit and all that went with it like the boots, a grand beard and hat, and I went down to Bewleys in Grafton Street to sign on.

I was well met when I arrived by two lovely ladies named Elizabeth and Maureen.

Now the deal was as follows.

I was Christmas Santa. My job was to meet the customers with their children whom I was to entertain. The fathers would give me a cheque for the Bewleys Charity Collection. From the word I got, I was a great success and management was delighted with my efforts.

I did not have to tell Essie anything about Santa's adventures, Nuala informed her about everything I was doing.

I got on real well with all the children. Looking back, it was a great, fulfilling way to spend my weeks before Christmas.

One of the days before Christmas Ronnie Drew came into the store to visit with me. I ended up by telling him who Santa was and Ronnie said, with his dry wit, "Sure, Jim, I knew you all along."

"You're kidding aren't you ?"

"Didn't I say, 'Jim' to you?" he asked me.

I said, "You did, Ronnie, you did."

"But I found out from Elizabeth my friend, who gave me the right story. She said, since Ronnie had asked her who Santa was, she gave him my name. He thanked me so much and said he didn't want to give his money to the wrong person."

It was a typical Ronnie Drew classic, God rest his soul.

One day the week before Christmas a couple of young guys came into the store. The crowd was enormous, all aisles packed with customers. I needn't tell you spirits were sky high. One of the lads had a guitar and he started to play. He said, "Give us a song", then turned to me and said, "come on, Santa".

So I obliged. "Why not," I said, "it's Christmas."

It was great, the laughter, the singing, everyone dancing. A great time was had by all in Bewleys and it was a happy Christmas to everyone with the spirit of Christmas reigning supreme.

The manager in Bewleys gave me an envelope which said, "A happy Christmas to you, Jim, thank you" and Nuala sent me a "thank you, Jim" note. All in all it was one great Christmas. That was my first meeting with Packard and I needn't tell you, dear friend, it was a lovely Christmas to remember.

A gentle man rang me on Christmas Eve to ask if I would do Santa for him. He had some presents for an orphanage in Harolds Cross that he gave aid to.

"I certainly will," I said to him. "I will be working but no matter, I can do it for you as well. After all, it's Christmas Eve." And you know, looking at those lovely young girls and shaking their hands brought a tear to my eye. When I thought how little we think of the simple things in life, as you say to yourself, as I did, you begin to wonder whatever will happen to those lovely young ladies on Christmas. I wonder how many of them will have good times and dear friends to look after them, to give them a kiss and hug and mother them when they would cry, or kiss away the night fears.

Just across the road from the Convent was my old haunt, Marymount Hall. It brought back more memories.

I said to my driver who was leaving me home to Tallaght, "You know, Pat, I'm absolutely drained. What a night it has been. It's opened up so much to me. You know, the poor things that we never even have time for, but you know, one day they will have their chances in life. All these lovely little angels will one day find their true happiness."

I got home to my family and said to Esther, "It was a wonderful Christmas Eve I got this day. It was a memorable day and my God is born today," for now it was after midnight and was now the Christmas Day.

I would be too late for Evening Mass but I would enjoy my Morning Mass, which would be something to look forward to.

So that was my first introduction to Hewlett Packard and I needn't tell you I loved it. All the family, Esther, myself, Dermot, Michael and Jacqueline, we all went together to Christmas Morning Mass and what a happy Christmas it turned out to be.

Chapter 52

Minding my Business

One day I was walking down home from my Church, The Holy Spirit, up in Perrystown.

A car pulled up beside me.

A young man stuck his head out of the car's window and in a loud voice he shouted to me, "Hello Sir."

I said hello back to him. I was a little bemused.

"You help me, please. I look for airport. I fly home."

He spoke in very broken English. This is, I'm sure you are aware, an art form in itself. I was a little taken back for a minute but then gained my composure.

"Okay Cisco," I said. "What is it, really? If it's the airport, it's out on the Naas Road."

He took off with a tirade of words. He kept on and on. He told me where he came from. It was Italy. Then he took out a leather coat. It was nice.

"I give this to you, sir. You are a nice man."

I said, "Thank you, that's real decent of you, I mean it."

Then he takes another coat from his car and gave the two coats to me. Then he took his I.D. card from his pocket. He continued to impress me with his sales talk. As a matter of fact he never stopped talking. I thought he had a dose of diarrhea of the mouth.

I still hadn't given him a penny for his coats.

I said to myself, 'All I lack is a leather whip'.

He must have heard me, he understood my English pretty well, for he immediately produced a whip. “Sir,” he said, “this is free for you with this coat.”

Now comes the pitch. This coat I could have for €250. I eventually got the message. The penny dropped.

A couple lads were collecting bins and watching us as we came abreast of them. I saw they were laughing.

One said to me, “I thought he had fooled you.”

“Was I lucky?” I asked. “I think so?”

“My friend here,” he said, pointing to the lad beside him, “got stuck with the coats, all three and the whip and – wait for it – he threw in a leather mask as well. Mister he has got to be the best dressed man on the job.”

This got a great laugh from the other men there.

I said, “He comes from Italy, or so his passport said.”

“Not at all,” the lad said, “sure he was born in Dolphin’s Barn. He was reared there all his life.”

I laughed. I had to. He was standing by his car and cracking his whip for all it was worth.

“I nearly got caught,” I said, “I’ll know the next time to keep walking.”

The men said to me, “I couldn’t imagine how he didn’t take you.”

“Simple,” I said, “a very logical reply to your question, I had no money.” This was true, I said to the man.

He was pleased for me and I was pleased for him as well.

“Don’t forget, if you meet him, crack your whip or his.”

Chapter 53

Santa, Bewleys, 2004

It's almost Christmas in 2004. I was down to Grafton Street today. I stopped by to Bewleys and had a think and a tear.

I think it's a foregone conclusion it's gone, it's sold and it's the past tense. So maybe I am a little sad about the closing of its doors. It has been a landmark on Grafton Street for so many years. Maybe it might be saved in some form, I don't know, but it will certainly be missed. Grafton Street has its share of cafes ready to take the business over. We'll see.

Being on Grafton Street at Christmas time reminds me of my Santa Christmas with them, just ten years ago. I worked pretty hard that Christmas but I can tell you there was a lot of money collected that holiday and it gave me a great feeling to be part of it all. So maybe I am a little sad about closing its doors.

When I played Santa for Mr. Bewley he would accept money donations from benefactors and present it to the travelling people. I thought this was most generous of him. But then the Bewley people were very good people. They were always through the years very good to their workers and charity was their middle name.

I remember Equity used Bewleys for film shoots I was on many of the shoots, all enjoyable times. There were many laughs with Joe Lynch, Dick Bergin, Miley and the cast of Glenroe, Cyril Cusack.

Whatever the final solution of Bewleys, the Bewleys were well liked, the family and the restaurant family. And so ends my Santa Christmas at Bewleys and an era on Grafton Street.

Chapter 54

Tallaght Hospital

This day in particular was a Monday, the 12th of April 2004 to be exact. I was to go to Tallaght Hospital this day, I had an appointment at eight o'clock and 45 minutes in the morning.

I wasn't in good form. I was tired. My appointment was regarding my prostate. "You may have it, you get it checked out," the doctor said to me. This I was doing so I was on my way. But I was very nervous, very much so. I had heard about it, the prostate, but the very name terrified me. Prostate cancer.

Essie gave me a lift up to the hospital. We stopped for a few seconds at the roundabout. I threw a kiss at her, it landed on her head. I knew she was worried about me. I was worried too, dear one.

Some time had lapsed since I had been there but it was still the same nice and clean place. There was a big poster at the front door saying, "Welcome to the New Medical Staff". Grey haired Mary from Packard was in Reception. She had been working there for a good many years. She had a lovely voice, was nice to listen to, always pleasant and popular with everyone. She was deep in conversation with a doctor. I didn't interrupt. Essie had taken off home so I was on my own.

I went upstairs to my appointment.

There was one man waiting to see the doctor. "Take a ticket," he said to me. I understood by the loudness of his voice that he was deaf. I was right, no big deal. He dozed off awhile after.

I took a ticket and stood in line. A stout girl sat down beside me. She was a friendly girl and we struck up a conversation. We got a bit friendly. Then her mobile rang. She held a conversation with someone. "Goodbye," she said to the person, "goodbye". She stood up and was gone, just like that. As she was going she said, "I might see you again."

I said, "Right you are, darling, mind how you go." Funny I said that.

She came back a short while later and never even said a word to me. She was with her husband and a young boy. I got the message. Her husband was a big guy anyway.

I was getting a bit restless. Time was getting on. I wanted to get myself sorted out.

I asked the young nurse to help me. She said she wasn't seeing the prostate patients, "but I'll enquire," she said.

I thanked her.

Sometime after, she came back. "I've been speaking to a doctor, he'll see you soon. Could you give me a urine sample?" she asked.

She handed me a little jar with a seal on it. I took it. She showed me a little room to go into. I shut the door and I tried to pass some water. Now, have you ever tried to pass water if it was needed? I can tell you it's the hardest thing to do. I tried and tried but it just wouldn't come.

She tapped on the door. "Are you ready, Mr. Smyth?"

I said, "Just a minute, nurse, I won't be long. Sorry."

I got a dribble out, not enough I said to myself.

"Fill it, Mr. Smyth please."

I was just about to come out with what was in it. I stuck the jar under the sink and filled it with water. I handed it to her. This pleased her. She smiled and said, "Thank you."

She brought me in to see the doctor. He was a young

man. He introduced himself. I forgot his name but it doesn't matter.

He sat me down on a small couch. The usual procedure, hand up your arse. It wasn't painful and it didn't take long. He took off the rubber glove he used, tossed it into the wastebasket and sat down facing me.

Then he proceeded to tell me about prostate cancer. He said, "You know prostate is not like other cancers, it doesn't take over your body and you disintegrate. You can live with it and you won't die from it. When I was examining you I found a hard surface and this was on the "elbow", on your left side. I'm sorry I have to tell you this. I bet when you came here this is not what you wanted to hear."

I said, "No doctor it wasn't, it certainly was not."

You know, I said to myself, I never fail to amaze myself. "What way do you feel now, James?"

I said, "I feel okay and I'm accepting what you are saying."

He looked at me. "I'm going to do a full prostate scan. Now you will have to give a blood sample and the nurse will make an appointment for you for the scan."

The nurse came over and took my arm. "Come with me, James, and I will fix an appointment for you." We went to another nurse who did all the paperwork.

"You will go down and give a blood sample." She gave me a card and I went downstairs where the blood bank was located. It was packed. I took a ticket and sat down. I was about forty behind and they were coming thick and fast. I was beginning to feel the strain now and I was starting to remember what the doctor had told me. I thought I was going to make it but it wasn't to be, and to cap it all he told me I had another hernia. That's all I needed. This is where it all started, in Tallaght Hospital.

Do you know, I was just about to go home when I noticed somebody was talking in my ear. I turned my head and looked into a bushy face.

"How is it? What's up with you?" He started a conversation with me. He started talking and he never stopped. He just kept on and on. He was from Tymon North. His name was Jim. His knowledge about the film business was unbelievable. "Did you know that there was an Irish Mafia in Hollywood? There was," he said, and called out the names, Jimmy Cagney, Pat O'Brien, Spencer Tracy and Clark Gable who was a gentleman.

I said, "After Jack Doyle got finished with him he wasn't much use."

"No way," he said, "they became great pals."

I agreed with him at this stage. I was trying to get away. But it was no use. I was taken prisoner. I was finished. I was ready to submit to him. He was doing my head in. I couldn't take any more. Just then he caught hold of my arm. "I ask you this," he said to this big, bald headed man, "What country western star won three Oscars?"

Everyone in the hall heard him ask the question. I had a fair idea but I couldn't name him. A few people got involved but no winners.

"I'll tell you," he said with a big smile on his face. "Walter Brennan," he said. He got a round of applause.

She called out, "Fifty-eight!"

I said, "Bingo!, I've a full house, I'm out of here," and I meant it.

I said to the nurse, "Thanks be to God, that guy out there was doing my head in."

She started to laugh. "You should have seen your face, it was priceless, the expressions on it. I remember when you worked here." She took my blood sample and said, "I'll send it upstairs. By the way, James, that man you were sitting with comes in every day. He never fails to get someone going."

I laughed with her now, it was funny, but I don't think life is all that funny. I have to return the end of August. This time they will insert a machine into me. The old years are coming upon me fast. But I'm still pushing them back and seem to be doing fine, day by day.